A CRITICAL ACCOUNT OF ARTICLE 106(2) TFEU

A Critical Account of Article 106(2) TFEU: Government Failure in Public Service Provision offers a sceptical perspective on how EU law applies to public services. Article 106(2) provides that other Treaty rules may be disapplied in order to sustain a Service of General Economic Interest (SGEI). In rhetorical terms, Article 106(2) is framed as a strict exception. As a result, Article 106(2) is often presented as a threat to Europe's public service tradition. This book challenges those shibboleths by using the concept of government failure. It is concerned with instances of government intervention that are unnecessary, generate avoidable inefficiencies, or that can be bettered so as to realise general interest goals more efficaciously. As an element of the government failure critique, a market feasibility test incorporating the concept of market failure is used to expose laxity in the review of general interests under Article 106(2). Complementing that, the process of disapplying other Treaty rules under Article 106(2) is shown to have evolved from being strict to being highly indulgent of SGEI providers, with a relatively recent but only partial correction post *Altmark*. Overall, the strict exception label for Article 106(2) does not hold. Moreover, it is contingent and presents no legitimate general interest related threat to the organisation and delivery of public services. A comprehensive re-orientation of Article 106(2) on issues of proof is required, as is greater reliance on market counterfactuals, and much more careful separation of objectives and means in SGEI operation and design. Through these measures, the toleration of government failure can be stemmed and Article 106(2)'s contingency reduced.

Volume 18 in the series Hart Studies in Competition Law

Hart Studies in Competition Law

Cross-Border EU Competition Law Actions
Edited by Mihail Danov, Florian Becker and Paul Beaumont

Competition Laws, Globalization and Legal Pluralism: China's Experience
Qianlan Wu

Joint Ventures and EU Competition Law
Luis Silva Morais

Sanctions in EU Competition Law: Principles and Practice
Michael Frese

Fairness in Antitrust: Protecting the Strong from the Weak
Adi Ayal

European Merger Remedies: Law and Policy
Dorte Hoeg

Media Ownership and Control: Law, Economics and Policy in an Indian and International Context
Suzanne Rab and Alison Sprague

The Interface between Competition and the Internal Market: Market Separation under Article 102 TFEU
Vasiliki Brisimi

Anti-Cartel Enforcement in a Contemporary Age: Leniency Religion
Edited by Caron Beaton-Wells and Christopher Tran

Public Procurement and the EU Competition Rules
Albert Sánchez Graells

The Concept of Abuse in EU Competition Law: Law and Economic Approaches
Pınar Akman

The Competitive Effects of Minority Shareholdings: Legal and Economic Issues
Panagiotis Fotis and Nikolaos Zevgolis

The More Economic Approach to EU Antitrust Law
Anne C Witt

Private Power, Online Information Flows and EU Law
Angela Daly

The Role of Competitors in the Enforcement of State Aid Law
Fernando Pastor-Merchante

The Legality of Bailouts and Buy Nationals: International Trade Law in a Crisis
Kamala Dawar

A Critical Account of Article 106(2) TFEU

Government Failure in Public Service Provision

Jarleth M Burke

•HART•
OXFORD • LONDON • NEW YORK • NEW DELHI • SYDNEY

HART PUBLISHING
Bloomsbury Publishing Plc
Kemp House, Chawley Park, Cumnor Hill, Oxford, OX2 9PH, UK

HART PUBLISHING, the Hart/Stag logo, BLOOMSBURY and the Diana logo are trademarks of Bloomsbury Publishing Plc

First published in Great Britain 2018

A catalogue record for this book is available from the British Library.

Library of Congress Cataloging-in-Publication data

Names: Burke, Jarleth M., author.

Title: A critical account of Article 106(2) TFEU : government failure in public service provision.

Description: Oxford [UK] ; Portland, Oregon : Hart Publishing, 2018. | Series: Hart studies in competition law ; 18 | Includes bibliographical references and index.

Identifiers: LCCN 2017051089 (print) | LCCN 2017051855 (ebook) | ISBN 9781509912742 (Epub) | ISBN 9781509912759 (hardback : alk. paper)

Subjects: LCSH: Restraint of trade—European Union countries. | Trade regulation—European Union countries.

Classification: LCC KJE6428 (ebook) | LCC KJE6428 .B87 2018 (print) | DDC 343.2408—dc23

LC record available at https://lccn.loc.gov/2017051089

ISBN: HB: 978-1-50991-275-9
ePDF: 978-1-50991-273-5
ePub: 978-1-50991-274-2

Typeset by Compuscript Ltd, Shannon

For the Idea of the European Union

'The legitimate object of government is to do for a community of people whatever they need to have done but cannot do at all, or cannot do so well for themselves in their separate and individual capacities. In all that people can individually do for themselves, government ought not to interfere.'

Abraham Lincoln (1854)

FOREWORD

This is a remarkable book about a remarkable area of law.

Undertakings entrusted with 'services of general economic interest' (SGEIs) are exempt under Article 106(2) TFEU from Treaty rules, including the rules on competition, insofar as those rules would obstruct the specific tasks imposed on them by Member State measures. No other provision of the EU Treaties allows Member States to exempt any entity from EU law. (In the United States the state action doctrine is similar). The EU rule has limitations. It applies only to 'undertakings' (and not to regulatory bodies or social insurance funds based on solidarity). It applies only when the national measures have clearly imposed specific obligations on a particular enterprise so that the need for exemption from Treaty rules can be assessed. It does not apply merely because the enterprise is providing useful or necessary products or services. There must be a clear reason why the exemption is needed.

In practice, Article 106(2) has been held to apply in a variety of situations, even on financial grounds. It has been held, for example, to permit a monopoly that was said to be necessary to allow cross-subsiding of inherently unprofitable operations, and a monopoly for a waste disposal company given for a period long enough to ensure that it could expect to make a profit on its large initial capital investment.

EU Member States need to rely on Article 106(2) only if the monopoly in question would not otherwise be permitted under EU law. However, in some cases the states have argued that the monopoly or other measure is so obviously permitted by Article 106(2) that the question whether it would otherwise be permissible need not be decided. In each case the state needs to show that the task imposed could not be carried out, satisfactorily or at all, without the monopoly, that is, that there is no less restrictive way of achieving the desired result. States may be free to define not only the objective to be achieved, but also the means by which it is to be obtained, and the quality, conditions and price to be aimed at or required.

The European Commission has never had a clear and comprehensive understanding of Article 106(2). The Commission has never even asked the Member States to provide complete lists of what they regard as SGEIs. The Commission has not enforced Article 106(2) vigorously: many of the cases on its interpretation have arisen in national courts. The Commission has not integrated its interpretation of Article 106(2) with its practice under State aid rules: it has never challenged a statutory monopoly on the grounds that a State aid would be a more transparent and more competitive solution, and one that would reduce the need for regulatory surveillance.

In this book Jarleth Burke traces changes in the interpretation and application of Article 106(2), using both law and economics, to try to answer a number of important questions. He also raises a variety of other issues that have not been dealt with, fully or at all, in the Commission's statements. Is the application of Article 106(2) justified only if there would otherwise be a 'market failure', and if so, in what sense? (In the related area of State aid, the Commission uses the phrase very loosely, sometimes apparently meaning that something thought desirable is not happening fast enough.) The phrase is not useful if it can be applied to every unsatisfactory feature of a product or service, or if Member States are entirely free to require higher standards or lower prices in order to justify an SGEI.

Is the monopoly or other restrictive measure appropriate and necessary to achieve the desired objective, or is it misconceived and an example of 'government failure', a less familiar economic concept for most lawyers? How strictly have the requirements of Article 106(2) been applied, and how strictly should they be insisted upon? Should the standard of review be based only on 'manifest error'? Should the justification for a monopoly be reconsidered at intervals, in the light of changes in technology, in economic knowledge or in economic conditions? If so, should the monopoly, if it is still justified, be awarded on the basis of competitive tender, open to enterprises from all Member States? What, if anything, does EU law say about how monopolies under Article 106(2) should be regulated and supervised? Is it realistic to expect the European Court of Justice, without much help from the Commission, to deal satisfactorily with the economic issues raised by questions from national courts, and is it realistic to expect national courts to deal satisfactorily with the same issues without the help of the Commission? Is it a 'government failure' to set up a monopoly without regulating it effectively, and if so, is it a breach of EU law? Is it discriminatory to leave a monopoly indefinitely in the hands of one company (always in practice a company of the State in question) when the monopoly was not originally awarded on the basis of competitive tenders?

The author concludes, rightly, that the law is so uncertain that it is not possible to answer all these questions with confidence. But in discussing them so fully he has thrown much light on a very important, difficult, and controversial area of law and shown usefully how much more there is for the Commission to do in this area. He has also shown some of the relationships between Article 106(2), on the one hand, and the EU rules on State aids and imperative requirements in the general interest, on the other. The legal and economic issues he has raised are likely to arise in most cases involving Article 106(2) and the book enriches the debate and illustrates its complexity. It is particularly valuable because it integrates the legal and economic issues and is therefore useful to both lawyers and economists.

Dr John Temple Lang

PREFACE

Article 106(2) of the Treaty on the Functioning of the European Union serves as a legal crucible for the resolution of critical debates that rage in most Western democracies concerning the proper role of government. It provides that any other Treaty rule may be set aside or disapplied if that is necessary to sustain a Service of General Economic Interest. Article 106(2) concerns fundamental questions about what services the state should regulate or organise rather than relying on market mechanisms. That is a knotty problem—if not a central arena of contest in the domestic political realm—and it assumes even greater levels of difficulty in a quasi-federal system such as the EU. The fact that from the outset the Treaty of Rome even made provision for resolution of those difficulties through what is now Article 106(2) is a prominent example of the foresight of the EU's founders. More importantly, although largely left in abeyance for a long time, Article 106(2) is now routinely engaged and the judicial power frequently tasked with coming up with nuanced solutions to very difficult questions. We are well past treating these as political questions beyond the rule of law.

This book is about government failure in the creation, prohibition and regulation of markets. By government failure, I am referring to unwarranted departures from market mechanisms, which includes situations where regulation seeks to achieve a legitimate (non-market-provided) outcome but where the means used disrupt the functioning of markets in ways that are avoidable. Coming out of the global financial crisis, the role and efficacy of markets and that of economics as explaining their operation is contested now in ways that have not occurred since the Great Depression. Nevertheless, there is reason to be cautious. Markets are the subterranean but fundamental building block of the EU. Where a decision is made to depart from them, then the alternatives and their consequences need in-depth consideration. While our understanding of market failure may be evolving, the limits of government must always be kept foremost in mind. As Coase observed, ultimately, these are questions of selecting the better institutional choices where imperfections are inevitable.[1]

The primary goal of this book is to show the extent to which government failure is apparent in the regulation of public services under Article 106(2). That exemption may not appear significant, but considering that under Article 106(2), cartels may be tolerated, abuses of dominant positions excused, and subsidies that

[1] Coase, R, 'The Regulated Industries; Discussion with Ernest W Williams, Jr' (1964) 54(3) *The American Economic Review* 192–97.

amount to State aid sanctioned, the importance of this exemption will be apparent. Article 106(2) exemplifies a political concern about public services that is unique. To put that in the context of the current political manoeuvring over Brexit, where the violability of free movement principles has featured as part of that debate, by its terms Article 106(2) permits departures from those requirements and indeed any other Treaty rule, albeit under supervised conditions.

This book is an extended study of the limits of government through the prism of Article 106(2). It is, however, very much intended as a positive contribution to an enduring debate. Anybody concerned about equality and redistribution should be equally concerned about government failure in public service provision. Greater efficiency increases the potential for redistribution where that is favoured and justified. The fact that this potential is overlooked frequently is a symptom of the underlying degree of government failure: provider power endemic and the general interest frequently subverted. That is the polar opposite of what Article 106(2) is about.

At a time when the EU appears to move from one existential crisis to the next, this book is in part a reminder of its achievements. Even though the overall thrust of this book is critical (in the sense of urging better), it covers a vital and sophisticated area of EU intervention. Such an achievement is apparent in the Treaty rules concerning public services, or services of general economic interest, the umbrella term under EU law. No other political system has made such a sustained and intellectually coherent effort to tackle the trade-off between efficiency and equity in the realm of state action as an element of competition policy and enforcement. Commentators have often pointed out the unique nature of the EU's State aid rules as an important innovation building on traditional antitrust rules pioneered in the United States.[2] The law on Article 106(2) is an even more impressive creation. Before we criticise, it is necessary to understand, and with that understanding comes appreciation. The potential to do even better still remains and in this book I focus on some of the practicalities of doing so.

The writing of this book would not have been possible without the influence of many people whom I have had the pleasure of learning from and working with on regulatory issues. In that regard I am especially grateful to Bernard Amory, Kevin Barrins, Jim Bergeron, Vincent Brophy, Prof Martin Cave, Nick Cotter, Dr Cathal Guiomard (DCU), John Gunnigan, Oliver Hogan, Janet Li, Prof Douglas Lichtman (UCLA), Helen Martin, Prof Linda Mulcahy (LSE), Dr Alison Oldale, Nigel Pleming QC, Bill Prasifka, Dr Andrew Scott (LSE), Dr John Temple Lang, Noel Travers SC, Alexandre Verheyden and Prof George Yarrow (RPI).

Dr John Temple Lang provided early encouragement for this work and has also written the incisive foreword to this book, for which I am most grateful. I would

[2] See generally, Santa Maria, A, *European Economic Law* 3rd edn (Wolters Kluwer, 2014) 477–80, who is somewhat ambivalent on the strategic value of the innovation, whatever its intellectual sophistication.

also like to thank Prof Pablo Íbañez Colomo for giving this book vital impetus at the London School of Economics, and for his constant attention and invaluable direction. I would also like to express my sincere thanks to Jose Luis Buendía Sierra and Leigh Hancher, each pre-eminent in this field, both for their observations on my work and for their encouragement to express myself fully. Similarly, this book would also not have been possible without Sinéad Maloney and her team at Hart, including Emily Braggins.

Finally, I must say a final thank you to my family in Mayo and Dublin, for all of their help and support. In particular, I would like to thank my parents, Michael and Anne, who made a crucial contribution in the early days to making this work possible. For Elliot and Linus who have been in our family since the beginning of this project, it has been so much more fun with you both on the team! Equally, none of this would have been possible without the constant understanding, support and patience of my wife, Susan. Grá chugat go deo!

Cape Canaveral
30 October 2017

CONTENTS

CASE LAW, COMMISSION DECISIONS, LEGISLATION, EU DOCUMENTS, OTHER DOCUMENTS

Case Law

EU Courts

EFTA Court Judgments

United States Court Judgments

European Commission Decisions

(By decision number)

EU Legislation

EU Notices, Recommendation, Reports and other Documents

National Official Documents

Other Papers and Documents

1

In the General Interest?

A. Introduction

This book is about failings in the organisation and provision of public services and how, in particular, they are not corrected by EU law. It explores government failure in public service provision through Article 106(2) of the Treaty on the Functioning of the European Union (TFEU).[1] Article 106(2) TFEU provides that any Treaty rule, including those concerning competition and free movement, may be disapplied for a service of general economic interest (SGEI). Although the concept of SGEI is wider that 'public services', the terms are used interchangeably very often. In very broad terms, the concept of government failure concerns situations where state interventions in markets are not necessary or are ineffectual in terms of the trade-off between cost and benefit, including as to competitive distortions.[2] It is most apparent in this context through inefficient delivery of public services.

Article 106(2) provides:

> Undertakings entrusted with the operation of services of general economic interest or having the character of a revenue-producing monopoly shall be subject to the rules contained in the Treaties, in particular to the rules on competition, in so far as the application of such rules does not obstruct the performance, in law or in fact, of the particular tasks assigned to them. The development of trade must not be affected to such an extent as would be contrary to the interests of the Union.

By its terms, Article 106(2) is concerned with mediating between all other Treaty provisions and the realisation by the Member States of objectives in the general interest. According to the Commission in 2000, Article 106(2) is the central provision for reconciling Member State and EU interests with respect to SGEIs.[3]

[1] This will be referred to as 'the TFEU' and 'the Treaty' throughout this book. This book concerns SGEIs and does not cover 'revenue producing monopolies'.

[2] See generally, Wolf Jr, C, 'A Theory of Nonmarket Failure: Framework for Implementation Analysis' (1979) 22(1) *Journal of Law and Economics* 107–39 and Le Grand J, 'The Theory of Government Failure' (1991) 21 *British Journal of Political Science* 424–42.

[3] Commission Communication [2001] OJ C17/04, p 4, §19. This formulation by the Commission appears to be an adapted version of the Court of Justice's observation in C-202/88 *France v Commission* [1991] ECR I-1223 to the effect that: 'In allowing derogations to be made from the general rules of the Treaty on certain conditions, that provision seeks to reconcile the Member State's interest in using certain undertakings, in particular in the public sector, as an instrument of economic or fiscal policy with the Community's interest in ensuring compliance with the rules of competition and the preservation of the unity of the Common Market', §12.

Echoing that view, in *Altmark*, Advocate General Léger identified Article 106(2) as the lynchpin provision within the Treaty for the reconciliation of economic and social goals, stating that

> Article [106] of the Treaty, and in particular Article [106(2)], is the central provision for reconciling the Community objectives, including those of competition and internal market freedoms on the one hand, with effective fulfilment of the mission of general economic interest entrusted by the public authorities on the other hand.[4]

The Court of Justice has frequently referred to Article 106(2) as a significant exception to the Treaty, and as such, one that is to be interpreted strictly. This began with the judgment of the Court in 1973 in *BRT v SABAM II*, and has been repeated at regular intervals ever since.[5] Although the initial characterisation of Article 106(2) as strict was particular to the entrustment requirement, it was confirmed as applying to Article 106(2) in all of its facets in 1997.[6] A generally strict disposition is an unsurprising reaction to a provision that by its terms may sanction the disapplication of any other Treaty provision.[7] Yet, as I will demonstrate, Article 106(2)'s application has evolved to the point where very significant instances and degrees of government failure are tolerated routinely. That indulgence operates through exemptions from fundamental Treaty provisions and takes effect in sub-optimal public service organisation and provision.

In its operation, Article 106(2) raises two distinct sets of challenges. The first is one of qualification, and it concerns what activities warrant treatment as SGEIs. Given that it is axiomatic that the Member States have a right of initiative over the formulation and scope of SGEIs, the question of the appropriate level of supervision by the EU has raised acute difficulties. That process is referred to as 'SGEI verification' in this book. The second is the question of whether and to what extent an exemption from other Treaty provisions is necessary once the existence of an SGEI is verified or goes uncontested. That is referred to as 'disapplication review' in this book.[8] As worded, there are no limits under Article 106(2) to what rules may be jettisoned, either in whole or in part, including those normally applying in relation to competition and free movement.

[4] Opinion of AG Léger of 19 March 2002 in C-280/00 *Altmark* [2003] ECR I-07747, §80.

[5] C-127/73 *BRT v SABAM II* [1974] ECR-313, §19. See also C-242/95 *GT-Link* [1997] ECR I-4449, §50 and C-340/99 *TNT Traco* [2000] ECR I-4109, §56.

[6] C-157/94 *Commission v Netherlands* [1997] ECR I-5699, §37.

[7] Baquero Cruz has pointed out that initially, the strict exception moniker was applied to the formal requirements of Art 106(2), in particular, with respect to the entrustment requirement, before morphing into a description for the operation of the provision in all of its facets (Baquero Cruz, J, 'Beyond Competition: Services of General Interest and European Community Law' in de Búrca (ed), *EU Law and the Welfare State: In Search of Solidarity* (Oxford University Press, 2005) 176.

[8] While there are some situations where the splitting of Art 106(2)'s operation between SGEI verification and disapplication review is difficult (especially where the framing of the intervention is inextricably bound up with the SGEI), this dichotomy does reflect the mechanical essentials of Art 106(2).

This work offers a legally driven but economics-informed demonstration of government failure in the operation of Article 106(2). The demonstration of government failure in SGEI verification takes place by focusing on the extent to which the feasibility of market provisioning is taken into account. That may require verification of whether there are any disabling market failures of other impediments to the realisation of the general interest. By contrast, the demonstration of government failure in disapplication review focuses on the extent to which the principles of transparency, necessity and efficiency are upheld when Article 106(2) is used to justify an exemption from other provisions of the Treaty. Those demonstrations are presaged by a detailed account of the extent to which Article 106(2)'s application is contested, its applicability undercut by competing Treaty derogation mechanisms, and in some cases its subordination. Collectively, those phenomena are referred to throughout this work as 'contingency', which I introduce as a new way of understanding the operation of Article 106(2).

The elements of this chapter are as follows. I first set out the nature of the problem of government failure in SGEI organisation and provision (abbreviated to 'provision' in this book). I then explain the mechanics of Article 106(2) in terms of its various tests, bearing in mind that it is framed with reference to an 'undertaking' entrusted with an SGEI. I then provide a primer on the concept of government failure and give an indication of the cost of government failure in the provision of SGEIs, both at the macro and the micro level. I conclude with a summary of the objectives, approach and elements of the overall work.

B. The Nature of the Problem

The classic situation where Article 106(2) comes into play typically involves a Member State deciding to intervene in an area of its economy, choosing a particular means to do so and being faced either in advance of implementation or after the fact with objections that competition has been ousted or distorted or that free movement has been adversely affected. Assuming that the subject matter of the intervention concerns an SGEI (the constellation of which is unlimited) then on paper Article 106(2) provides the framework for resolution of those concerns and challenges. As part of that process, attention will come to bear not just on the nature and legitimacy of the Member State intervention, but also on the means that are chosen to bring about particular outcomes.

The debate concerning the qualification of services as SGEIs and in turn their effect on the operation of other Treaty provisions has been an enduring political and legal controversy in EU law. In part, that is because the demarcation between state and market is continuously in flux, with SGEIs often positioned at their intersection. Leading commentators on Article 106(2) have described it as 'a flashpoint for the tensions resulting from the shifting balance between the regime for undertakings subject to the competition rules, and the public interest exceptions thereto'.[9] In less dramatic but equally revealing terms, the Court of Justice has explained that

> Article [106(2)] seeks to reconcile the Member States' interest in using certain undertakings, in particular in the public sector, as an instrument of economic or fiscal policy with the Community's interest in ensuring compliance with the rules on competition and the preservation of the unity of the common market.[10]

The case law on what amounts to an SGEI is disparate and in some respects confused.[11] This is not altogether surprising considering that the Treaty simply refers to 'services of general economic interest' without further elaboration.[12] On several occasions, the European Courts have asserted the lack of controlling principles over the concept of SGEI. In 2008 the General Court sought to summarise the position concerning the nature of eligible general interests in *BUPA* as follows: 'there is no clear and precise regulatory definition of the concept of an SGEI mission and no established legal concept definitively fixing the conditions that must be satisfied …'.[13] Inevitably perhaps, given the claimed lack of controlling principles, it has been held that Member States are only subject to control for manifest error in deciding that a particular service is an SGEI.[14] That raises the vexed issue of how supervision for manifest error works in practice, since even marginal control presupposes some limiting principles, however attenuated.

The position with respect to disapplication review, namely the process by which a decision is taken under Article 106(2) that other Treaty rules need not be complied with has proven to be equally problematic. Article 106(2) has been the subject of a myriad of irreconcilable claims. It has been argued that it does not necessarily incorporate necessity review and alternatively, that necessity review under Article 106(2) is effectively equivalent to the position with respect to derogations from the fundamental Treaty freedoms.[15] At the same time, the intensity of proportionality review is extensively debated with claims that the least restrictive means must be deployed, and counterclaims that even if it must, that

[9] See, Sauter, W and Schepel, H, '"State" and "Market" in the Competition and Free Movement Case Law of the EU Courts' (2007) 024 *TILEC Discussion Paper* 124.

[10] C-159/94 *Commission v France* [1997] ECR I-5815, §55.

[11] Cases are characterised by cursory analysis of whether there is an SGEI, with a tendency towards declaratory statements by the Court of Justice. See, for example, C-320/91 *Corbeau* [1993] ECR I 2533, §14 and C-475/99 *Ambulanz Glöckner* [2001] ECR I-8089, §55, where the Court makes peremptory findings accepting postal and ambulance services respectively as SGEIs.

[12] Usually both the EU Courts and the Commission tend, where possible, to avoid trying to take any position on whether a particular activity is an SGEI. See Buendía Sierra JL, 'Article 106—Exclusive or Special Rights and other Anti-Competitive State Measures' in Faull and Nikpay (eds), *The EU Law of Competition*, 3rd edn (Oxford University Press, 2014) 850.

[13] T-289/03 *BUPA* [2008] ECR-81, §165. By way of disclosure, the author acted as one of BUPA's counsel in that case and in the prior administrative procedure before the European Commission.

[14] T-17/02 *Fred Olsen* [2005] ECR II-2031, §216. See also T-289/03 *BUPA*, §166.

[15] The former is argued for in Baquero Cruz (n 7) 195–96. As to the latter, see *Livret A et Livret Bleu*, Commission Decision of 10 May 2007, 2110 final, §146.

requirement applies exceptionally, only.[16] Complicating matters further is the interchanging of terminology and inconsistency in its use, most particularly as between necessity and proportionality review under Article 106(2).

An interesting example of the complexity and sensitivity of what comes under the microscope of Article 106(2) is provided by social housing. Surprisingly perhaps, this field has been the subject of a number of interventions by the European Commission and by the EFTA (European Free Trade Association) Court.[17] The decision of the European Commission in *Dutch Social Housing* is revealing both as to the sensitivity of SGEI verification and disapplication review, which in that matter were fungible to a degree.[18] Dutch housing associations were the recipients of direct and indirect support ranging from special access to land through to favourable state-backed lending and guarantees. The Netherlands was planning €750 million in additional support for this sector over 10 years through loan grants and guarantees for housing foundations. In the background there were allegations of significant competitive distortions in the private rental sector. Those concerns were based on claims of diversification by social housing foundations into other activities, resulting in housing associations competing to provide higher-end accommodation at deflated prices.

In discussions with the Commission concerning the existing system and the planned aid, the Netherlands took the position that although the housing was social, it was not necessarily confined to the assistance of people based on financial circumstances. The Dutch authorities considered that they could take into account the desirability of ensuring a spread of ages and means so as to avoid ghettoisation. A seeming obstacle in that regard was the 2005 SGEI Decision, which created an unlimited exemption for social housing activities, qualified as an SGEI by the Member State.[19] As against that, recital 16 limited eligibility to 'solvability' constraints, suggesting that aspects of Dutch policy could not be accommodated within the 2005 decision. Nevertheless, following negotiations, the Commission

[16] This difficulty is by no means unique to Art 106(2). For a comprehensive but succinct overview of this problem generally, including as to the position concerning SGEIs, see Sauter, W, 'Proportionality in EU Law—a Balancing Act' (2013) *Cambridge Yearbook of European Legal Studies* 439–66.

[17] *Dutch Social Housing* C(2009) 9963 final. Judgment of the EFTA Court in Case E-4/97 *Norwegian Bankers' Association v EFTA Surveillance Authority* of 3 March 1999 and Case E-9/04 *The Bankers' and Securities' Dealers Association of Iceland v EFTA Surveillance Authority* of 7 April 2006. In both cases the EFTA Court applied Art 59(2) of the EFTA Agreement, which is modelled on Art 106(2). In E-4/97, the EFTA Court upheld the SGEI claim but annulled the underpinning EFTA decision by reason of a failure to consider the development of trade requirement adequately. See §§67–70. In E-9/04, the EFTA Court again upheld the underlying SGEI, but annulled the decisions, this time on doubts concerning proportionality, which it found to warrant a full investigation. These were focused on open-ended eligibility criteria, and as such, might be better understood as going to the validity of the underlying SGEI. See §§77–79.

[18] State Aid No E/2005 and N 642/2009—*Dutch Social Housing* C(2009) 9963 final. On 30 August 2010, the Commission adopted Decision C(2010) 5841 final, relating to State aid E 2/2005, which amended the previous decision with respect to guarantees.

[19] See Commission Decision 2005/842/EC of 28 November 2005. Art 2(1)(b) appeared to give the Member States SGEI designation decision to the Member State, entirely.

agreed that Article 106(2) applied, but only after significant alterations to eligibility criteria. In addition to agreeing to cap the income level for qualification for social housing by reference to the trigger for other entitlements under the Dutch welfare system, the Netherlands also agreed that 90 per cent of rented accommodation would be allocated to persons with taxable income below a specified amount, meaning that only 10 per cent could be allocated based on other criteria, which were required to be transparent and determined in advance.

The Commission's stance has been criticised on the basis of insufficient deference to the Member State's choices as to domestic social policy.[20] In particular, there is the problem of how to trade off the relative weightings of a policy as between redistributive and other goals. What, for example, would the position have been if the Netherlands had insisted on much higher allocation levels that were not income determined? Would it have been sufficient if the criteria were objective and somehow constraining or would it have mattered if by way of achieving a balanced social mix, that alternative basis of allocation was entirely open? In reality, it may have been impossible for the Dutch government to achieve the reforms that were definitely necessary to a certain degree without the Commission's stance. This would not be the first case of the solution to domestic government failure having to be seen to come from Brussels, if only to give it extra political heft, while providing a convenient alibi for a Member State government.[21]

C. The Mechanics of Article 106(2)

1. Services of General Economic Interest

On its face, the task of interpreting Article 106(2), and in particular the concept of SGEI, appears to be similar to the challenge faced by the Court when interpreting the concept of 'State aid' in Article 107 or the term 'undertaking' as the lynchpin concept for the Treaty rules on competition. There is, however, a particular

[20] See, Drijber, 'SGEI and Social Housing, Presentation at "One Year of Application of the New Package for Services of General Economic Interest"' Academy of European Law, Trier, 15 March 2013, notes on file with author and elements of the conference summarised in Hoornaert, L, Conference Report, *European State Aid Law Quarterly* 4 (2013) 773–77.

[21] The fact that the Netherlands offered to specify and limit eligibilities proved to be a significant point in a subsequent challenge before the General Court (following a reversal of an inadmissibility ruling) in T-202/10 *Stichting Woonlinie v Commission* ECLI:EU:T:2015:287. The General Court not only refused to attribute eligibility restrictions to the Commission as an element of control for manifest error, but went further and declined to treat the Commission as having implicitly found that the pre-existing system could not qualify as an SGEI on the basis of manifest error. See §§54–63. The General Court's judgment was annulled and again remitted to it in a further appeal to the Court in C-414/15 P *Stichting Woonlinie* ECLI:EU:C:2017:215. The Court emphasised that ultimately commitments were made binding and accepted by the Commission and that given the monitoring system for existing aids the General Court was wrong not to deal with claims by the beneficiaries that the Commission had abused its powers by effectively requiring a new definition of social housing when no manifest error with respect to its previous specification had been disclosed.

challenge presented by Article 106(2) given that the term 'general economic interest' is inherently open ended.[22] As a matter of practicality, Member States are usually responsible for the organisation of public services that frequently qualify as SGEIs. In addition, the concept is necessarily dynamic, giving evolving social, economic and technological conditions.[23] SGEI policy may exhibit preferences that are unique to certain Member States, in particular concerning the achievement of distributional or cohesion objectives. As such, arguments for a 'national' or 'communautaire' approach to the concept of SGEI appear to be finely balanced.[24] While the communautaire approach to SGEI definition has never been in the ascendancy, it has been necessary to stipulate at least some minimal level of control over Member State SGEI claims. That has taken the form of the manifest error test.[25] The challenge is that to be meaningful, that test needs to have some substantive content, in respect of which neither the Commission nor the European Courts have been forthcoming.

In line with the open-ended nature of the general interest capable of qualification under Article 106(2), there has been little judicial guidance as to the essential attributes of an SGEI. Writing in 1999, Hancher maintained that the Court has never offered a general definition and prefers a 'casuistic approach', a position that has not changed all that much since then.[26] Exceptionally, the Court's 1991 judgment in *Porto di Genova* hints at a possible market failure perspective informing its approach to SGEI claims.[27] The context was a dispute over the allocation of exclusive loading and unloading rights for cargo at that port, which was argued to be an SGEI. The Court rejected the claim summarily on the basis that this activity did not 'exhibit special characteristics as compared with the general economic interest of other economic activities …'.[28] In conventional terms *Porto di Genova* might also be understood as referring to activity that on

[22] There are some parallels between this question and the issue in US constitutional law about whether activity is sufficiently affected by a public interest so as to justify certain kinds of intervention. See in that regard *Munn v Illinois* 94 U.S. 113 (1876) 126–127, which relies on old English precedent as to whether a matter is exclusively one *juris privati*. Interestingly, in that case the Court's underlying concern appeared to relate to the possible exercise of market power. That was regarded as a sufficient public interest to avoid a taking claim with respect to property rights. US law, however, recognises a distinction between classic police powers (which, significantly, are taken to include licensing and authorisation) and other regulatory interventions, including price regulation, which in the *Lochner* era were more at risk of invalidation. See *Lochner v New York*, 198 U.S. 45 (1905). That position was significantly diluted after the New Deal.

[23] C-18/88 *GB-Inno-BM* [1991] ECR I-5941, §16.

[24] Buendía Sierra argues that the tension between the 'national' and '*communautaire*' approaches to SGEI definition is more notional than real, while noting a pronounced tendency on the part of the European Courts to accommodate Member State claims with respect to the existence of SGEIs. See Buendía Sierra JL, *Exclusive Rights and State Monopolies under EC Law* (Oxford University Press, 2000) 279–83.

[25] This, it should be noted, is the standard applied by the Commission to Member State SGEI claims in the context of State aid assessment. While subsequent review by the General Court of those decisions is also on the basis of that standard, in practice that review needs to be fuller if it is to be meaningful.

[26] Hancher, L, 'Community State, State, and Market' in Craig and de Búrca (eds), *The Evolution of EU Law* (Oxford University Press, 1999) 726.

[27] C-179/90 *Porto di Genova* [1991] ECR I-5889.

[28] ibid, §27.

account of a particular regulatory overlay, for example a requirement of service provision on uniform terms, qualifies as an SGEI. Alternatively, in referring to special characteristics of dock services, the Court may also have been alluding to the lack of inherent market failures in that activity that prevent their operation at optimum efficiency. Despite regular quotation in subsequent case law, the Court's pithy comparison in *Porto di Genova* has never been elaborated upon.[29]

Part of the reason for the Court not having expanded upon the meaning of 'special characteristics' can be understood on the basis that in many cases the acknowledgment of a particular intervention as being in the general interest may be a costless concession on the part of the Commission or the European Courts. An agnostic or at least accommodating approach to SGEI qualification may appear to be justified, especially in those cases where by reason of the lack of entrustment, Article 106(2) is ultimately found not to apply. Separately, both the Commission and the European Courts may prefer to concentrate scrutiny on the questions of necessity and proportionality. There are, however, significant dangers inherent in such an approach, not least since those tests are not as such concerned with verifying the existence or extent of an SGEI.[30] As a result, a distortion of competition may be permitted to some extent, even when there is no justification whatsoever for such an approach.

Finally, over time, the Court of Justice has also pioneered an approach to SGEI qualification based on the delivery of sufficient 'public' benefits, classically fulfilled by the making available of services on a ubiquitous basis. It entails that a generally identifiable portion of the population can avail itself of the SGEI. It reached its apotheosis in telecommunications in the form of Universal Service Obligations (USOs), typically comprising the provision of a basic level of service on a national basis subject to uniform terms. Despite that, and in the face of arguments that public benefits must be national in scope, both the Commission and the General Court, in particular, have sought to move away from a blanket universality requirement. As a result, the Commission has emphasised that an SGEI claim is perfectly viable, even where the service in question is local or regional.[31] There does, however, appear to be a minimum requirement as to standardised availability within the intended class of beneficiaries. That is reflected in the judgment of the General Court in *BUPA*, where it emphasised that all market participants were under a general obligation to contract, subject to meeting minimum requirements.[32] As a result, it did not matter that only half of the population availed itself of cover.[33]

[29] See, for example, C-266/96 *Corsica Ferries France* [1998] ECR I-3949, §45; T-157/01 *Danske Busvognmænd* [2004] ECR II-917, §84; C-1/12 *OTOC*, ECLI:EU:C:2013:127, §105.

[30] See Buendía Sierra (n 24) 280.

[31] This stems necessarily from the recognition of the role of local and regional governments in organising SGEIs within their functional areas. See White Paper on Services of General Interest, 12.05.2004, COM (2004) 374 final, sections 2.3, 3.1, 4.2.

[32] T-289/03 *BUPA* [2008] ECR II-81, §§163, 172.

[33] ibid, §§186–87.

2. Entrustment with Particular Tasks

The formal requirement, namely that there be an act of public authority, is evidential in nature since it assists with the isolation of particular tasks.[34] Marenco has maintained that 'the word "entrusted" further restricts the scope of the exception in so far as it requires that the Member States concerned should have mandated the undertaking for the operation of the service, in order to achieve specific results'.[35] Interpreted in this way, the key features of entrustment are specificity and compulsion brought about through an act of public authority. Constraining these requirements is the fact that SGEI organisation is the product of complex political, institutional and historical considerations. The modern regulatory state operates in a myriad of different ways, with responsibility for SGEI organisation frequently undertaken at different levels of government, and with many SGEIs organised locally.[36] In the light of that reality, both the Commission and the Court of Justice have approached the requirement for an act of public authority pragmatically, provided that the public authority is acting in an official capacity.[37] In its judgment in the *Electricity and Gas Cases*, the Court confirmed that neither legislation nor regulation was required for entrustment to be valid.[38]

Given the variety of governance models underpinning SGEI organisation, there are also very significant limitations on the ability of EU law to supervise the steps leading to entrustment. Consistent with that, the General Court has taken an equally pragmatic view of the iterative process that is likely to underpin entrustment.[39] That is best represented by its judgment in *Fred Olsen* in 2002.[40] There, the General Court refused to accept claims that entrustment had not been properly undertaken simply because the SGEI had its origins in a proposal from the entity subsequently selected as the service provider. The General Court reasoned that since the entrusted undertaking had (by necessity) to agree to be bound by the concession, it was unavoidably involved in the entrustment process. That did not mean that there was no longer an underlying public act.[41] The limited potential for penetrating the process behind entrustment is also apparent in light of the requirement put in place in the post-*Altmark* SGEI packages. Under the 2011 SGEI

[34] The requirement for an act of public authority was first stipulated in C-127/73 *BRT v SABAM II*, §20.

[35] Marenco, G, 'Public Sector and Community Law' (1983) 20 *CML Rev:* 495–527, 517.

[36] See Communication from the Commission, Services of General Interest in Europe, 11.09.1996, COM (96) 443 final, §9.

[37] See Buendía Sierra (n 12) 851.

[38] See among them, C-159/94 *Commission v France*, §66.

[39] For the argument that entrustment and the concept of SGEI have become impermissibly bound up with each other, see Wehlander, C, *Services of General Economic Interest as a Constitutional Concept in EU Law* (Springer, 2016) section 5.2.2.

[40] T-17/02 *Fred Olsen* [2005] ECR II-2031.

[41] ibid, §188.

Framework, Member States are simply 'encouraged' to consult widely with respect to the formulation of the SGEI mission.[42]

Instead of focusing on the entrustment process or taking a rigid view of the subsequent evidential act, a principal concern under EU law has been as to the verification of compulsion. As a result, both the Commission and the Court have ruled out mere approval or authorisation of specific activities as amounting to entrustment.[43] In *GVL* the Court emphasised the nature of supervision as decisive.[44] While the entrustment criterion was also the subject of extended debate before the General Court in *BUPA*, one of its conclusions, namely that sectoral legislation was capable of amounting to entrustment, is hardly controversial, even if that entailed some implicit rowing back on the position going back to *GVL*.[45]

3. Necessity

The use of the word 'obstruct' serves as the touchstone for determining the degree of incompatibility that must arise between the application of those rules and provision of a particular SGEI. As such, this is interpreted as the necessity test under Article 106(2).[46] Under its terms, Treaty rules may only be set aside 'in so far' as this is necessary, a phrase that seems to incorporate a proportionality standard. The difficulty of separating necessity and proportionality review stems from the fact that necessity review involves a consideration of the requirement for a given intervention. By contrast, proportionality review may identify a number of alternatives, each of which may be said to be necessary in a 'but for' sense (i.e. without it the SGEI would go unfulfilled) but where the distortive effects are very different. As a result, the question of necessity is always means specific, even if that is not always apparent in the deployment of Article 106(2).

The critical challenge presented by the necessity test is the degree of jeopardy that must be encountered by the SGEI provider in the fulfilment of the particular tasks that are assigned to it before the disapplication of other Treaty rules is regarded as warranted. The difficulty of the assessment is exemplified by the *Electricity and Gas Cases*.[47] These were enforcement proceedings against the Netherlands, Italy, France and Spain concerning exclusive production, import and export rights for electricity, and in one case, gas. The Court held that it would be sufficient to show

[42] European Union Framework for State Aid in the Form of Public Service Compensation [2012] OJ C8/03, §12.

[43] Commission Decision 85/77/EEC, *Uniform Eurocheques* [1985] OJ L35/43, §29.

[44] C-7/82 *GVL* [1983] ECR 483, §41. This upheld Commission Decision 81/1030/EEC.

[45] T-289/03 *BUPA* [2008] ECR II-81, §177–79.

[46] See, for example, the opinion of AG Léger in C-438/02 *Hanner* [2005] ECR I-4551, §§140–41, where he locates the necessity test in the use of the word 'obstruct' in Art 106(2) and the proportionality test in the words 'in so far as'.

[47] C-157/94 *Commission v Netherlands* [1997] ECR I-5699, C-158/94 *Commission v Italy* [1997] ECR I-5789, C-159/94 *Commission v France* [1997] ECR I-5815, C-160/94 *Commission v Spain* [1997] ECR I-5851.

that without the measures at issue, it would not be possible for the incumbents to perform the particular tasks assigned to them.[48] That did not entail proving that without the contested measure they would not be viable.[49] The Commission had argued that the defendants needed to demonstrate some type of financial imperilment absent the contested bans or less restrictive alternatives.[50]

It will be apparent that ultimately questions of necessity turn on complex financial assessments. The obstruction test is only capable of very rigorous deployment where reliable evidence gives the reviewing institution the necessary confidence that the effect of its intervention will not materially impact underlying SGEI provision. SGEIs are often important public services where an exacting assessment of necessity may be regarded as possibly compromising the continuity of essential services. That risk may have been a very significant subtext to the judgments of the Court of Justice in the *Electricity and Gas Cases*. These issues are considered further in Chapters 3 and 6.

4. Proportionality

The proportionality element of Article 106(2) is reflected in the words 'in so far as' since it is specified that the competition and other Treaty rules should only be displaced to the extent that it is necessary for the performance of the particular tasks.[51] In the opinion of former Competition Commissioner Karel Van Miert, proportionality review is usually the single most important issue in SGEI cases.[52] The express language of Article 106(2) appears to make some type of proportionality review inevitable, with debate focused on whether the standard is the same as for free movement or is *sui generis*. Consistent with that, Buendía Sierra has advanced the case for a global proportionality standard identical to that operating in the context of free movement, but with less rigorous scrutiny of special or exclusive rights.[53] By contrast, advancing a provocative and distinctly minority viewpoint, Baquereo Cruz has questioned whether proportionality review is actually a

[48] C-159/94 *Commission v France*, §95.

[49] ibid, §52.

[50] ibid, §93. With the benefit of hindsight, this was both unnecessary and unwise, especially considering likely judicial concern as to whether continuity of supply might be affected by striking down the national monopolies.

[51] Van Bael and Bellis suggest that the literal wording of the provision supports a construction that something beyond mere necessity (ie, without the measure at issue would the SGEI be assured?) but that the nature of the extra element is context specific. See Van Bael and Bellis, *Competition Law of the European Union*, 5th edn (Kluwer, 2010) 940–42.

[52] According to former Competition Commissioner Karel Van Miert, 'Le problème de l'article [106(2] du traité, s'il existe, est celui du contrôle de la proportionalité des moyens utilisés par les États membres ou par les entreprises pour assurer leur missions du intérêt général. La définition de ces missions n'a presque jamais fait l'objet de controverses'. Reproduced in Sauter and Schepel (n 9) from the original, 'Les mission d'interet general et l'article 90§2 du Traité CE dans la politique de la Commission' (1997) 2 *Il diritto dell'economia* 277, 280–81.

[53] See Buendía Sierra (n 12) 854–64.

prerequisite of Article 106(2) scrutiny in all cases.[54] He characterise the exemption as more of an 'on-off switch' and disapproves of any reflexive attribution of standard necessity and proportionality controls to its operation. Despite that, the case law evidences the existence of a distinct proportionality requirement, in the sense of focusing on alternative means, although as will be explored in detail in Chapter 6, there are many instances where proportionality review is missing from the Article 106(2) analysis. Based on those cases where proportionality review is at least referred to, there appears to be at least two standards. One of these is predicated on the adoption of the least restrictive means.[55] The alternative does not require this, provided that a selection is made among reasonable alternatives and as a result is not manifestly disproportionate.

Despite the Court of Justice's seeming insistence on less restrictive alternatives in *Dusseldorp*, on other occasions it has taken a deferential stance, even when presented with evidence that less restrictive alternatives may have achieved the general interest objective. That, for example, was the position in *Albany*, which concerned the provision of supplemental insurance cover in respect of which affiliation to designated sectoral funds had been made compulsory.[56] There, Advocate General Jacobs drew attention to evidence suggesting that in other sectors, general interest objectives akin to those imposed on the fund in *Albany* were being fulfilled on the basis of managed competition as opposed to the conferral of exclusive rights.[57] By contrast, in deferring to the means chosen, the Court emphasised the measure of discretion that the Member States had with respect to the operation of their social security systems.[58]

5. The Effect on the Development of Trade

The second sentence of Article 106(2) provides that 'the development of trade must not be affected to such an extent as would be contrary to the interests of the Union'. Leaving aside the difficulty of interpreting this sentence, there appears to be an in-built conflict between it and the first sentence of Article 106(2).[59] The latter is concerned with identifying to what extent Treaty rules, including those affecting trade, need to be curtailed in order to sustain a particular SGEI. If that determination is made, it is difficult to see what useful purpose is served by the final sentence of Article 106(2). Contrary to that, if it serves a distinct purpose

[54] Baquero Cruz (n 7) 195–96.

[55] See Buendía Sierra (n 24) 303–04.

[56] C-67/96 *Albany* [1999] ECR I-5751.

[57] Opinion of AG Jacobs in Joined Cases C-67/96 *Albany*; C-115/97 *Brentjens* [1999] ECR I-6025; and, C-219/97 *Drijvede Bokken* [1999] ECR I-6121 of 28 January 1999, §432.

[58] ibid, §122.

[59] There is also the difficult issue of the impact of the second sentence on the direct effect of Art 106(2), which is considered in Chapter 4. See in that regard a detailed consideration in Buendía Sierra (n 24) 346–52.

then that is not very apparent. As will be considered in Chapter 4, it was a factor in inhibiting the direct effect of Article 106(2).

In the *Electricity and Gas Cases* the Court reprimanded the Commission for having failed to outline how the development of trade might have been affected by the impugned restrictions.[60] Since the judgments in the *Electricity and Gas Cases* there has been no real judicial guidance on the meaning of the last sentence of Article 106(2).[61] As summarised by Advocate General Léger in *Wouters*, several Advocates General have tried to give some sense of what is entailed but that has not gone much beyond indications that the curtailment of Treaty rules should not have a 'substantial effect on intra-Community trade'.[62] For its part, however, occasionally the Commission has deployed the final sentence of Article 106(2) in a dynamic way, in particular by requiring the adjustment of mechanisms (for example reviewing the SGEI against ongoing market developments) as a condition of its approval of State aid.[63] Separately, the Commission has invoked the final sentence as justification for making non-compliance with secondary law lead to State aid being denied the benefit of Article 106(2).[64]

D. The Essence of Government Failure and its Cost

1. A Primer on the Concept of Government Failure

According to Winston, '[g]overnment failure ... arises when government has created inefficiencies because it should not have intervened (in the market) in the first place, or when it could have solved a given problem or set of problems more efficiently, that is by generating greater net benefits'.[65] Central to government failure in an economic context are concerns about both the efficiency and efficaciousness of interventions having regard to the underlying objectives, whether aimed at the resolution of classic market failures or the achievement of distributional goals.

Government failure, which is sometimes referred to as 'non-market failure', is a diverse school of scholarship, with political, economic and political economy strands. The most prominent of these is the political economy branch in the form

[60] §111.

[61] It is elaborated upon in very general terms in Commission Decision 91/50/EEC *Isselcentrale*, §47. It was also considered in *BUPA*, but only in a perfunctory way. See T-289/03 *BUPA*, §308.

[62] C-309/99 *Wouters* [2002] I-1577, Opinion of AG Léger, §166.

[63] For example, Commission Decision 2002/149/EC, *SNCM*, where the Commission stipulated that the nature of the PSO obligations be reassessed (and likely reduced) in the light of the greater provision of competing services. See §§117ff.

[64] See sections 18 and 19 of the 2011 SGEI Framework [2012] OJ C8/03. Although this was published in 2012, consistent with its title, this is referred to as the '2011 SGEI Framework' throughout this book.

[65] Winston, C, *Government Failure versus Market Failure* (AEI-Brookings Joint Centre for Regulatory Studies, 2006) 2–3.

of public choice theory.[66] It focuses on the underlying causes and manifestations of government failure and the probable divergence of democratically determined interventions from the economic prescriptions for the correction of market failure. Those are the situations recognised in neo-classic economics where markets either do not exist or where they do not perform at optimum efficiency. The public choice inspired strand of government failure involves the application of economic techniques to political decision making, was pioneered by the Virginia School, and formerly led by Buchanan and Tullock.[67] The Virginia School demonstrated how self-interest and the power of special interests within the political system might interfere with the realisation of general interest goals.[68] As such, it was very much concerned with explaining how self-interested actions by political actors can lead to wasteful intervention.

By contrast, the 'rent seeking' school of public choice focuses on the demonstration, quantification and study of the private benefits that may be extracted from political tampering with the operation of markets. It is best represented by Krueger, whose pioneering work showed that import quotas would, when the welfare loss of rent seeking is taken into account (i.e. lobbying both lawful and unlawful for a slice of the quota), equal that of a tariff system leading to the equivalent level of imports.[69] Krueger's work gave rise to a substantial literature on rent seeking and in particular how entrepreneurial effort comes to be wasted by seeking selective advantage within a system where competition takes place to enjoy the spoils of state restriction on competition.

In this book the concept of government failure is economic in nature and it focuses on the micro-economic aspects through an examination of the optimality of SGEI organisation and provision. Waste in public service provision through productive inefficiency is a significant problem. While productive inefficiency is one aspect of the problem, too often sight is lost of the fact that the underlying architecture of a public service may be highly sub-optimal. In that sense, productive efficiency can be something of a static concept that is configuration specific. As a result, the two other types of efficiency at the centre of economic analysis, namely allocative and dynamic efficiency, are part of this government failure critique of SGEI provision. Allocative efficiency is concerned with the convergence of price towards marginal cost, while dynamic efficiency concerns the capacity to break the efficiency frontier through new technology and modes of organisation. For those concerns to be reflected in the scrutiny of public services, the design of the SGEI and the relationship of means and objective must be interrogated very carefully.

[66] See generally, Velijanovski C, 'Economic Approaches to Regulation' in Baldwin, Cave and Lodge (eds), *The Oxford Handbook of Regulation* (Oxford University Press, 2010).

[67] For a general introduction to public choice, see Besley, T, *Principled Agents? The Political Economy of Good Government* (Oxford University Press, 2007).

[68] See, for example, Buchanan, J and Vanberg, V, 'The Politicisation of Market Failure' (1988) 57 *Public Choice* 101–13.

[69] Krueger, A, 'The Political Economy of the Rent Seeking Society' (1974) 64(3) *The American Economic Review* 291–303.

2. The Cost of Government Failure

As will be set out in Chapter 3, in particular, the system of controls operated under Article 106(2) is a matter of considerable legal complexity. In the face of that detail it is easy to lose sight of the underlying purpose, or to be more precise, the goal of controlling departures from the default fulfilment of the general interest through market mechanisms. The predominant purpose of SGEI organisation and provision is the pursuit of distributional objectives. Therefore, the extent to which the link between sub-optimal (including inefficient) SGEI provision and the better fulfilment of distributional goals is missed or deliberately disregarded is surprising. In fact, so ubiquitous is the provider-inspired and -determined account of public service provisions that arguments that more people could be better served or assisted at less cost are frequently missing from the debate. Instead, the provider perspective invariably converts private interests (those of the responsible organisation, their employees and political backers) into a putative public concern usually directed at opposing reform as yet another 'neoliberal' imposition. Certain constitutional additions at EU level, which are considered in Chapter 3, are stand-out examples of the success of that posture.

This work focuses on those public services that are treated as SGEIs, but I will also argue that many more should come within Article 106(2) with a view to controlling government failure. Many public services are provided by vertically integrated operators using outmoded service delivery models, more still are entirely unaccountable as to the nature of their output. Several have managed to avoid meaningful quality commitments while maximising monopoly pricing offset by tax-generated subsidies. Apart from sectors where there has been EU legislative intervention, many public services provided in Europe are not even the subject of the most rudimentary economic regulation. Frequently, there are no meaningful price controls but instead only ad hoc bartering as part of both periodic and opportunistic adjustments to prices. Often prices are set to extract monopoly rents, not expressed as profit but instead dissipated through gold plating and excessive remuneration.[70] In this context, it is difficult to emulate the observation of Rand and Entwistle that '[t]o reject the pursuit of efficiency as somehow anathema to the aims of government, is to ignore the interplay between democratic values and the hard facts of budgetary constraint and scarce resources that characterise the practice of public administration'.[71]

It is difficult to procure accurate figures on how much inefficiency in public service provision is costing European economies but there is reason to consider that it may be very considerable. Work by the European Central Bank has attempted to quantify the welfare loss attributable to inefficiency and in particular has estimated

[70] See Averch, J and Johnson, J, 'Behaviour of the Firm Under Regulatory Constraint' (1962) 52(5) *American Economic Review* 1052–69.

[71] Rand, A, and Entwistle T, *Public Service Efficiency: Reframing the Debate* (Routledge, 2014) 4.

the relative distortionary effects of associated tax-raising measures.[72] Although not offered as a reliable quantification of the actual loss, based on estimates for Portugal alone, the enormity of what is at stake is readily apparent. While the study finds that the distortive effects of funding taxes is very material relative to the underlying inefficiency, the data used to arrive at that conclusion with reference to input and output inefficiency in public service provision is striking. For 2000, the average input efficiency for 15 EU Member States was calculated such that 38.9 per cent more resources were being used on public sector output than necessary to provide the same level of public services.[73] While that data set is relatively old, it will be recalled that it comes in the wake of the first big wave of liberalisation, which saw the opening up of the telecommunications, postal and energy sectors, previously major bastions of public service provision.

What is considered at the macro level is perhaps the most convincing illustration of what is going wrong in public service provision. Yet, it is at the level of the individual that sub-optimal organisation and delivery of public service bites the most. Inefficiency will inevitably mean that individuals whom society has made a deliberate decision to assist may be entirely excluded from a service or find that it is provided on conditions that fail to meet their basic needs. Article 106(2) is by no means implicated in all or even most of that failure, but it is an important part of the overall equation. It offers a very interesting window into the underlying problem of government failure, primarily in terms of its interrogation of the delivery architecture and associated restriction of competition or distortions in trade inherent in the operation of public services. The concern to secure widely available, high-quality public services is taken as an uncontroversial political objective in many EU Member States. It is, however, very telling that perhaps the most penetrating analysis of the optimality or efficaciousness of what is planned or being done occurs not in national legislatures but often in Brussels and ultimately in Luxembourg.

E. This Book

1. Objectives

This book pioneers a new understanding of Article 106(2) in the 'law and economics' tradition. In particular, it proposes an understanding of a provision that in its deployment condones significant instances and degrees of

[72] European Central Bank, 'Excess Burden and the Cost of Inefficiency in Public Service Provision', Working Paper Series, no. 601/April 2006.

[73] This data was adapted from Alfonso, A, Schuknecht, L and Tanzi, V, 'Public Sector Efficiency: An International Comparison' (2005) 123(3–4) *Public Choice* 321–47. The underlying assessment appears broader than just public services and is definitely wider than SGEIs.

government failure. I aim to cut through the formalism that has obscured the understanding of Article 106(2) by combining a critical reading of the exception with an economics-informed deconstruction of its operation. In short, the justification for using a government failure approach is to be found in a teleological reading of the competition rules and a straightforward reading of Article 106(2)'s express terms. I propose an understanding of this derogation mechanism that is a direct challenge to form based accounts of Article 106(2) that tend to obscure the nature and extent of underlying government failure.

A curious feature of Article 106(2) is the number of myths and misconceptions that complicate its operation and cloud its comprehension. Article 106(2) is said to be strict and it is also claimed to be central, yet as to the verification of SGEIs, the General Court said that there are no controlling principles, while also acquiescing in the Commission's supervision on the basis of manifest error appraisal.[74] Intuitively, it may seem that all of these claims cannot hold true simultaneously, yet they remain largely unchallenged. In this book I do precisely that. Through the exposition of the nature and extent of government failure under Article 106(2), I will actively question concerns that EU law, and in particular the over-zealous application of Article 106(2), has jeopardised the provision of public services. Instead, I will argue that the operation of Article 106(2) permits significant inefficiency in SGEI provision, thereby subverting the achievement of distributional objectives frequently at the core of public services. That central finding is the basis of proposals that I make for the reorientation of Article 106(2) and related law.

2. Approach

I use a structured law and economics-type approach in order to expose the laxity of Article 106(2). That is accomplished under the rubric of government failure, which for these purposes is necessarily *sui generis* in its construction, but which is faithful to the fundamental concerns raised by the literature on government failure. More particularly government failure is concerned with both the justification for interventions in markets and separately, the nature of particular intervention, including the possibility of more efficacious alternatives.[75] These are the critical questions that arise in the application of Article 106(2). In this book I draw on fundamental precepts of the scholarship on government failure to construct a version of government failure that can be used to interrogate Article 106(2) in a meaningful way. My focus is very much on the 'how' of government failure, but with exposure of the 'why' where that can be discerned with conviction. That is not altogether obvious or apparent in many instances, but nevertheless, certain alignments in terms of interests and outcomes are apparent. In that regard, greater

[74] T-289/03 *BUPA* [2008] ECR II-81, §165.
[75] See generally, Wolf, Jr (n 2) 107–39 and Le Grand (n 2) 424–42.

focus and insistence on transparency, particularly in the formulation of policy, may be the best disinfectant from a government failure perspective.

Government failure scholarship is focused on whether government intervention in an economy is warranted and effective in the sense of being fit for purpose. I argue that it is axiomatic that the justification for any given action be tested based on how a market does and will perform relative to a specified objective that is outcome defined. This is what I refer to as 'market feasibility'. If markets are delivering on the relevant general interest (ie, political objectives), or are set to do so within a relatively short period, or are to or may do so to a significant degree, then there is no case for intervention. Certainly, that is what one might expect the position to be with respect to SGEI verification under Article 106(2). Although at first blush, market feasibility may appear to be market counterfactual testing, the proposed approach ranges more widely and may necessitate the identification of disabling market failures. In addition, the question may need to be asked whether even with intervention a given objective may be realised feasibly to any significant extent.

There may, of course, be a range of situations where on account of pre-existing conditions, markets will not perform optimally or may even fail to exist entirely. Neoclassical economics provides a comprehensive account of those problems (where allocative, productive and dynamic efficiency is not achieved) through the theory of market failure.[76] As a result, an important line of inquiry in SGEI verification is to determine whether non-realisation of a particular general interest objective is by reason of the existence of a disabling market failure. This work incorporates the concept of market failure as a critical element of the overall exposition of government failure.

Aspects of the tests that he then goes on to advocate may be taken to reflect a concern to avoid government failure through an emphasis on competitive solutions. In his 2008 normative account of Article 106(2), Sauter suggests that market failure 'and/or government failure' would be a logical starting point in defining the scope of the SGEI and USO obligations.[77] While aspects of the tests that he then goes on to advocate may be taken to reflect a concern to avoid government failures (in particular, the emphasis on the implementation of competitive solutions), they are not tested against case law and practice under Article 106(2). Separately, Hancher and Sauter have suggested possible reliance on the concept of government failure for the purposes of proportionality review, but that is in the context of the free movement derogations.[78] Finally, Ølykke and Møllgaard's 2013 account of what an SGEI is also raises the possible relevance of government failure with respect to the pursuit of the most efficient policy for SGEI delivery but is not taken forward

[76] See generally, Ledyard, J, 'Market Failure', in Durlauf and Blume (eds), *The New Palgrave Dictionary of Economics* (online edition, 2008).

[77] Sauter, W, 'Services of General Economic Interest and Universal Service in EU Law' (2008) 33(2) *European Law Review* 167–93, 167.

[78] Hancher, L and Sauter, W, 'One Step Beyond? From Sodemare to Docmorris: The EU's Freedom of Establishment Case Law Concerning Health Care' (2010) 47 *CML Rev* 117–46, 144.

by them considering their principal focus.[79] This and other SGEI-related analytical theories are considered in detail in Chapter 3.

A key characteristic of this work is the adaption of government failure scholarship to the mechanics of Article 106(2). That is especially necessary for the exposure of government failure in disapplication review. Government failure scholarship is diffuse and is more weighted towards the modelling and diagnosis of underlying causes of failure (particularly in the correction of market failures) having regard to political incentives than with cataloguing its instances.[80] In comparison with market failure theory, which this work subsumes within a broader market feasibility test, the demonstration of government failure in disapplication review has required greater adaption to the peculiarities of Article 106(2)[81] Despite that, the experience from State aid, and in particular the theoretical underpinnings of the Refined Economic Approach (REA) provide an example of a very closely related field where a concern to prevent and mitigate government failure is manifest.

Through exposing the extent of government failure in Article 106(2), this work will debunk the myth of Article 106(2) as a strict exception. Despite Article 106(2) being routinely styled as such, it will become apparent that absolute strictness was never possible. Even when a lesser but still exacting form of strictness was feasible, judicial timidity took hold, in the process leading to greater and greater degrees of market failure being tolerated in respect of public services under Article 106(2). More recently and in the light of detailed implementation of the *Altmark* criteria by the Commission, a concern to prevent and mitigate government failure is more apparent. Nevertheless, considerable weaknesses remain, which will only ever be resolved if the political deliberations around SGEI organisation and delivery are much more faithful to the specification and safeguarding of the general interest. That is precisely what Article 106(2) requires.

3. Elements

Given the centrality of government failure to this work, the next chapter is an extended consideration of that concept, relevant scholarship and suggested adaptions of it so as to inquire into the extent of government failure under Article 106(2). That is then laid beside a consideration of the scope and purpose of Article 106(2)'s inclusion in a wider Treaty scheme that presupposes market mechanisms as a default. That grounds my fundamental argument that in teleological terms, Article 106(2) makes most sense if understood as a constitutional guard against government failure. I then take that contention forward to demonstrate how SGEI verification makes most sense if approached on the basis

[79] Ølykke, G and Møllgaard, P, 'What is a Service of General Economic Interest?' (1 Dec 2013) Online *European Journal of Law and Economics*, section 2.7.

[80] For an exposition of suboptimal political correction of a negative externality using the tax system, see Buchanan J, 'Market Failure and Political Failure' (1988) 8(1) *Cato Journal* 1–13.

[81] As a result, it is questionable whether government failure constitutes a unitary 'theory'.

of testing market feasibility, including, if relevant, the investigation of possible market failures. Supplementing this, the task of disapplication review within a government failure construct requires particular adaption to the mechanics of Article 106(2). I tackle this thorough the identification of transparency and proof, necessity and proportionality, and finally, efficiency, in order to reveal the nature of the underlying failures.

I then provide 'internal' and 'external' accounts of Article 106(2) in Chapters 3 and 4, respectively. These provide essential background for the detailed exposition of government failure toleration under Article 106(2) that follows. By an internal account of Article 106(2), I am referring to a stand-alone consideration of the provision. In providing an internal account, which includes an exposition of the mechanics of Article 106(2), I also address just how politically contested Article 106(2) has been for so long. By contrast with that, the external account of Article 106(2) dissects the interaction of Article 106(2) with other TFEU derogation mechanisms. The external account of Article 106(2) demonstrates the ways in which Article 106(2) is sidelined by other Treaty derogation mechanisms and by judicial inventions such as the exercise of public authority and the solidarity exemption. The external account discloses the ubiquitous contingency of Article 106(2). Overall, it is not surprising that a provision mired in that kind of institutional and constitutional controversy should tolerate so much government failure in its operation.

In Chapter 5 I demonstrate government failure in SGEI verification by focusing on the general position under Article 106(2) as well as by means of a particular focus on telecommunications, environmental protection and broadcasting. Those sectors were chosen because of the mix of efficiency- and distributional-type issues that arise when SGEI claims are made. In Chapter 6 I provide a demonstration of government failure in disapplication review. It divides the operation of Article 106(2) into three broad phases demarcated by the *Corbeau* and *Altmark* judgments. In *Corbeau* the Court of Justice was confronted with how the delivery of a traditional SGEI, namely postal services, should be balanced with the accommodation of competitive entry. Within those phases the treatment of transparency, the demonstration of necessity and efficiency concerns are all tracked under Article 106(2) with a view to highlighting the extent to which government failure is tolerated in its operation.

Finally, in Chapter 7, I draw together the major findings of this work. It includes suggestions for a possible reorientation in Article 106(2) (and related law), and a redefinition of what SGEIs entail, if it is to operate as a more effective check on government failure in the organisation and delivery of public services.

2

The Pathology of Government Failure

A. Introduction

By its terms Article 106(2) discloses a concern that in reconciling the operation of market forces and public service provision Member States may strike that balance in ways that are inimical to the interests of the EU. Since in essence Article 106(2) is concerned with how markets or their operation are ousted or their outcomes adjusted, it invites a detailed understanding of the limits of both markets and intervention.

The limits of markets may be understood from a number of different perspectives. One starting point is to consider what neoclassical economic thought identified as shortcomings that would make their full efficiency potential elusive. That takes the form of the theory of market failure, which, as will be considered, creates a relatively limited set of reasons for state intervention so that efficiency is maximised. Alternatively, in the socialist tradition, the potential for significant differences between people in terms of income and resources is identified as a key equality failing. In the form of a planned economy, the issue was reduced to deciding what economic outcomes should be, with production and regulation then organised and structured so as to attempt to bring those outcomes about. Much more representative of mainstream European political consensus is an intermediate approach that takes or assumes markets as a default form of economic organisation but which, based on political deliberations, intervenes in certain situations to secure specific outcomes.

The limits of intervention in markets can be understood by reference to the concept of government failure. In very general terms, government failure is concerned with how government interventions in any sphere of its activities are ineffectual or suboptimal.[1] In the economic sphere, it may result in avoidable inefficiencies, often arising from the exclusion or restriction of competition. Separately, excess resources may be consumed in the realisation of the underlying objective. Very frequently those imperfections undermine the efficacy or scope of the underlying objective, which in many cases may be distributional. In that

[1] For a general introduction to the concept of government failure, see Orbach, B, 'What Is Government Failure?' (2013) online, 30(44) *Yale Journal on Regulation*.

regard, and as I will demonstrate, government failure scholarship with a focus on microeconomic issues ranges more widely than an assessment of government efforts to resolve classic market failures. That is important considering the range of general interests capable of being accommodated under Article 106(2), which in many cases encompass the pursuit of distributional or cohesion goals.

Considering the function of Article 106(2), the fundamental question that arises concerns how well it performs that role, or more precisely, how effectively is it deployed to that end. It is something of a paradox that such a scientific questioning of the operation of Article 106(2) has not taken place. Aspects of the debate concerning the applicable proportionality standard under Article 106(2) touch upon government failure-type concerns, but in the main they are concerned with developing positive accounts of a body of judgments that are not easily reconciled. More ominously, the lack of a government failure critique of Article 106(2) might be put down to the extent to which its operation has deviated from its intended purpose in mitigation of government failure

The elements of this chapter are as follows. I first provide an introduction to the concept of government failure and its connection to market failure. I then develop the constitutional argument, both teleological and literal, for why the mitigation of government failure within a market default economic system is the defining purpose of Article 106(2). That is followed by a closer interrogation of various government failure accounts. I then tackle the issue of how to test for government failure in both SGEI verification and disapplication review, having considered the risks of government failure that are particular to Article 106(2) and the limits of government failure scholarship having regard to its particular requirements.

B. Government Failure and Market Failure

The theory of market failure is an economic account of when market-derived outcomes depart from an economic version of the general interest, namely aggregate economic efficiency. That is frequently referred to as welfare maximisation, under which allocative, productive and dynamic efficiency are maximised. It is concerned with achieving the greatest economy-wide utility for consumers and producers.[2] Market failure is concerned with departures from the idealised conditions in which a full complement of markets are present and operating optimally so as to maximise efficiency.[3] Its complementarity to government failure stems from the elementary proposition that there is at least a role for government to the extent that the correction of market failures requires state action.

[2] See generally, Ledyard, J, 'Market Failure' in Durlauf and Blume (eds), *The New Palgrave Dictionary of Economics* (online edition, 2008).

[3] As to the claim that government failure is a part analogue to market failure, see Dollery, B and Worthington, A, 'The Evaluation of Public Policy: Normative Economic Theories of Government Failure' (1996) 7(1) *Journal of Interdisciplinary Economics* 27–39.

The theory of market failure has its origins in neoclassical economic thinking on the characteristics of a perfectly competitive economy.[4] A perfectly competitive economy is, inter alia, predicated on a large number of utility-maximising consumers and profit-maximising producers. In an economy that is competitive across all markets, a pattern of consumption and production emerges so as to set prices such that it is not possible to make anybody else better off without making some other participant worse off, so called Pareto optimality. Under those idealised conditions, total welfare is maximised.[5] Total welfare is the sum of the consumer and producer surplus. Consumer surplus is the difference between what a consumer pays and what they would have been prepared to pay in a given transaction. Producer surplus is the difference between what a producer is paid and what it would have been prepared to accept in a given transaction. Whether it is conceived of as the maximisation of total welfare or, as it is also referred to, the achievement of Pareto optimality, competitive markets are tendered as maximising efficiency. Alternatively, they are said to maximise total welfare.

Market failure identifies a number of situations where the operation of markets is either negatively impacted from an efficiency perspective, or where markets do not exist at all, both resulting in a departure from the idealised outcomes calculated using General Equilibrium Theory at the end of the nineteenth century. Under it a broad mathematical framework with a complete set of markets could be hypothesised. Through modelling, General Equilibrium Theory established how a simulated perfectly competitive economy might be capable of simultaneously clearing all markets, thereby maximising total welfare.[6] That work reached a zenith in the 1950s with the development of the Arrow-Debreu-McKenzie Model (ADM Model).[7] This proved the existence of an economy-wide competitive equilibrium, or in other words, systemic Pareto optimality using the ADM Model.[8]

General equilibrium models make a number of simplifying assumptions, several of which are very significant for present purposes. First, they assume a complete set of markets, with all necessary property rights. Second, they proceed on the basis that consumers and producers maximise benefits and minimise costs, respectively. Third, they hypothesise that markets are fully competitive (ie, no market power), with prices and related information known by all firms and consumers. Fourth, they assume that there are no transaction costs associated with

[4] The classic account is to be found in Bator, F, 'The Anatomy of Market Failure' (1958) 72(3) *The Quarterly Journal of Economics* 351–79.

[5] See generally, Mankiw, G, *Principles of Economics*, 4th edn (South-Western College Publishers, 2006), ch 7.

[6] In practice many markets do not clear, the employment market being the most prominent example. Frequently, wages do not fall to equalise supply and demand, the result being unemployment.

[7] In General Equilibrium Models, consumers have an initial allocation of goods and services and they are allocated a utility function tracking the satisfaction that they derive from purchases. See Bewley, T, *General Equilibrium, Overlapping Generations Models and Optimal Growth Theory* (Harvard University Press, 2007) ch 1.

[8] For a discussion of General Equilibrium Theory, see Backhouse, R, *The Penguin History of Economics* (Penguin Books, 2002) 254–62.

trades. The existence of market failures can in some respects be understood as departures from the optimised condition of an ADM Model.

Among the principal examples usually included in orthodox accounts of market failures are externalities, public goods, information asymmetries, natural monopoly, and market power. These are considered in greater detail later in this chapter but the following are the fundamentals. Externalities refer to those situations where the full benefits or dis-benefits of a transaction are not confined to the parties to it such as to prevent its occurrence. Public goods are goods or services which, because of peculiar delivery and consumption characteristics, are not likely to be provided efficiently (or at all) by market mechanisms. Information asymmetries refer to impediments to efficient bargaining by virtue of parties not possessing the same essential information. Natural monopoly refers to a situation in which a product or service is provided at least cost to society by a single provider. Finally, market power is concerned with those situations where firms have the ability to determine prices in their own right rather than being price takers. Each of these and other forms of market failure are considered in more detail below. In addition, consideration will be given to merit goods. Merit goods refer to goods the consumption of which confers greater benefits on society than revealed by consumer-expressed preferences.[9] Although merit goods fall outside the standard neoclassical paradigm of market failure, they are sometimes included within it, which can be rationalised on the basis that guaranteeing their provision may increase total welfare.

Although the theory of market failure is heavily implicated in my exposition of government failure, the breadth of application that is accommodated within government failure means that it is an ideal umbrella framework to use to demonstrate government failure under Article 106(2). In addition, a meaningful assessment of government failure under Article 106(2) is not just concerned with the legitimacy of the impugned general interest. It must extend to disapplication review in respect of which elements of government failure scholarship can be used to ground an interrogative approach. By contrast, and as will be addressed in greater detail below, market failure theory does have a number of specified remedies but they are particular to the market failure in question and, being efficiency constrained, are of limited practical use when considering disapplication review.

C. The Constitutional Grounding for Government Failure Control Under Article 106(2)

It is elementary that the approach to the interpretation of Article 106(2) needs to be located within the basic architecture of the Treaty and in particular its default reliance on market mechanisms. From the outset, the EU was able to effectively

[9] While merit goods are capable of being understood as a special case of information asymmetries, there is often an element of positive externalities also operating.

piggyback on Member State recognition, in particular through their legal systems, of the mechanisms key to the operation of a market economy. That is so even though the extent of public involvement in those economies was very diverse from the outset and continues to exhibit significant variety.[10] The constant manifestation of the default nature of market mechanisms under the constitutional order has been the competition rules and, maybe even more fundamentally, the free movement rules, which in part presuppose the existence of national markets to be progressively expanded through the elimination of trade barriers.

The case for a market-centric analysis of Article 106(2) is also inherent in its position within the Treaty and by reason of its specific formulation. Although Article 106(2) is more than just an exception to Article 106(1), it is significant that Article 106(1) includes a specific obligation prohibiting the introduction of measures violating the Treaty rules with respect to public undertakings and the holders of special or exclusive rights. Equally, Article 106(2) begins by affirming the application in principle of Treaty rules to SGEI providers. That is then followed by a very specific balancing mechanism in the residual portions of Article 106(2). As a result, Article 106(2) is concerned with the trade-off between market mechanisms (exemplified by the competition and free movement rules) and the pursuit of general interest objectives. As the Court of Justice explained in 1975:

> [T]he Treaty includes various provisions relating to infringements of the normal functioning of the competition system by actions on the part of the State. This in particular is the purpose of Article [106] to the extent to which it lays down a particular system in favour of undertakings entrusted with the operation of services of general economic interest ...[11]

Although recourse to markets, as a default form of economic organisation, remains hardwired into the Treaty, constitutional change has qualified the position somewhat.[12] That is reflected in the reference to 'a highly competitive social market economy' in Article 3(3) TEU.[13] Despite that, reliance on market mechanisms remains an embedded feature of the constitutional order. Article 120 TFEU requires the Member States to 'act in accordance with the principle of an open market economy with free competition, favouring an efficient allocation of resources' in compliance with the principles of Article 119 TFEU. That provision stipulates that in respect of exclusive competences, the activities of the EU and the Member States are to be conducted in accordance with the principles of 'an open market economy with free competition'.

[10] See generally, Nugent, N, *The Government and Politics of the European Community* (Macmillan, 1991) 42–45.

[11] C-94/74 *IGAV v ENCC* [1975] ECR II-699, §§33, 34.

[12] On the mixed economic constitution of the EU, see Sauter, W, 'Public Services and the Internal Market: Building Blocks or Persistent Irritant?' (2014) 022 *TILEC Discussion Paper* 7–8.

[13] On the process of evolution towards a social market economy, and more generally on the 'open' nature of the economic constitution, see Devroe, W and Cleynenbreugel, P, 'Observations on Economic Governance and the Search for a European Economic Constitution' in Schiek, Liebert and Schneider (eds), *European Economic and Social Constitutionalism after the Treaty of Lisbon* (Cambridge University Press, 2011) 95–120.

The constitutional bridge from markets to government, and in turn an acknowledgment of the risk of government failure, is created by the express wording of the conditional portions of Article 106(2). Of course, the mechanical objective of its authors was to provide a potential exemption from any Treaty rule with respect to services of general economic interest. The concern for government failure is evident in the creation of the mechanism and in its literal terms. The concern is not with SGEI providers per se, but with the 'particular task' assigned to them. Moreover, that concern is engaged only where the regular application of other Treaty rules would 'obstruct' and not just make more complex or difficult the performance of those tasks in law or in fact.

The fact that the form of government failure implicated by Article 106(2) is of the kind that jeopardises the operation of the internal market, including adherence to the application of the free movement and competition rules, does not affect its characterisation as such. While there is of course a jurisdictional limit, namely that a prior violation of a Treaty rule, usually predicated on a cross-border dimension, must first arise before Article 106(2) is engaged, the concern to mitigate government failure for EU purposes suffices to bring about the potential rectification of government failure within the Member States' own political systems. Where EU law is not engaged then the potential for this corrective disappears, meaning that Article 106(2) is not a potential corrective for all government failures with respect to SGEIs, although it will be in cases where the requisite level of materiality to engage EU law is reached.

D. Approaches to Government Failure

There are five principal approaches to government failure that are potentially relevant for present purposes. The first was developed by Wolf during the 1970s and 1980s and is a comprehensive account of government failure in production.[14] The second is that proposed by Le Grand in the early 1990s, which is largely a critique of Wolf.[15] The third is Vining and Weimer's theory of government production failures, which also hails from the early 1990s.[16] As Vining and Weimer's theory of government failure focuses on government production only (narrowly defined), it

[14] See Wolf Jr, C, 'A Theory of Nonmarket Failure: Framework for Implementation Analysis' (1979) 22(1) *Journal of Law and Economics* 107–39; Wolf, Jr, C, 'Markets or Governments: Choosing Between Imperfect Alternatives' (Sep 1986) N-2505-SF, *A Rand Note, prepared for the Alfred P. Sloan Foundation*; and, Wolf Jr, C, 'Market and Non-Market Failures: Comparison and Assessment' (1987) 7(1) *Journal of Public Policy* 43–70. Wolf takes a generally broad view of production so as to encompass more traditional state supply.

[15] Le Grand, 'The Theory of Government Failure' (1991) 21(4) *British Journal of Political Science* 424–42.

[16] Vining, A and Weimer, D, 'Government Supply and Government Production Failure: A Framework Based on Contestability' (1990) 10(1) *Journal of Public Policy* 1–22.

is not considered further for present purposes.[17] The fourth is the 2007 exposition of the Refined Economic Approach (REA) to State aid enforcement authored by Friederiszick, Röller and Verouden.[18] Röller et al's work is not a theoretical account of government failure, but it is a practical normative prescription with a concern to prevent government failure at its core.[19] In light of practicality and its likely relevance, if only by reason of overlap and analogy, Röller et al's REA is considered in extended detail. Finally, there is Dolfsma's 2011 account of typologies of government failure, which he derives from legal philosophy.[20] The core of Dolfsma's claim is the dimensioning of rules, either as too general, specific, arbitrary or conflict creating, and he applies it to selected topics but it is not a general synthesis of how over-generality, excess specificity or arbitrariness can be assessed in a way that is translatable to Article 106(2).[21]

1. Wolf's Theory of Government Failure

Wolf's analysis is directed at identifying certain anomalies in the conditions of supply and demand that lead to government failure in production.[22] This is key to the analogy with market failure. According to Wolf, government supply is characterised by four basic attributes.[23] The first concerns the difficulty of measuring or evaluating outputs leading instead to a focus on inputs. Secondly, government supply is often monopolistic, leading to inefficiency. Thirdly, many government outputs are subject to peculiar production uncertainties. Fourthly, government activity usually lacks a success measure analogous to profit and losses within markets. On the demand side, Wolf identifies five factors as driving demand for government intervention.[24] The first factor is greater awareness of the limitations of markets. The second is the heightened power of special interest groups. The third concerns the particular incentives of politicians to be seen to solve social problems. The fourth is the emphasis on the short term having regard to the electoral cycle. The fifth concerns the frequent

[17] Production is defined by Vining and Weimer as the securing of goods either through production or contracting for use or distribution by government, ibid, 4.

[18] Friederiszick, W, Röller, LH and Verouden V, 'European State Aid Control: an Economic Framework' in Buccirossi (ed), *Handbook of Antitrust Economics* (MIT Press, 2008).

[19] Although the REA was formally presented in 2005, considering the likely dispositive contribution of Röller et al (as members of the Competition Directorate's economic service) to its adoption as well as their fuller exposition of its rationale, it seems appropriate to credit them with the specification of the REA.

[20] Dolfsma, W, 'Government Failure—Four Types' (2011) XLV(3) *Journal of Economic Issues* 593.

[21] In effect, Dolfsma provides an underpinning ad hoc economic rationale for why different systems of rules, eg intellectual property rights, may be overbroad as well as creating conflict with competition rules or their underpinning standards.

[22] In this he appears to be heavily influenced by Stigler's account of economic regulation. See, for example, Stigler, G, 'A Theory of Government Regulation' (1971) 2(1) *Bell Journal of Economics* 3–21.

[23] See Wolf Jr, 'Market and Non-Market Failures' (n 14) 60–63.

[24] ibid, 54–60.

disconnect between the beneficiaries of particular interventions and those who incur the costs.

Against those conditions of supply and demand, Wolf proposes four major categories of government failure.[25] The first he terms 'internalities', which are driven by private motives that he suggests are derived from government not facing an external market constraint. Redundant costs are Wolf's second form of government failure and they relate to productive inefficiency caused by the lack of competition. Wolf's third form of government failure is the derived externality, which he explains as an unintended effect not foreseen or properly understood when the original market failure prompted an intervention. As with their market failure theory antecedents, these externalities can be positive or negative. Wolf's final category of government failure is distributional inequity. While he accepts that conventional market failure theory focuses only on efficiency-derived problems, he identifies inequities in terms of privilege and power as a distinct form of government failure. With respect to the prevention of government failures, Wolf provides only generalised comment on the desirability of market-based solutions.

2. Le Grand's Critique of Wolf

Le Grand's chief criticism of Wolf is that he pays insufficient attention to the precise form of government intervention, which can range from production through to regulation. As a result, Le Grand engages in a high-level analysis of the efficiency and equity effects of government intervention by reference to their three principal forms: provision, taxation or subsidy, and regulation. With respect to provision, unsurprisingly, Le Grand finds that the degree of competition has a significant bearing on efficiency. With respect to taxes and subsidies, he cites likely departures from allocative and productive efficiency.[26] With respect to regulation, Le Grand hypothesises that a government acting in the public interest that was perfectly informed might be able to determine an efficient allocation of a good or a service. That potential is offset, however, by the significant information asymmetries that it usually faces. In addition, Le Grand refers to the possibility of industry capture, and the potential for sectoral interests to eventually emasculate the general interest. Both of those problems are enduring government failure concerns.

With respect to equity generally, Le Grand argues that there is no prior reason to assume that government provision will be equitable or inequitable, but that there may be consequences for income given that profits from government ownership accrue to taxpayers generally. As to subsidies, according to Le Grand, the degree of equity is a function of successful targeting to ensure a minimum quantity for all. That depends on the eligibility criteria for assistance. Overall, a comparison is only meaningful considering the nature of distribution prior to the intervention.

[25] ibid, 63–67.
[26] Le Grand (n 15) 436.

With respect to regulation, Le Grand observes that regulation of quality or entry may have significant distributional consequences if it raises prices. As with the case of the efficiency properties of regulation, outcomes are affected by information asymmetries and the potential for regulatory capture.

3. Röller et al's Refined Economic Approach for State Aid

The REA was first proposed in the Commission's 2005 State Aid Action Plan (SAAP), which, among other things, suggested greater reliance on the concept of market failure and other economic concepts for the purpose of compatibility review under Article 107(3)(c).[27] Although the REA as ultimately reflected in the SAAP was issued as a Commission document, a subsequent paper by Friederiszick, Röller and Verouden provides an overall justification for the REA based on the mitigation of government failures, an underpinning that is less apparent in the SAAP.[28] Given that at the time it was authored Röller was the Chief Economist at DG Competition, it will be referred to as 'Röller et al's' REA.

Röller et al identify the rationales for State aid both in terms of efficiency and equity, and—in an orthodox economic approach—treat the resolution of market failures as efficiency directed.[29] They also emphasise the potential for economic analysis to illuminate what they appear to assume is an inevitable efficiency loss inherent in the pursuit of distributional policies.[30] Separately, they address the limits of State aid policy and raise the issue of government failure, including its potential ineffectuality in raising total welfare due to features of the political system.[31] As a result, the potential of procedural safeguards to help mitigate government failures is emphasised. Röller et al then turn to the specification of elements of an REA, which incorporates a balancing test between positive features and distortionary effects.

On the positive side, Röller et al propose three considerations as part of assessing the compatibility of an intervention falling within the State aid rules. First, a measure should address a market failure or other objective of common interest. In turn, the second test is comprised of three limbs, namely that the appropriate policy instrument is used; that it produces an incentive effect; and that this could not be achieved with less aid. These are expressly attributed to the concern to

[27] Brussels 7.6.2005, COM (2005) 107 final, §§22–23.

[28] Friederiszick, Röller and Verouden (n 18). An outline of their approach is contained in a June 2005 presentation by two of the authors at the LEAR Conference on Advances in the Economics of Competition Law, Rome, 23–25 June 2005. That took place only a number of weeks after the publication of the SAAP. See also on the same issues, Friederiszick, W, Röller, LH and Verouden, V, 'EC State Aid Control: An Economic Perspective' in Rydelski (ed), *The EC State Aid Regime; Distortive Effects of State Aid on Competition and Trade* (Cambridge University Press, 2006) ch 8, 145–82.

[29] Friederiszick, Röller and Verouden (n 18) 632–33.

[30] ibid, 634–36.

[31] ibid, 637.

address the problem of government failure.[32] With respect to the appropriateness of the instrument, while Röller et al make the point that another policy option outside of State aid may be more appropriate, the normative prescription is that 'at minimum alternative measures outside State aid should be assessed'.[33] This may be an instance of practical normativity considering the Member States' presumptive discretion over policy choices.[34] The second limb of the second test in relation to incentivisation introduces a requirement for counterfactual analysis. The third limb of the second test is an inquiry as to whether the same change in behaviour could be produced with less aid.

The third consideration proposed by Röller et al is the assessment of the overall balance, taking the effect on competition and trade as a composite standard. To that end, a variety of circumstances are documented illustrating possible forms of anti-competitive effects, such as support for inefficient production and exclusion. There is no suggestion of any hierarchy within these 'theories of harm'. Instead, it is proposed that the gravity of the specific distortion should be determined by reference to a consideration of three subsidiary questions: the procedural context for the award of the aid, the market characteristics, and the amount and type of aid. The first question incorporates a qualified presumption that the transparency of the award process may give some comfort as to the minimisation of competitive distortions. The second is a consideration of the market structure. The final question reflects the variety of forms of aid, and in turn their magnitude as significant drivers of distortive effects. Röller et al do not give any indication as to when the overall balancing exercise should tip in favour of prohibition as a result of a material distortion of competition having an effect on trade.[35]

Röller et al's REA was not included in fully adumbrated form in the SAAP. Nevertheless, in subsequent guidance the overall balancing tests described above made their way into the framework for compatibility assessment. That has not been without significant objections and concerns. Kaupa has argued that Röller et al's claim that the pursuit of equity inevitably has a trade-off in terms of efficiency is generally unproven and is highly context specific.[36] Separately, Buendía Sierra and Smulders have raised concerns that the REA reflects a view of State aid enforcement as an appendage of competition law to be applied within a common

[32] ibid, under 'Assessing the Benefits'.

[33] ibid, 650.

[34] A review of the policy choices considered and an assessment of their advantages is called for in the 2009 Commission Staff Common Principles for An Economic Assessment of the Compatibility of State Aid under Article 87(3). Note, however, the specific opposition of the UK on this point. See letter to Mr H. Drabbe from the UK Permanent Representation of 6 July 2009.

[35] Unsurprisingly, the Commission's 2008 Vademecum on State Aid indicates that a large number of negative indicators need to be offset by a high level of positives. 30 September 2008, 12.

[36] See Kaupa, C, 'The More Economic Approach—A Reform Based on Ideology' (2009) 3 *European State Aid Law Quarterly* 311–322, 317. This criticism also draws attention to the fact that even if Röller et al are correct, the Commission faces significant legitimacy problems in seeking to supervise or second-guess any such trade off. That is acknowledged as ultimately a political question. See Friederiszick, Röller and Verouden (n 18) 636.

analytical framework.[37] Instead, they identify the concern to ensure a level playing field in the internal market as crucial.[38] To that end, they maintain that the State aid rules are directed at the prevention of subsidy wars.[39] As such, they argue that the body of State aid rules is not really a framework for controlling Member State economic errors. Nevertheless, they see in the more positive elements of the REA tools that may assist the Member States in being more efficient in the use of their resources, even if that is not of direct assistance to the Commission in furtherance of the ultimate rationale of the State aid rules.

It will be apparent that Röller et al have provided the most likely candidate framework (albeit requiring adaption) to reveal the extent of government failure in SGEI design, organisation and delivery. Their work focuses on a closely related Treaty provision and it appears to engage with the essential issues that arise in the operation of Article 106(2). Nevertheless, there are important differences, not least because Röller at al provide a prescription for less government failure in State aid review while my concern is with demonstrating the extent of government failure with respect to SGEIs. That concern is most acute with respect to disapplication review, where the particular evolution of Article 106(2) must be taken into account. In addition, there is a need to delve further into the stipulation by Röller at al that in State aid review, the initial task is to verify the existence of a market failure or of some other of common interest.

E. Government Failure Under Article 106(2)

1. The Risk of Government Failure in SGEI Formulation

The relevance of government failure with respect to SGEIs stems from their political and social contexts and the particular challenges presented for governments by the pursuit of distributional and cohesion objectives. As such, SGEI formulation and delivery may serve as something of an open laboratory for the observation of government failure. Although significant government failure scholarship is focused on the potential for failures in production, similar challenges arise with respect to the regulation of markets so as to deliver SGEIs. From a government failure perspective, three types of difficulty appear to be especially acute with respect to the framing and delivery of SGEIs. The first is information problems, the second

[37] Buendía Sierra, JL and Smulders, B, 'The Limited Role of the "Refined Economic Approach" in Achieving the Objectives of State Aid Control: Time for Some Realism' *EC State Aid Law, Liber Amicorum in Honour of Francisco Santaolalla* (Kluwer, 2008) 9–11.

[38] Buendía Sierra and Smulders also raise doubts as to the possible elasticity of the concept of market failures, ibid, 15–16.

[39] ibid, 8–9.

stems from possible shortcomings in the political systems underpinning SGEI formulation, and the third concerns the challenge of efficiency, particularly in the context of achieving distributional objectives. Although each factor is considered separately, they are fungible in many respects.

The problem of information deficits is a significant challenge for government in terms of implementing distributionally motivated policies.[40] Firms that are entrusted with SGEIs will readily understand that opacity is often in their interest. Frequently, the SGEI-entrusted provider is the only source of the actual information necessary to understand a range of salient issues such as cost of service provision, the need for exclusive rights, or the justification for a particular pricing strategy.[41] Adding to the information challenges, SGEIs are common in network industries, frequently requiring specialist technical knowledge for effective market design and regulation. Expertise may gravitate towards the SGEI-entrusted firms, sometimes making it difficult for government to sustain crucial technical competence.[42] This in turn may increase the risk of regulatory capture. As a result, SGEI organisation and delivery entails unique principal-agency problems going beyond traditional government welfare programmes.[43]

A second principal difficulty concerning SGEIs is that often their organisation and provision is the result of a complex interaction of technological, historical and social circumstances mediated through ad hoc political bargaining. Complicating matters, the electoral system may create incentives to be seen to confer eligibilities or entitlements to public services even when market provision is at least adequate or has not been tested.[44] Furthermore, political processes have a bias for the pursuit of redistribution objectives through regulation rather than taxation and direct financing.[45] Moreover, under the Treaty, Member States' entitlement to public ownership of undertakings is respected. Historically, almost all SGEIs were provided through public undertakings. Frequently, they were large employers with corresponding political clout. From a government failure perspective, those circumstances create a risk that the welfare of the entity providing the SGEI may emasculate the determination of what is in the general interest. In Member States where SGEI providers have significant political influence, that risk may be elevated.

[40] See Le Grand (n 15) 438.

[41] As to that concern, see Nicolaides, P, 'Compensation for Public Service Obligations: the Floodgates of State Aid' (2003) *European Competition Law Review* 24(11), 561–73, with reference to C-53/00 *Ferring* [2001] ECR I-9067.

[42] This may be exacerbated by EU requirements to operate national regulatory authorities in which case both government and the regulator may be competing for a very small number of people.

[43] There is in fact a double principal-agent problem, in that the population delegates to elected politicians and, in turn, government (frequently) delegates the delivery of public services to separate entities. See generally, Lane, J, 'The Principal-Agent Approach to Politics: Policy Implementation and Public Policy-Making' (2013) 3(2) *Open Journal of Political Science* 85–89.

[44] As to this possibility, see Shepsle, K and Weingast, B, 'Political Solutions to Market Problems' (1984) 78 *American Political Science Review* 417–34.

[45] See Posner, R, 'Taxation by Regulation' (1971) 2(1) *The Bell Journal of Economics and Management Science* 22–50.

The third difficulty stemming from the peculiar nature of SGEIs is the risk of inefficiency. The causes are multifaceted and cannot be automatically attributed to the fact that many SGEIs are provided by public undertakings, not least considering that there is competition for some SGEIs. Nevertheless, public ownership may open up political routes that allow for special pleading on behalf of public providers, including their employees, or more generally allow their representative organisations to assume an outsized influence.[46] In addition, peculiar difficulties may arise from the nature of general interest objectives that predominate in SGEIs, namely the pursuit of distributional and cohesion goals. Unsurprisingly, the focus of political debate will usually be on the formulation and specification of the underlying eligibilities or entitlements. Given that emphasis, questions of efficiency may be regarded as a secondary consideration, frequently relegated to specialist regulators. The difficulty is that efficiency considerations are inherent in SGEI design and the associated market structure, which in line with their significance are often determined through the political process. Legislators may not, however, have access to information on a range of alternatives with different degrees of efficaciousness in terms of the realisation of the underlying general interest goals. As a result, typically regulatory controls are focused on minimising productive inefficiency but may still result in greater aggregate inefficiency (ie a total welfare loss) than would arise if different means were chosen for SGEI delivery.[47] In addition, the problem of the 'soft budget constraint' looms large.[48] In particular, it may lead to systematic over-compensation for SGEI providers.

2. Diagnosing Government Failure in SGEI Verification

(a) Context

While it may appear attractive to test for government failure through checking whether SGEI claims are only upheld with respect to one or more of the forms of market failure previously identified, that is hardly adequate. A crucial limitation of the market failure critique is its focus on efficiency only. Even within an economic

[46] Interventions such as New Public Management (NPM), namely incentivising and directing management to behave as if a service is provided under competitive conditions, may have some impact on efficiency, but it is too far removed from Art 106(2)'s operation to assess its significance. It is, however, likely that if under the 2012 SGEI Framework, Member States propose efficiency measures, realising them may require the deployment of NPM initiatives.

[47] Even where they do, the effects of productive inefficiency in terms of qualifying eligibility or in reducing the benefits accruing to beneficiaries may not have as much prominence in political debates as might be expected.

[48] See generally, Kornai, J, Maskin, E and Rolan, G, 'Understanding the Soft Budget Constraint' (2003) 41(4) *Journal of Economic Literature* 1085–136. They have summarised the phenomenon as concerning a funder's willingness to provide more compensation or support for output *ex post* than it had been willing to do *ex ante*. Its essential drivers are expectation on one side and a predilection on the other.

system based on markets as a default, there are no prior limits on the variety of general interests that may be invoked under Article 106(2). The orthodox view of market failure is that it is confined to total welfare maximisation and in that way distributional concerns or other non-equity-motivated concerns are separate matters.

That separation of efficiency and equity was formalised by the ADM Model, which was subsequently used to derive two principles that have come to be known as the 'Fundamental Theorems of Welfare Economics'.[49] The First Welfare Theorem states that subject to some specific assumptions, and a general assumption about the absence of any market failures, an economy-wide competitive equilibrium is Pareto efficient. That in substance is the defining efficiency claim of competitive markets. A converse of the First Welfare Theorem is the Second Welfare Theorem, which holds that any Pareto-efficient outcome can be brought about by way of lump-sum taxes and payments so as to redistribute wealth among consumers. According to Stiglitz, in effect, the Second Welfare Theorem brings about the formal separation of efficiency and distributional concerns.[50] It does so by setting distributional issues to one side in favour of an initial prioritisation of total welfare maximisation.[51] This, as will be considered, has significant implications considering the policy objectives typically pursued for SGEIs.

Despite the obvious inadequacy of a market failure paradigm to offer an all-encompassing explanation of SGEI verification, nevertheless it is likely that situations will arise where the existence of a market failure (or an argument that is tantamount to that) is at the core of a claim, usually by a Member State, that an SGEI exists. As such, it is important that there is certainty as to what constitutes a market failure as well as the evidence that is necessary to underpin such a claim. The latter is a task that is complicated in at least two ways. First, despite being a term of art in neoclassical economics that is efficiency specific, the term 'market failure' has a much wider vernacular use in business, and more especially political discourse, where it can mean any number of things. Often its use is on the basis that some distributional or other equity goal is not being realised. From a government failure perspective, even the language of 'market failure' has the potential to be hijacked, in particular if there is political kudos on offer from appearing to solve through intervention something that has been framed as a 'market failure'. As a result of these difficulties, it is important to have a deeper and more coherent understanding of each of the various forms of market failure.

[49] Leon Walras undertook the pioneering work on General Equilibrium Theory. Arrow and Debreu took this forward before further final refinements by McKenzie. See Backhouse (n 8) 169–72.

[50] Stiglitz, J, 'The Invisible Hand and Modern Welfare Economics' (Mar 1991) *National Bureau of Economic Research, Working paper* no. 3641, 4.

[51] This is exemplified by Musgrave's working hypothesis that distributional issues are a matter for a separate branch of government. See Musgrave, M, 'A Multiple Theory of Budget Determination' (1956/57) New Series, Bd.17, H. 3 *FinanzArchiv/Public Finance Analysis* 333–43.

(b) Forms of Market Failure

Externalities

Externalities arise where all of the benefits or harms associated with activity do not accrue to whoever performs it. As such, externalities can either be positive or negative. An example of a positive externality is the incremental benefit to all users of a communications network when another user is added. An example of a negative externality is pollution from a factory affecting nearby residents. Pigou refined the concept of externalities by introducing the concepts of marginal private costs and marginal private benefits. He demonstrated that the presence of externalities resulted in a divergence between private and social benefits, or alternatively, private and social costs.[52] In the presence of either, total welfare is not maximised. In the case of a positive externality, an insufficient quantity of the service or good is provided. The opposite holds true for a negative externality, where a product or service is produced to excess, in the process failing to maximise total welfare.

With respect to solutions to the problems of externalities, economic debate has focused on their prevalence as well as on the most effective means for their elimination. The solution to positive and negative externalities offered by Pigou was to propose the alignment of private and social costs. In respect of negative externalities this is a tax, while for positive externalities it is some form of subsidy. The effect of either form of intervention is to establish a new equilibrium and in turn to maximise total welfare. This is what is referred to as 'internalising' the cost or benefit of the externality. The other likely governmental responses to either type of externality are a redefinition of legal structures (and possibly the allocation of property rights) or direct regulation, including, possibly, prohibition.[53] Many externalities are sufficiently trivial to be ignored, or alternatively may be mitigated by market work-arounds.

Public Goods

Public goods are those goods and services for which the exclusion of consumers is not feasible and where each incremental act of consumption does not reduce the residual quantity. The problem of excludability refers to the fact that sometimes it is difficult to prevent certain persons from the consumption or enjoyment of a good or a service even though they are unwilling to pay. The inability to keep out free riders will inevitably lead to some goods and services not being provided. Some goods can or will be provided even if exclusion is not perfect, but for others complete excludability is essential. Non-excludability is the pre-eminent cause of market failure in public goods. The second characteristic of public goods is that they are non-rivalrous in consumption. The fact that incremental consumption has no bearing on the residual quantity confounds the price system since ordinarily each act

[52] Backhouse (n 8) 273–74.
[53] Buchanan, J and Vanberg, V, 'The Politicisation of Market Failure' (1988) 57 *Public Choice* 101–13.

of consumption reduces the available supply. There are situations where non-rivalry in consumption applies, but only up to a certain point, in which case the problem of congestion may become relevant. Not all public goods are both non-excludable and non-rivalrous in consumption. These are referred to as 'impure' public goods.

Conventional examples of public goods include the provision of national defence and the operation of lighthouses.[54] Some kinds of information are regarded as pure public goods. The outcome of fundamental scientific research is one such example.[55] Once knowledge of it is passed from any one person to another, its subsequent retransmission is virtually uncontrollable. Similarly, any one person's knowledge of this information has absolutely no bearing on its availability for another. The first coherent explanation of public goods is to be found in a 1954 work of Samuelson.[56] His work focused on what have come to be referred to as pure public goods: namely those situations where the characteristics of both non-excludability and non-rivalry are present. Samuelson's conclusion was that: 'no decentralised price system can serve to determine optimally, these levels of collective consumption'.[57] By contrast, private goods are neither non-excludable nor non-rivalrous in consumption.

The classification of a good or a service as a public good has usually been treated as unavoidably making the case for government intervention. Since the problem of non-excludability is one of free riding, the obvious solution is to use coercive tax powers to ensure adequate funding and in turn provision. Historically, the arguments for a tax-based solution to the provision of public goods (so as to overcome the problem of excludability) in part explain significant state provision of public goods, not least in Europe.[58] If a good or service is also non-rivalrous in consumption, then the case for government provision becomes very compelling, although determining the optimal level of output (from an efficiency perspective) remains highly problematic.

Information Asymmetries

This refers to a situation where market actors do not have the same type of information for the purposes of a particular transaction. In orthodox accounts,

[54] Stiglitz argues that the realisation that information is very different from other commodities and is in fact a public good was 'the fundamental breakthrough in the economics of information'. See Stiglitz, J, 'The Contribution of the Economics of Information to Twentieth Century Economics' (2000) 115(4) *The Quarterly Journal of Economics* 1448.

[55] For a comprehensive account of knowledge as a public good see, Stiglitz, J, 'Knowledge as a Global Public Good' in Inge, Grunberg and Stern (eds), *Global Public Goods: International Cooperation in the 21st Century*, United Nations Development Programme (New York, 1999).

[56] Samuleson, P, 'The Pure Theory of Public Expenditure' (1954) 36 *Review of Economics and Statistics* 387.

[57] ibid, 388.

[58] This by itself would appear to be something of a non sequitur since although the state may need to take the lead in commissioning and financing the provision of public goods, that does not seem to preclude the possibility of private provision. See Hayek, FA, *The Constitution of Liberty* (Routledge reprint, 2010) 155.

the essential concern is a relative and not an absolute one. Related problems are those of adverse selection and moral hazard.[59] Adverse selection is the tendency of certain types of contract to attract individuals who are the least profitable. Moral hazard refers to a phenomenon whereby certain interventions intended to obviate a particular risk or harm may have the opposite effect in practice. Information asymmetries arise in many areas of economic activity, most especially where service providers have special knowledge or expertise relevant to purchasing decisions. The related problems of adverse selection and information asymmetry are especially acute in the field of insurance.

The absence of information asymmetries is a fundamental assumption of General Equilibrium Theory. It was not until a 1970 paper by Akerlof that the problem of information asymmetry and the associated difficulty of adverse selection was the subject of comprehensive formal treatment.[60] Using the stylised example of the market for second-hand cars, Akerlof models a scenario in which, because of the problem of judging quality in advance, market prices fall to those of the inferior cars, with the potential for no trades at all.[61] It is possible to conceive of both private and government solutions to the problem of information asymmetries. In many cases private solutions (such as agreements on standard, guarantees, quality certification etc) can overcome this form of market failure. Despite that, the resolution of many information asymmetry problems, such as weights and measures, are left to government. This may be largely for historical reasons although there might be reason to expect higher degrees of impartiality and consistency from government where it has no direct pecuniary interest in the market in question. Problems associated with adverse selection are more difficult to overcome effectively using private means. Sometimes they are the subjects of significant regulatory intervention such as 'must buy' rules for certain products. By contrast, moral hazard problems may be overcome, at least to some degree, by private means such as excess rules of the kind common in the insurance sector.

Natural Monopoly

A natural monopoly arises when the total social costs are minimised by having one firm serve the entire market. As a result, only a single provider will be profitable.[62]

[59] For an extended argument as to the pervasiveness and significance of information asymmetries, see Stiglitz (n 54) 1441–78.

[60] Akerlof, G, 'The Market for "Lemons"; Quality Uncertainty and the Market Mechanism' (1970) 84(3) *The Quarterly Journal of Economics* 488–500.

[61] Akerlof acknowledges that this is not the case in practice for many markets, even with significant information asymmetries, including that for second-hand cars. This he selected on the basis of its ease of understanding as opposed to its realism or importance. Ibid, 489.

[62] Examples of natural monopoly, although not referred to as such, feature in the writing of Adam Smith, in more conceptual terms in those of JS Mill, before being initially rendered in the neoclassical tradition by Edgeworth in the early 20th century. See generally, Mosca, M, 'On the Origins of the Concept of Natural Monopoly: Economies of Scale and Competition' (2006) 15(2) *The European Journal of the Theory of Economic Thought* 317–53.

As summarised by Posner, natural monopoly is not about the number of sellers in a market, but instead concerns the relationship between demand and the technology of supply.[63] Since a natural monopoly may result in monopoly provision, it is also a form of market failure given that it is a departure from conditions of perfect competition. Natural monopolies are often characterised by increasing returns to scale, usually in the presence of significant fixed costs. Work led by Baumol in the late 1970s demonstrated that in a multi-product setting the presence of scale economies was not a necessary or sufficient condition for natural monopoly to pertain in that context.[64] What matters is subadditivity, a situation where the cost of total output is less than the sum of the cost of those outputs separately produced. As a result, Baumol argued that the verification of the condition of natural monopoly is more difficult than previously understood.[65] In a more direct challenge to the phenomenon, the Austrian School tradition in economics has criticised natural monopoly theory as entirely unsound and developed *ex post facto* to justify grants of exclusive rights resulting from political bartering.[66] Separately, Posner has argued that given technological change and evolving consumer preferences, natural monopolies are not likely to last long enough to warrant direct intervention.[67]

By definition, and unlike many other forms of market failure, there is no scope for private action to mitigate the negative effects of natural monopoly, which will include all of the shortcomings of regular monopoly as to price, efficiency and innovation. Traditionally, the existence of natural monopoly has often been used to justify the grant of exclusive rights to a particular firm, backed up by a prohibition on competing activities. Historically, that approach was exemplified by the utilities. The more modern response to natural monopoly is some form of economic regulation targeting the natural monopoly element but with no legal barriers to entry. Usually, the focus of such regulation is to mitigate the effects of monopoly pricing and to implement distributional goals. Initially, the US forged the way with rate of return regulation, which was eventually heavily criticised.[68] Following work by Littlechild and Beesley in the 1980s, rate of return regulation using price caps was pioneered in the UK.[69] That offered the potential to limit market power, to create efficiency incentives and to prevent 'rate shocks' at the advent of liberalisation.

[63] Posner, R, 'Natural Monopoly and its Regulation' (1969) 21(3) *Stanford Law Review* 548.

[64] Baumol, W, 'On the Proper Cost Tests for Natural Monopoly in a Multi-product Industry' (1977) 76 *American Economic Review* 809.

[65] It would also seem to follow that true natural monopolies are less likely to be encountered in multi-product settings.

[66] In particular, see DiLorenzo, J, 'The Myth of Natural Monopoly' (1996) 9(2) *The Review of Austrian Economics* 43.

[67] Posner (n 63) 643.

[68] ibid, 592–606, includes an extended critique of rate of return regulation in particular.

[69] See Littlechild, S, 'Privatisation, Competition and Regulation' (2000) *Institute of Economic Affairs* Occasional Paper 110, for a discussion of the lead-up to the introduction of price cap regulation in the UK.

Market Power

Closely related to the problem of natural monopoly is that of market power. In classic form, the concept of market power entails the ability to maintain prices above competitive levels, although this conception of the problem is limited to allocative and productive efficiency concerns.[70] Market power can be equally inimical to dynamic efficiency over time given reduced incentives to innovate. Problems associated with market power have long been regarded as a source of market failure and instances of market power may be quite common. Despite that, interventions directed at market power tend to be relatively limited for a number of reasons. First, while perfectly atomistic competition would exclude any market power, workable competition based on a more limited number of firms may produce broadly comparable results. Second, and perhaps more fundamentally, the existence of market power may provide a crucial incentive for further entry, provided that this is not foreclosed through regulatory constraints or exclusionary business practices. Accordingly, the focus of intervention is often on removing those obstacles, bearing in mind that technological and other innovation will frequently redefine those challenges. Finally, the control of market power entails price regulation in many instances, which requires considerable resources to administer.

The Special Case of Merit Goods

A merit good is one whose consumption is regarded as conferring wider benefits beyond those reflected in the preferences of a particular consumer.[71] The concept of merit goods, as pioneered by Musgrave, is based on a deliberate departure from the consumer sovereignty paradigm reflected in the *homus economicus* assumption of the individual as best placed to maximise personal utility.[72] As acknowledged by its originator, the decision on what is a merit good can be arrived at through a number of distinct lines of justification. Musgrave himself locates the strongest justification in situations where community values supplant the usual consumer sovereignty paradigm characteristic of markets.[73] In some respects, the concept of merit goods can be understood as an externality-driven problem, but one where, by contrast with public goods, the externality obscures the consumer's purchasing preferences as opposed to the incentives of producers to provide, which is typically the case for a public good arising through non-excludability.[74] As a result, the

[70] See *Oxford Dictionary of Economics*, 3rd edn (Oxford University Press, 2009) 284.

[71] ibid, 290.

[72] Musgrave (n 51) 33–43.

[73] The concept of merit goods, although accessible in vernacular terms, suffers from very significant indeterminacy in terms of its theoretical justification. Musgrave himself acknowledges this and offers a number of candidate justifications before settling upon the community values account as the most persuasive. See Musgrave, M, 'Merit Goods', *New Palgrave Dictionary of Economics* (Basingstoke, 2008).

[74] Considering further the security implication of broadcasting, state monopolies, although by no means necessary, are nevertheless an unsurprising outcome.

output of certain goods is assumed to be suboptimal. Television output in the form of public service broadcasting (PSB) is usually regarded as a classic merit good.[75]

3. Market Feasibility as the Critical Government Failure Concern in SGEI Verification

There will be cases where a Member State points to the existence of a market failure as a reason for a particular intervention and in turn seeks to argue that corresponding obligations constitute an SGEI. Occasionally, situations arise where a market failure is claimed to exist that must be corrected, at the same time as delivering on a distributional goal. In other instances, and often these will likely predominate under Article 106(2), the Member State may make no market failure claim and none may arise on the facts, but instead it may wish to achieve a distribution or cohesion-type goal. As a result, for present purposes the demonstration of government failure in SGEI verification must go beyond a market failure paradigm and instead focus more generally on market feasibility. By that, I mean that a number of different elements should come together for the purpose of SGEI verification. First, it involves checking the extent to which a market is *ex ante* capable of delivering on specified general interest goals either fully or substantially, either immediately or in the short term. That entails clarity on what precisely the general interest is, at least in terms of gauging the differences from prevailing market outcomes.[76] Separately, it may be necessary to verify that no disabling market failures arise since, in the most extreme case, they are capable of preventing the very existence of markets. Furthermore, even where the underlying basis for intervention is distributional it is worth inquiring whether there are market failures which could be addressed at lower social costs than the proposed intervention so as to bring about the underlying goal. In practice, a lower social cost will have to be estimated by reference to heuristics based on the relative restrictiveness on competition or distortion of trade of various forms of intervention.

Invariably, any intervention comes with administrative and compliance costs, separate and apart from possible spill-over effects more generally. For example, a firm in a multi-service market that is subsidised so as to support one particular output as an SGEI may therefore realise a significant competitive advantage in terms of its ability to compete more generally. As a result, the disparity between general interest-determined outcomes and market outcomes should be material

[75] This issue is the subject of further consideration in Chapter 5.

[76] The judgment of the Court in C-159/94 *Commission v France* is a prominent example of various stylised delivery characteristics being individually assessed in terms of whether they mandated departures from outcomes that might otherwise have pertained under *ex ante* market conditions. See §§72–89.

and discernible before an SGEI is recognised. That might be treated as axiomatic or a proposition that is so self-evident that it hardly requires stating, but as will be considered in Chapter 5, the nature of the service in question and its idiosyncratic value for the political classes can mean that a market feasibility approach to framing an SGEI is bypassed and needs judicial correction.

In addition to the nature or terms of a service, questions of the time should also form part of the analysis. There will be situations where it is clear that a market is not delivering on politically desired outcomes and where it is sufficiently static that no major improvements are envisaged. There will, however, be situations where that is not the case, most especially where a market is nascent or displaying dynamic qualities even if it is underdeveloped. When mobile technology was launched for the first time, no provider could have argued credibly for the treatment of the basic voice service as an SGEI given market incentives in terms of ubiquitous network coverage. Subsequent experience has shown that under fairly lightly regulated market conditions competitive rivalry drove widespread availability on relatively affordable terms. As such, the time interval may be relevant in respect of which the question of the materiality of the waiting period for the realisation of political goals is undoubtedly a difficult question. In practice that might be linked to the electoral cycle.

Keeping all of those considerations in mind, I will demonstrate the extent of government failure in SGEI verification by focusing on telecommunications, environmental protection and broadcasting. These have been selected for a number of reasons. First, all three are regarded as manifesting many classic market failures. Secondly, in both the telecommunications and broadcasting sectors, distributional and other general interest objectives loom large. Thirdly, environmental protection and broadcasting have seen specific constitutional change bearing on SGEI verification. In each, questions as to the feasibility of markets and concerning the underpinning dynamics and how they affect the framing of SGEIs abound. As such, they provide a useful opportunity for comparative analysis in the light of the political tensions surrounding SGEIs. Overall, these sectors raise a myriad of issues under Article 106(2), not least as to government failure.

4. Diagnosing Government Failure in Disapplication Review

(a) Limitations of Government Failure Theories for the Purposes of Disapplication Review

It will be recalled that disapplication review is the process by which, using Article 106(2), an exemption is granted from other Treaty rules. The relevance of government failure concepts for understanding Article 106(2) stems from the relative rigidity of market failure compared to the diffuse nature of government failure scholarship. While market failure theory offers a number of remedies for some of its manifestations, considering the variety of SGEIs (and their underpinning objectives), practical government failure accounts (such as that of Röller et al) explicitly recognise the pursuit of distributional goals. Despite that, government failure scholarship has been the subject of many critiques and objections.[77] Given the preponderance of that scholarship in the form of challenges to public choice scholarship, much of that criticism is not directly relevant for present purposes. Similarly, objections to government failure accounts on the basis that it sets a gold standard for government intervention not capable of being satisfied in practice (thereby unduly restraining government) are not a constraint for positive analysis, although they clearly matter for the purpose of making any normative claim. It is worth noting, however, that the more nuanced insights into what is likely to be a perpetual debate on the role of government and markets have emphasised that the critical question frequently entails a choice of alternatives that are all imperfect to some degree.[78] That, if anything, reinforces the case for recourse to economic analysis to the extent that it exposes the limitations of both markets and governments.

It is, however, at the level of specifics that difficulties arise concerning recourse to government failure theory for a practical purpose. Writing generally as to the indeterminacy of the concept, Orbach notes 'Neither the prevalence of studies of government failures nor the use of the phrase "government failure" necessarily says much about the standard of "failure"'.[79] This is to be contrasted with the seeming fixity of purpose exhibited by market failure theory.[80] Market failure has the great advantage of focusing on the identification of conditions giving rise to a departure from an economy-wide general equilibrium. Scholarship in that field has always enjoyed a constancy of purpose focused only on efficiency, based on a total welfare standard. Separately, since forms of market failure are fairly coherent and stable, testing for market failure can proceed directly based on the presence or otherwise of its various manifestations.[81]

By contrast, direct recourse to government failure scholarship presents a greater challenge for present purposes. As has been explored, the principal theoretical accounts of the nature of government failure focus only on production. While Wolf offers incidental prescriptions in mitigation of market failure, they are production specific and not likely to illuminate disapplication review under Article 106(2).[82] At most, he offers insights into possible shortcomings in the provision of public

[77] See, for example, Block, F, 'The Roles of the State in the Economy' in Smelser and Swedberg (eds), *The Handbook of Economic Sociology* (Princeton University Press, 1994), 691.

[78] See Coase, R, 'The Regulated Industries; Discussion, with Ernest W Williams, Jr.' (1964) 54(3) *The American Economic Review*, Papers and Proceedings of the Seventy-sixth Annual Meeting of the American Economic Association 192–97.

[79] Orbach (n 1).

[80] On the attractiveness of the market failure synthesis generally and also a critical account, see Bozeman, B, 'Public-Value Failure: When Efficient Markets May Not Do' (2002) 62(2) *Public Administration Review* 145–61.

[81] It is the case that this then becomes a qualitative exercise based on factual verification, but arguably that is unavoidable given the difficulty of quantifying market failures. See LECG, Comments on DG Competition's Draft Common Principles, 11 June 2009, 6–7.

[82] Wolf Jr, 'A Theory of NonMarket Failure' (n 14) 136–137.

services. While Le Grand correctly focuses attention on the form of government intervention as important to the nature of outcomes, his analysis does not penetrate to the design of market regulation of the kind often implicated in Article 106(2) cases. More generally, the scholarship on government failure (especially the public choice variety) is concerned with explaining the how and why of government failures, frequently with very particularised demonstrations of the phenomena, such as rent seeking. Even when it ranges more broadly to critique regulation generally, its essential insights require adaption for the purpose of assessing disapplication review under Article 106(2).[83]

Given the impossibility of direct testing, the question arises whether, as was the case for Article 107 through the adoption of the REA, it is possible to assemble a similar government failure-inspired construct for interrogating Article 106(2). That would appear to be feasible considering the broad congruency of general and common interest goals under Article 106(2) and Article 107(3)(c) respectively, and the similarity of the underlying control mechanisms. In this regard, it is important to acknowledge the normative nature of the REA versus the principal purpose of using government failure in this instance, which is as a way of assessing government failure disapplication review. Fiedziuk has argued that REA is capable of adaption for the purpose of reviewing PSO compensation under Article 106(2).[84] That, however, is subject to an important limitation in that her claim (which is also normative) is limited to the treatment of PSO compensation. For present purposes, a variety of interventions capable of falling under Article 106(2) need to be tested from a government failure perspective. In order to do so, it is proposed to draw on the particular susceptibilities of SGEIs to government failures outlined in the preceding subsection in the light of the established legal mechanics of disapplication review under Article 106(2).

(b) Adapting Insights from Government Failure to Assess Disapplication Review

Considering the particular challenges that are presented by SGEIs, it is necessary to focus on those aspects of the operation of Article 106(2) that may be the most revealing with respect to government failures. As explored in Chapter 1, the conventional treatment of Article 106(2) is predicated on six elements. That includes the existence of SGEIs. As a result, and apart from entrustment, the principal residual element of Article 106(2) is necessity and proportionality review, the dominant view being that the development of trade criterion in the second sentence is an aspect of that overall review.[85] I will pursue a government failure

[83] There are many prominent theories of government regulation, including that of Stigler. See, for example, Stigler (n 22).

[84] Fiedziuk, N, 'Towards a More Refined Economic Approach to Services of General Economic Interest' (2010) 16(2) *European Public Law* 271–88.

[85] See Buendía Sierra, JL, *Exclusive Rights and State Monopolies under EC Law* (Oxford University Press, 2000) 351.

critique of necessity and proportionality in Chapter 6 on the basis of considering the strictness of the obstruction requirement, whether less restrictive means are considered, and the extent to which the general interest can be determined independently of the interests of the SGEI provider.

In addition to a consideration of necessity and proportionality, two fundamental issues, namely that of information problems and efficiency, will be considered. They may be said to be both antecedent to and consequential upon the issues of necessity and proportionality, respectively. Informational constraints are ubiquitous in the formulation and regulation of SGEIs.[86] They undercut everything from the evidence sustaining claims for exclusive rights through to the proof of the level of funding required to sustain a universal service. In broader terms, one of the interrogative parameters to be deployed in Chapter 6 will be framed in composite terms as transparency and proof. That is so as to encompass legislative and other interventions requiring the production of certain information, and the consequences (if any) of not complying with such requirements. In addition, given that disapplication review typically takes place within a legal procedure, it will also include the question of proof, the allocation of burdens, and the drawing of appropriate inferences. As typified by the *Electricity and Gas Cases*, those matters are frequently dispositive in SGEI cases.

The third main issue that will be considered as part of the assessment of disapplication review from a government failure perspective is that of efficiency. In government failure scholarship it is axiomatic that government interventions be well targeted and cost-effective, as well as minimising waste, otherwise the underlying distributional goal is subverted, at least to some degree.[87] Questions of efficiency transcend almost all aspects of the operation of Article 106(2) and are centrally implicated in the choices of the Member State. Inevitably, this leads to questions as to whether Member State ascendancy in SGEI definition necessarily precludes efficiency review or whether disapplication should be conditioned on some minimum level of efficiency. Perhaps less fundamental, but still relevant for the overall consideration of efficiency, are questions as to the feasibility of higher levels of productive efficiency, taking Member States' structuring of SGEI delivery as a given. Here, too, information issues are heavily implicated, highlighting once more the interconnectedness of all of these matters.

In summary, government failure in disapplication review will be assessed by tracking the evolution in the strictness of three parameters, namely transparency and proof, necessity and proportionality, and efficiency. That will be undertaken with respect to three distinct periods, given the possible variability of the underlying positions over time. The first phase runs from the earliest Article 106(2) cases up

[86] In that regard, it is notable that enduring information problems are inherent in the design of the State aid procedures. See Neven, D and Verouden, V, 'Towards a More Refined Economic Approach in State Aid Control' in Mederer, Peraresi and Van Hoof (eds), *EU Competition Law—Volume IV: State Aid* (Claeys & Casteels, 2008).

[87] See Winston, C, *Government Failure versus Market Failure* (AEI-Brookings Joint Centre for Regulatory Studies, 2006) 75, who frames this as a failure to optimise social welfare.

to the period just before the *Corbeau* judgment of the Court of Justice. *Corbeau* is proposed as a demarcation point on the basis that it was the first case where the Court was confronted by and directly engaged with the very difficult question of disapplication review for distributional and cohesion objectives. The second phase runs from *Corbeau* up to just before the *Altmark* judgment of the Court. *Altmark* is proposed as a demarcation point both because of its general implications for Article 106(2), and more generally because of the subsequent interventions on the part of the Commission in the form of the Monti-Kroes and Almunia Packages. In respect of both regimes, the implications for disapplication review, albeit confined to the funding of PSOs, are very considerable. As such, the third phase runs from the *Altmark* judgment up to the present.

F. Conclusions

While in high-level terms the relevance of government failure will be readily apparent, the development of a method of identifying its occurrence is a more complicated task. Nevertheless, the Treaty provides a lodestar not easily eclipsed, namely reliance on markets as a default system of economic organisation. In the current constitutional order that is not just a default, it is expressly hardwired into the Treaty scheme. As a result, the investigation of market feasibility is axiomatic for the revelation of government failure in SGEI verification. On the other hand, the exposure of government failure in disapplication review is a more *sui generis* challenge. Nevertheless, what I propose is faithful to the market *grundnorm*, is informed by the government failure scholarship and is adapted to the mechanical tasks necessitated by the wording of Article 106(2). Equipped with these instruments, I will proceed to extract the nature of government failure in SGEI verification and disapplication review in Chapters 5 and 6, respectively. Before that, however, it is necessary to provide a much fuller account of the actual operation of Article 106(2) from the internal and external perspectives. In addition, those accounts, which are set out in Chapters 3 and 4, respectively, provide essential context for the demonstration of government failure to come.

3

The Contestation and Indeterminacy of Article 106(2)

A. Introduction

Article 106(2) is an enigma. On the one hand, it is said to be an indispensable mediation mechanism between market and non-market objectives.[1] On the other hand, in respect of the qualification of activities as SGEIs, the General Court has declared that there are no controlling principles.[2] Overlaying its application, there have been serious political difficulties and consequential constitutional changes. The operation of Article 106(2) is incendiary in nature and, as one leading commentator has put it, difficulties have been encountered at almost every turn.[3] This chapter establishes the wider political and constitutional context, and considers certain academic accounts of the exemption. In overall terms, this chapter explores the indeterminacy of Article 106(2) as driven by its political contestation. That goes to the core of Article 106(2)'s ability to be operated as an effective brake on government failure.

The elements of this chapter are as follows. In the next section, I consider the wider political, constitutional and administrative landscape on which SGEIs have been a principal point of contention for some time. That includes details of how the debates surrounding Article 106(2) framed the approach of the Commission as well as how that interacted with constitutional change and efforts at more generalised legislative interventions concerning SGEIs. Following that I explore relevant conceptual accounts of Article 106(2). That exercise is not intended to be an exhaustive critique of the voluminous legal literature in the field. Instead, the focus is on identifying overarching explanations of Article 106(2) bearing on its clarity and coherence with reference to SGEI verification and disapplication review.

[1] See AG Léger in C-280/00 *Altmark* [2003] ECR I-7747.

[2] T-289/03 *BUPA* [2008] ECR II-81, §165.

[3] Ross, M, 'Article 16 E.C. and Services of General Interest: From Derogation to Obligation?' (2000) 25(1) *European Law Review* 22–38, 23.

B. The Political, Constitutional and Administrative Battleground

1. The Trigger—Article 106(3)

Under Article 106(3), the Commission is given the power to adopt Directives and Decisions 'where necessary' in order to give effect to the provisions of Article 106, including Article 106(2). Crucially, that power is exercisable without the formal involvement of either the Council or the European Parliament. The Commission's first use of its general legislative power under Article 106(3) did not occur until 1980, when it adopted what came to be referred to as the Transparency Directive.[4] Significantly, the Court of Justice rejected a challenge to the Commission recourse to Article 106(3). In particular, it refused to treat the availability of the regular legislative process as precluding recourse to that mechanism.[5] As a result, the Commission was given the green light to deploy Article 106(3) more ambitiously.

The first significant use of the Commission's Article 106(3) powers in a way that directly concerned Article 106(2) was to begin the liberalisation of the telecommunications sector. That began with the adoption of Directive 88/301 on Terminal Equipment.[6] The Terminal Directive forced the Member State to end exclusive rights over the sale and connection of telephone handsets. In recital 11 of the Terminal Equipment Directive, the Commission had asserted, baldly, that Article 106(2) did not apply and that in any event, if it did, exclusive rights over equipment would not jeopardise universal telecommunications networks. A challenge to this Directive was also unsuccessful. Rejecting the argument that the adoption of the Terminal Equipment Directive was tantamount to findings of Treaty violation by the Member States, the Court held that Article 106(3) permits the Commission to 'specify in general terms the obligations arising from Article [106(1)]'.[7]

Victory on the Terminal Directive emboldened the Commission to press forward with the liberalisation of telecommunications services. That endeavour was fraught with much greater risks. Unlike the case of equipment, the Commission could not assume that the abolition of exclusive rights would not have any impact on the ability of incumbents to continue providing universal service. Most incumbents had highly unbalanced tariffs with significant cost under-recovery for local calls being financed in part through monopoly profits on international

[4] Directive 80/723/EEC.

[5] Joined Cases 188/80, 189/80 and 190/80, *France, Italy and the UK v Commission* [1982] ECR 2545.

[6] C-202/88 *France v Commission* [1991] ECR I-1223. For a detailed discussion of the constitutional issues at stake, see Brothwood, M, 'The Court of Justice on Article 90 of the EEC Treaty' (1983) 20 *CML Rev* 335–46.

[7] ibid, §17.

calling.[8] Despite this, through the Telecommunications Services Directive, the Commission decided that all fixed services other than the provision of voice telephony should be liberalised.[9] Inevitably, several Member States brought a challenge. In substance the Commission's recourse to Article 106(3) was validated, yet again.[10] Subsequently, the Commission set a date for full liberalisation of 1 January 1998, subject to possible derogations.[11]

The political implications of the Commission's actions in telecommunications were significant. Dissenting Member States argued that, by proceeding unilaterally, the Commission had acted in an anti-democratic manner. Of special concern to the Member States must have been the Commission's implicit assessment of the burden of SGEI obligations for incumbents since that was the driver for determining the scope of exclusive rights. Recourse to Article 106(3) to liberalise telecommunications had one immediate and several long-term effects. The almost instant effect was the Commission being forced to promise that it would not rely on its Article 106(3) power without extended dialogue with the Council and the Economic and Social Committee.[12] Some Member States took this as precluding further reliance on Article 106(3) without their consent.[13] The more enduring effect was to focus intense political attention on the scope of Article 106(2).

Separately, and in what came to be a hugely significant decision, when tackling electricity liberalisation, the Commission prioritised enforcement proceedings rather than persevering with the adoption of a liberalising Article 106(3) Directive.[14] Although the Commission initially proposed an Article 106(3) Directive to open up the electricity and gas sectors, subsequently it changed course and instead presented this as a proposal for a Council Directive in February 1992.[15] In parallel, it brought enforcement proceedings in the *Electricity and Gas*

[8] For a review of this and other challenges faced by incumbents in the four largest Member States, see Thatcher, M, 'The Europeanisation of Regulation. The Case of Telecommunications' (Oct 1999) RSC No. 99/22 *European University Institute Working Paper.*

[9] Art 2 of Directive 90/388/EEC of 28 June 1990 on Competition in the Markets for Telecommunications Services. At recital 22, the Commission indicated that during 1992 it would reconsider the need for any special or exclusive rights.

[10] C-271/90 *Spain & others v Commission* [1992] ECR I-5883. The Commission's requirement for contractual termination was struck down on the basis that there was no evidence as to how the Member States had required or encouraged such arrangements. Its definition of special rights was invalidated because of its vagueness. See §§25 and 31 respectively.

[11] Directive 96/19 amending Directive 90/388/EEC with regard to the Implementation of Full Competition with Respect to Telecommunications Markets.

[12] Described in the Commission's XXVth Report on Competition Policy, 1995, §100.

[13] For a principal–agent comparison of the liberalisation of telecommunications and electricity, see Schmidt, S, 'Commission Activism: Subsuming Telecommunications and Electricity under European Competition Law' (2011) 5(1) *Journal of European Public Policy* 169–184. Schmidt traces the compromise on consultative recourse to Art 106(3) to a December 1989 Council meeting at which Directive 90/388/EEC was agreed. See ibid, 175.

[14] Schmidt, ibid, attributes the Commission's comparative timidity in electricity to the less clear-cut economic case for liberalisation, political divisions within the Commission itself and, in the main, unified opposition from the Member States, led by France.

[15] ibid, 177.

Cases against France, Spain, Italy and the Netherlands on the basis that import and export restrictions for electricity and gas violated the free movement rules. The Commission's probable strategy was to use a legal victory, or at least the prospect of it, to set the context for a political negotiation with the Council for the phased opening up of the electricity sector. As referred to above, the Commission lost the *Electricity and Gas Cases* although France eventually led the Member States to agree on a Council Directive before the handing down of judgments in those cases.[16] The outcome of the *Electricity and Gas Cases* only served to demonstrate the onerous nature of the burden of proof on the Commission in bringing forward evidence of the practicality of less restrictive means.

2. An Evolving Constitutional Position for SGEIs

Partly in response to the Commission's recourse to Article 106(3), Article 106(2) has been the subject of a number of Treaty changes, reflecting the underlying contestation of its application. A common feature of all of these addenda is their oblique nature, with no direct amendments to Article 106(2) as such, but instead, efforts to adjust its deployment through collateral and often incoherent constitutional accretions. Nevertheless, those changes have had a number of concrete effects, including sector-specific adjustments to the application of Article 106(2), the formalisation of SGEIs around stylised delivery characteristics and, most importantly, the emergence of the manifest error standard for SGEI control.

(a) Article 16 Treaty Establishing the European Community

The first constitutional changes with respect to SGEIs came with the introduction in the Treaty Establishing the European Community (TEC) of a new Article 16, which became effective on 1 May 1999.[17] It reveals greater sensitivity on the part of the Member States to the role of Article 106(2), given their experience in both telecommunications and electricity. Article 16 provided, without prejudice to certain other Treaty provisions, including the competition rules, that:

> [G]iven the place occupied by services of general economic interest in the shared values of the Union as well as their role in promoting social and territorial cohesion, the Community and the Member States, each within their respective powers and within the scope of the application of this Treaty, shall take care that such services operate on the basis of principles and conditions, which enable them to fulfil their tasks.

In addition, Article 16 was also subject to a Protocol affirming that its adoption was without prejudice to the then existing Article 106(2) *acquis* as regards the principle

[16] Directive 96/92/EC.

[17] The Treaty of Amsterdam was signed on 2 October 1997 based on negotiations initiated at Messina on 2 June 1995. Judgments in the *Electricity and Gas Cases* were not handed down until 23 October 1997.

of 'equality of treatment, quality and continuity of service'.[18] Despite a prominent role played by France in securing Article 16, its adoption underwhelmed many French parliamentarians, who referred to it as a 'consolation'.[19] Nevertheless, the Protocol underlined the need for special sensitivity with respect to SGEI verification, even if the precise nature of that deference was unspecified.

For its part, the General Court in particular has been careful to acknowledge Article 16 and in a number of instances to deploy it, largely for rhetorical effect.[20] Several Advocates General have interpreted it as signalling the need for greater deference to the Member States, most especially in relation to the qualification of SGEIs.[21] In *TNT Traco*, Advocate General Alber advised that Article 16 was 'an expression of a fundamental value judgment in Community law'.[22] For Advocate General Jacobs in *Ambulanz Glöckner*, the insertion of Article 16 drove the conclusion that providers of emergency ambulance services were entrusted with an SGEI.[23] As such, Article 16 provided a justificatory gloss. Seen in the round, however, it says everything and nothing, although it has been argued that it provides a basis for a positive entitlement to a bundle of SGEI rights.[24]

(b) The Public Service Broadcasting Protocol to the Amsterdam Treaty

The Amsterdam Treaty also inserted a Protocol into the TEC in relation to public service broadcasting. In a number of decisions in the 1990s the Commission had begun to take a more probing approach to scrutinising the nature and extent of public service obligations imposed mainly on Member State-owned or -controlled providers of television programming.[25] Partly in response, and after significant lobbying by the European Broadcasting Union, the Member States agreed to a Protocol on Public Service Broadcasting.[26] It states as follows:

> The provisions of the Treaty establishing the European Community shall be without prejudice to the competence of Member States to provide for the funding of public

[18] Declaration on Article 7d of the Treaty Establishing the European Community [1997] OJ C340/1 133.

[19] 'La France a néanmoins obtenu une consolation, avec l'insertion par le traité d'Amsterdam d'un article 16 nouveau', Rapport d'information fait au nom de la Délégation du Sénat pour l'Union européenne sur les services d'intérêt general en Europe (No. 82, 2000–2001) of November 2000, Rapporteur Hubert Haenel, p 20.

[20] In T-289/03 *BUPA* [2008] ECR II-81, it is referred to by the General Court as affecting 'in a general manner' the qualification of Member State interventions as SGEIs. See §167.

[21] According to AG Maduro, it provides a point of reference for the interpretation of Art 106(2). See C-205/03 P *FENIN* [2006] ECR I-6295, fn. 35 of his opinion.

[22] C-340/99 *TNT Traco* [2001] ECR I-4109, §94.

[23] Opinion of AG Jacobs, C-475/99 *Ambulanz Glöckner* [2001] ECR I-8089, §175.

[24] Prosser has argued that rather than being viewed as determinative of the balance of power, Art 16 might instead be understood as creating a new basis for constituting positive obligations in favour of the citizens in respect of SGEIs. See Prosser, T, 'Services of General Interest in Community Law: From Single Market to Citizenship Rights' Lecture, Seminariale tenuta il 15 dic. 2003 presso il Dipartimento di Diritto dell'Economomia, dell'Università degli Studi di Roma, La Sapienza.

[25] See Commission Decision 91/130/EEC and Commission Decision 93/403/EEC, both concerning the European Broadcasting Union.

[26] See Donders, K, 'State Aid and Public Service Broadcasting—How Future Proof is the Remit of Public Broadcasting Organisations?' (2009) 1 *Institute for European Studies Working Paper* 12.

> service broadcasting insofar as such funding is granted to broadcasting organisations for the fulfilment of the public service remit as conferred, defined and organised by each Member State, and insofar as such funding does not affect trading conditions and competition in the Community to an extent which would be contrary to the common interest, while the realisation of the remit of that public service shall be taken into account.[27]

Although displaying some of the compromise characteristics of Article 16 TEC, the terms of the Protocol are somewhat more pointed. It is a *sui generis* rule for public service broadcasting. Its primary purpose seems to be to deflect active Commission intervention with respect to supervision of the definition of public service remits in the field of broadcasting.[28] It also appears to restrict the Commission's ability to control ensuing distortions of trade and competition.[29] The Protocol came about though direct political actions by public service broadcasters who managed to enlist the support of the European Parliament for their purposes.[30] In government failure terms, that is an intriguing coalition, constituted by providers and a category of users with a particular set of incentives in terms of access to and coverage by the PSBs.[31] The aspirations of those broadcasters for the Protocol are well summed up by a 1998 statement from the European Broadcasting Union legal department claiming that 'far from requiring even so much as a minimum standard or level of definition of public broadcasting, the Protocol definitely does not prescribe that there must be "clearly defined public service obligations"'.[32] As will be explored in greater detail in Chapter 5, by and large the Protocol has been interpreted in that way. More specifically, it has driven a more general ousting of recourse to market outcomes as the benchmark for defining public service remits in the field.

(c) The Treaty Establishing a Constitution for Europe (TECE)

Unsurprisingly, SGEIs were also to be accorded further treatment in the TECE. Article III-122 of the TECE cautioned the EU and Member States to 'take care that

[27] [1997] OJ C340, p 109.

[28] Unlike Art 16, the Protocol is not stated to be without prejudice to Art 106(2) or other Treaty provisions. It was also the subject of a follow-up resolution by the Council on 25 January 1999 emphasising the importance of allowing public service content to move on to new delivery platforms. See [1999] OJ C30/01.

[29] An attempt to argue that it also entirely precluded the application of the *Altmark* criteria to the issue of advantage under the State aid rules was rejected in T-674/11 *TV Danmark v Commission* [2015] EU:T:2015:684, §§60–62. The General Court did confirm that the first *Altmark* criterion would be applied in the light of the Protocol, no doubt because of the assimilation of the SGEI and public service obligation concepts.

[30] See Katsirea, I, *Public Broadcasting Law: A Comparative Examination of Public Service Obligations in Six Member States* (Wolters Kluwer, 2008) 325.

[31] Some are less concerned by that combination and treat the Protocol as an act of political courage in the face of rapacious commercialism. In that regard, see Raboy, M and Price, W, *Public Service Broadcasting in Transition: A Documentary Reader* (Kluwer Law International, 2003) 32. At best this represents 'incentive-free' analysis of the situation disconnected from any consideration of the ultimate consequences.

[32] European Broadcasting Union, The Public Service Broadcasting Remit: Today and Tomorrow, 29 April 1998.

such services operate on the basis of principles and conditions, in particular economic and financial conditions, which enable them to fulfil their missions', adding that 'European laws shall establish these principles and set these conditions without prejudice to the competence of Member States, in compliance with the constitution, to provide, to commission and to fund such services'. Again, the drafting was ambiguous but with a renewed emphasis on the right of initiative of the Member States. In substance, it is difficult to distinguish Article III-122 from Article 16 introduced by the Amsterdam Treaty. While the Commission's 2004 White Paper on Services of General Interest welcomed Article III-122, it did so on the basis that it would clarify the basis for further action on SGEIs, even though the provision appears to direct legislative intervention at EU level to the issue of funding SGEIs as opposed to their specification.[33] Ultimately, the demise of the TECE at the hands of French and Dutch voters meant that Article III-122 never became effective, but nevertheless its orientation would influence later constitutional change.

(d) Article 14 of the TFEU Introduced by the Treaty of Lisbon

Unsurprisingly, SGEIs also featured in the debate leading up to the adoption of the Treaty of Lisbon. Again, it was a case of ambiguous incremental development. The new Article 14 TFEU, which replaced Article 16 provides that:

> Without prejudice to Article 4 of the Treaty on European Union or to Articles 93, 106 and 107 of this Treaty, and given the place occupied by services of general economic interest in the shared values of the Union as well as their role in promoting social and territorial cohesion, the Union and the Member States, each within their respective powers and within the scope of application of the Treaties, shall take care that such services operate on the basis of principles and conditions, particularly economic and financial conditions, which enable them to fulfil their missions. The European Parliament and the Council, acting by means of regulations in accordance with the ordinary legislative procedure, shall establish these principles and set these conditions without prejudice to the competence of Member States, in compliance with the Treaties, to provide, to commission and to fund such services.

Although it repeats the language on cohesion from Article 16 TEC, perhaps the most significant feature of this provision is the clarification of legislative competence in favour of the Parliament and Council. It is also noteworthy that in line with Article III-122 of the defunct TECE, this competence appears to be limited to those things that sustain SGEIs, and in particular their financing arrangements. How that is to be squared with powers to legislate generally with respect to matters affecting SGEIs (and not just their financing) that have been carried forward is far from clear.[34] In addition, the final proviso emphasises that the definition of the scope and content of SGEIs is for the Member States.

[33] COM (2004) 374 final, section 14.

[34] See generally, Buendía Sierra, JL, 'Writing Straight with Crooked Lines: Competition Policy and Services of General Economic Interest' in Biondi and Eekout, with Ripley (eds), *EU Law after Lisbon*, (Oxford University Press, 2012) 347–66.

(e) Protocol 26 to the Treaty of Lisbon

Consistent with the approach taken in the Amsterdam Treaty on SGEIs, the Treaty of Lisbon also came with a Protocol. Once more this continued the political debate by Treaty addendum. It appears that Dutch apprehension in relation to the treatment of social housing by the Commission was central to its inclusion.[35] Confusingly, while Protocol 26 is styled as referring to services of general interest (without the qualifier 'economic'), the substantive content refers mainly to SGEIs even though its stated effects are expressed with reference only to Article 14 and not Article 106(2). It provides as follows in the operative parts:

Article 1

> The shared values of the Union in respect of services of general economic interest within the meaning of Article 14 of the Treaty on the Functioning of the European Union include in particular:
>
> — the essential role and the wide discretion of national, regional and local authorities in providing, commissioning and organising services of general economic interest as closely as possible to the needs of the users;
> — the diversity between various services of general economic interest and the differences in the needs and preferences of users that may result from different geographical, social or cultural situations;
> — a high level of quality, safety and affordability, equal treatment and the promotion of universal access and of user rights.

Article 2

> The provisions of the Treaties do not affect in any way the competence of Member States to provide, commission and organise non-economic services of general interest.

Although it draws heavily on Commission soft law guidance in relation to SGEIs and earlier Court judgments, the Protocol appears to have the very clear objective of reining in the Commission.[36] The Protocol seeks to put beyond doubt that the formulation of those general interest concerns is a matter for Member States within their constitutional orders and that the Commission should not assume that the position will or should be uniform across the Member States. In addition to the terms of the Treaty of Lisbon, its entry into force in 2009 also initiated the terms of the Charter on Fundamental Rights. In Article 36 the Charter included yet another Delphic formulation concerning SGEIs. It provides that:

> The Union recognises and respects access to services of general economic interest as provided for in the national laws and practices, in accordance with the Treaty establishing the European Community, in order to promote the social and territorial cohesion of the Union.[37]

[35] See Opinion of the European Economic and Social Committee on the Affordability of SGEIs, 11.06.2014 [2014] OJ C177, pp 24–32, fn 1.

[36] For good measure there was yet another protocol inserted in relation to public service broadcasting. Protocol 29 is a restatement of the Protocol on Broadcasting introduced by the Amsterdam Treaty.

[37] See [2000] C364/01 for the initial version as promulgated.

While the issue of whether the Charter is a possible source of directly effective rights may still be in doubt, it is clear that at the very least it acts as a restraint on the EU institutional actors in the exercise of their powers and prerogatives.[38] This may ultimately act as a bar to certain Commission interventions through emphasising the primacy of the Members States in the determination of the general interest.[39] A relatively recent example in that regard is the 2016 judgment of the Court in *ANODE*, which concerned a referral from the French Conseil D'État in relation to the operation of a system of price regulation for tariffs to consumers and small business users for gas.[40] A previous judgment of the Court in *Federutility* had identified the various controlling criteria that apply to interventions directed at ousting market-determined prices under Directive 2009/73, which has as its objective the creation of an internal market with respect to gas.[41] At issue in the case was both the legitimacy of the claimed basis for intervention as well as the means adopted by France to do so. In essence, the French law provided for the regulator to propose tariffs (which applied to the incumbent and certain other providers, but not all) for ministerial approval, which were permitted to cover a range of costs. The regulated tariffs were caps, with providers free to price below them subject to default predation rules for dominant firms.

With respect to the objective to be achieved by the intervention, France sought to justify it by reference to security of supply as well as to territorial cohesion. With respect to territorial cohesion, what precisely France had in mind was not entirely clear. Under the Code de l'énergie territorial cohesion seemed to relate to universal access to energy, ie ubiquitous geographic service availability. Moreover, as Advocate General Mengozzi pointed out, the referring Court's questions treated territorial cohesion as distinct from ensuring that price was maintained at a reasonable level.[42] Nevertheless, it is possible to consider that a concern about affordability might arise for certain remote areas if prices were to reflect transmission costs in particular, which is ultimately how the Court proceeded to conceive of the problem. Advocate General Mengozzi considered that the concern to ensure territorial cohesion was reflected in Article 3(3) of the Directive in so far as it permitted measures to 'protect customers in remote areas who are connected to the gas system'.[43]

For its part, the Court was receptive to the Advocate General's prompting that the 'new context' for SGEIs operating by virtue of Article 14 and Protocol 26 tipped the balance in favour of permitting France to further the goal of territorial

[38] See Art 51 of the Charter.

[39] Despite that, it is notable that the promotion of social and territorial cohesion is framed with reference to the Union and not the Member States.

[40] C-121/15 *ANODE v Premier ministre et autres* ECLI:EU:C:2016:638.

[41] Directive 2009/73/EC concerning Common Rules for the Internal Market in Natural Gas of 13 July 2009.

[42] Opinion of 12 April 2016, ECLI:EU:C:2016:637, §42. That had been recognised as a distinct objective in *Federutility*.

[43] Ibid. §57.

cohesion under Article 3(2) of the Directive.[44] That provision makes express reference to Article 106(2) while identifying certain bases for intervention in gas markets. As such, we see the effect of constitutional change at the margin since it is by no means clear that the basis for intervention in this case was properly thought out at all. If anything, the measure, which resulted in price caps for several (but not all) providers, was aimed at the goal of affordability. By way of trying to overcome the fact that only some firms were regulated, the French government had claimed that the regulated price tended to set a reference ceiling for non-regulated firms.[45]

3. The Commission's SGEI Containment Strategy

Despite the Court having confirmed its power to do so, until the aftermath of *Altmark*, the Commission never used its Article 106(3) powers to establish any broad principles concerning SGEIs, either in terms of their definition, substantive content or supervision. Instead, the Commission issued a stream of soft law instruments in the form of several communications, a Green Paper, a White Paper and numerous ad hoc reports and communications.[46] In addition to clarifying certain issues, while occasionally introducing new uncertainties, the Commission has used these publications to attempt to keep political concern in check.[47]

(a) The Commission's Soft Law Guidance

The Commission's conceptualisation of SGEIs has evolved over time through soft law instruments. There has, however, been no definitive clarification of the SGEI concept in technical terms. The Commission's first containment effort in the field of SGEIs was its 1996 Communication on Services of General Interest in Europe.[48] The very title signals a presentational innovation on the part of the Commission, which was to distinguish between SGEIs and Services of General Interest (SGIs). The latter comprised what it defined as 'market and non-market services that the public authorities class as being of general interest and subject to specific public service obligations'.[49] In other words, SGIs comprise SGEIs provided by

[44] §40.

[45] While the Court by way of disapplication review was very critical of the departure from competitive prices brought about by the caps, given the costs that were allowable, it seems almost certain that the regulator was recommending tariffs using a variation on a rate-of-return-type model. See Chapter 6 for a fuller consideration of disapplication review in this case.

[46] Commission activity even extended to the issuance of an intriguingly entitled 'Non Paper on Services of General Economic Interest and State Aid', 12 November 2002.

[47] According to Sauter, the Commission's strategy can be conceived of as 'Drowning discord in a stream of communication …': Sauter, W, *Public Services in EU Law* (Cambridge University Press, 2015) 27.

[48] COM (1996) 443 final of 11.09.1996.

[49] ibid, p 2.

undertakings as well as public services provided otherwise. The Commission also acknowledged that the term 'public service' was itself ambiguous.[50] Separately, the Commission was careful to note the importance of subsidiarity, which it maintained would allow the Member States considerable discretion in the implementation of specified general interest objectives, particularly in the electricity sector.[51]

The Commission's 2000 Communication on Service of General Interest represented a significant evolution in its approach to SGEIs.[52] Pointedly, and presumably concerned to show its adaption to the enlarged constitutional landscape, the second sentence of the 2000 Communication makes reference to the then new Article 16 of the TEC. SGEIs are defined as 'services that are different from ordinary services in that public authorities consider they need to be provided even when the market may not have sufficient incentives to do so'.[53] While this is not styled as a 'market failure' approach, it has some of those connotations. In addition, the 2000 Communication is very significant for the Commission's voluntary adoption of the 'manifest error' control standard for the supervision of SGEI claims.[54] Although clearly offered to the Member States to give comfort on SGEI definition, there are no specifics provided as to how this standard might work in practice.

The Commission followed up in 2001 with a Report to the Laeken Summit.[55] Significantly, for the first time, the language of 'market failure' was used to explain certain interventions by public authorities.[56] In emphasising the possible underperformance of markets in some cases, the Commission provided three different bases for intervention.[57] The first concerned those cases where 'the individual or the market fail to appropriately value all benefits' of a particular activity.[58] Education was cited as an example. The second category concerned 'the desire by society to ensure the provision and use of "merit" goods and "club" goods', with museums cited as an example. The third category was a catchall and refers to services that society determines should be available to everybody. This report was not, however, tendered as soft law guidance.[59] Ultimately, this conceptual framework was not taken forward or developed by the Commission as part of the subsequent White Paper on SGIs, or for that matter in copious follow-up documents.[60]

[50] ibid.
[51] ibid, p 10. This was a clear acknowledgment of the sensitivity of its interventions in that sector.
[52] COM (2000) 580 final of 20.09.2000.
[53] ibid, §14.
[54] ibid, §22.
[55] COM (2001) 598 final.
[56] The margin note to §3 of the Introduction is: 'Public sector intervention in cases of market failure'.
[57] COM (2001) 598 final, §3.
[58] This corresponds to the concept of a positive externality, a classic market failure.
[59] §6 confirms that it does not replace the 1996 or 2000 Communications.
[60] There is a passing reference to market failures in the context of insurance in the 2003 Green Paper on Services of General Interest. See COM (2003) 270 final, §62(e).

(b) Avoiding a Framework Directive

A principal objective of the Commission in its publication of prolific guidance on SGEIs was the concern to avoid a 'Framework Directive'. While it is difficult to be certain what such a Directive might have included, it appears that certain political actors envisaged that it might define the concept of SGEI with greater precision, or possibly provide for more lenient treatment of SGEIs, not least with respect to supporting measures. The political battle over a Framework Directive reached a high point in the mid-2000s, having started as a demand for an SGEI 'charter', it was eventually supplanted by calls for a Framework Directive.[61] The call for a charter first appeared in a 1995 CEEP (an association of public undertakings in Europe) study that proposed a new Treaty provision on SGEIs that would have cut back on the scope of Article 106(2).[62]

EU institutional actors were more cautious.[63] While broadly welcoming the 2000 Communication, in plenary session the Parliament fell short of calling for the adoption of a Framework Directive on SGEIs.[64] In 2002, following up on a commitment contained in its Laeken Report, the Commission issued a terse communication on the possibility of a Framework Directive. It moved away from that on the basis that it was preparing a Green Paper.[65] In its subsequent Green Paper, while the Commission appeared to be open to the possibility of a Framework Directive, it pointed out that Article 16 TEC would not provide a legal basis for such a measure. It also emphasised the challenge that would be presented in trying to draft a measure based 'on the common denominator of different services with very different characteristics'.[66]

Subsequently, Parliament was to become explicit in its overall opposition to a framework law. In responding to the 2003 Green Paper on Services of General Interest, it argued that a Framework Directive could not accommodate the diversity of SGEIs and would lead to confusion concerning its relationship with already adopted sectoral regulation.[67] Parliament also maintained that a Framework Directive would cut across what it regarded as the exclusive competence of the

[61] Buendía Sierra, L, *Exclusive Rights and State Monopolies under EC Law* (Oxford University Press, 2000) 330–31.

[62] CEEP, *Concurrence et Service Public* (Masson/Armand Colin, 1995, 1995).

[63] See by way of commentary on the CEEP proposals, Editorial Comment, 'Public Service Obligations: A Blessing or a Liability?, (1996) 33 CMLR 395–400. The CEEP case for limiting Art 106(2) appears to have been offset by the Second Report of the Advisory Group on Competitiveness calling for further competition in utilities subject to the maintenance of universal service.

[64] European Parliament Resolution of 13.11.2001 (2002/C 140 E/002).

[65] Communication from the Commission to the Council, the European Parliament, the Economic and Social Committee and the Committee of the Regions on the Status of Work on the Examination of a Proposal for a Framework Directive on Services of General Interest, COM (2002) 0689 final.

[66] Green Paper on Services of General Interest, COM (2003) 270 final, §40.

[67] European Parliament, Report on the Green Paper on Services of General Interest, (COM(2003) 270—2003/2152(INI)), §11. The Commission identified the then Art 95 TEC as a potential legal basis, but claimed that it could not be availed of to demarcate between SGEIs and SEIs.

Member States to define SGEIs.[68] By the time the Commission adopted its 2004 White Paper on Services of General Interest, it ruled out a Framework Directive on the basis that it was anticipated that the TECE would enter into force and that it was possible that under it, new legislation for SGEIs might emerge.[69] In 2007, in continuing to reject the case for a Framework Directive, the Commission claimed that what came to be Protocol 26 to the Treaty of Lisbon was a 'new, transparent and reliable framework at the level of the Treaty' with respect to SGIs.[70]

(c) Stylising Services of General Economic Interest

Despite the Commission's prodigious output by way of soft law guidance, Sauter has argued that the net effect has been 'harmless'.[71] While the assembly of materials over time has brought forward surprisingly few innovations, there have been subtle but meaningful effects. That is most apparent in the formalisation of SGEIs around a number of stylised delivery characteristics. They include universality, continuity, non-discrimination and affordability. While these are typical characteristics of 'universal service' or 'public service' obligations, they have become part of the standard SGEI discourse and have been used to ground arguments that to qualify as an SGEI, activity must at minimum have several of these characteristics.[72] An emphasis on stylised delivery characteristics is understandable, not least because they have a very strong correspondence to elements of the French service public tradition and effectively embody many of the tenets of the *Loi Rolland* conception of public services.[73]

In its 2003 Green Paper on SGEIs, the Commission gave prominent attention to what it introduced as a 'common set of obligations' underpinning SGEIs in so far as they were then regulated at European level.[74] The Commission acknowledged the undesirability of 'a single comprehensive European definition', but nevertheless identified universal service, continuity, quality of service, affordability, and user and consumer protection as core features of SGEI provision. These were simply an amalgam of obligations from the regulation of the telecommunications, electricity

[68] §18.

[69] White Paper on Services of General Interest. COM(2004) 374 final, p.6,11.

[70] Communication of the Commission to the European Parliament, the Council, the European Economic and Social Committee and the Committee of the Regions, A Single Market for 21st Century Europe, COM (2007) 724 final, p 10. See also the accompanying Commission Staff Working Document, Progress since the 2004 White Paper on Services of General Interest, SEC (2007)1515.

[71] Sauter, W, 'Services of General Economic Interest and Universal Service in EU Law' (2008) 33(2) *European Law Review* 167–93, 171. See also, Sauter, W, 'Services of General Economic Interest (SGEI) and Universal Service Obligations (USO) as an EU Law Framework for Curative Health Care' (2007) 029 *TILEC Discussion Paper 9* where he says: 'In substance, there is no relevant change: the entire debate on services of general economic interest can be seen as a holding exercise by the Commission, intended to diffuse political tension on this topic, without having much of an impact on the scope or meaning of services of general economic interest', TILEC DP (2007-029) 9.

[72] See Ross, M, *A Healthy Approach to Services of General Economic Interest? The BUPA Judgment of the Court of First Instance* (2009) 34(1) *European Law Review* 127–40.

[73] See generally, Guglielmi G, *Une Introduction au Droit du Service Public.*

[74] Green Paper on Services of General Interest, 21.05.03, COM (2003) 270 final, p 16.

and postal sectors. Each one of these concepts is fraught with difficulties, however, some of which are acknowledged by the Commission. Consider, for example, the issue of continuity of supply for electricity. The Commission acknowledged in the Green Paper that there might be situations where a provider has adequate incentives not to interrupt supply absent any compulsion.[75] Take the other exemplar of an SGEI, namely 'affordability'. The Commission cites telecommunications regulation as having pioneered the concept but whether a particular price intervention has that effect depends on the content of the method of price regulation deployed. In the *Electricity and Gas Cases*, France sought to rely on what it claimed was an obligation of the incumbent to supply at lowest cost. The obligation in question was interrogated by the Court, which held that it did not in fact guarantee least cost supply.[76] Separately, the Commission's reliance in its Green Paper on 'universal service' as a general obligation omits any specific reference to how absolute or extensive supply obligations need to be for that purpose.

The difficulties become even more acute when comparing the other general obligations, 'quality of service' and 'user and consumer protection'. In line with the *GVL* distinction between general regulation and sector-specific requirements, with respect to 'user and consumer' protection, the Commission emphasises a distinction between 'horizontal consumer protection rules' and those that are distinctly applicable to a particular sector.[77] In respect of quality of service, however, the Commission relied on specific obligations taken mainly from telecommunications and postal liberalisation, such as safety regulation and billing requirements, which in substance appear to fit more readily in the category of general regulation and in turn outside the realm of an SGEI. Certainly, these do not appear to be the kind of negation of a fundamental commercial freedom of the type emphasised by the General Court in *BUPA*.[78]

The subsequent White Paper noted that there was division on the adoption of a common set of obligations at EU level and even more diluted support for the Commission's suggestions for additional obligations. Yet, despite the apparent rejection of the common obligations approach, the earlier, more discursive parts of the White Paper retain general language emphasising the importance of universal service, security, safety and quality provision.[79] Although the stylised delivery characteristics approach was not carried forward formally, it has an obvious attraction for interlocutors in the various political and legal debates on SGEIs that remain current. This approach, however, has several shortcomings, not least being that it tends to ossify the concept of SGEI. In essence, stylised delivery characteristics are just a generalised way of describing particular tasks. As a result, recourse to

[75] §50.

[76] *Electricity and Gas Cases* [1997] ECR I-5851, §81. The Commission rightly questioned whether a general requirement for productive efficiency could be regarded as an SGEI.

[77] Green Paper on Services of Economic Interest, COM (2003) 270 final, §62; Case-7/82 *GVL* [1983] ECR 483.

[78] T-289/03 *BUPA* [2008] ECR II-81, §190.

[79] COM (2004) 374 final, pp7–11.

them may turn the validation of SGEI claims into quasi-semantic debates about whether the characteristics of service delivery take pre-ordained forms.

4. Manifest Error and the Problem of Legitimacy

As previously referred to, the manifest error standard for SGEI supervision was included in the Commission's 2000 Communication on Services of General Interest.[80] It is perhaps the most significant move by the Commission as part of its overall containment strategy with respect to SGEIs. No authority or analysis was supplied in the 2000 Communication in support of the manifest error standard. Neither does it appear to have been pre-dated by any Commission decisions in individual cases expressly applying that supervision standard. As a result, it might be best understood as the Commission wishing to be seen to respond to the Member States in the light of Article 16 TEC. The manifest error standard appears to disavow any prior limits by both respecting the Member State's right of initiative as well as attaching strong prima facie validity to any assertion by a Member State that a particular activity has general interest significance.

(a) Judicial Approval

Relatively early in the case law on Article 106(2), there was a suggestion that the qualification of an activity as an SGEI entailed significant discretion on the part of Member States. The Court's judgment in *Sacchi* appeared to leave it to the Member States to decide what constitutes an SGEI.[81] That is an enigmatic judgment, in which the Court refers to Member States making the decision to 'treat' particular activities as SGEIs.[82] The use of this word suggests that it was for the Member State to determine what qualifies as an SGEI (in this case broadcasting and advertising), a proposition that did not go unchallenged.[83] Subsequently, in *GEMO* Advocate General Jacobs advanced the argument for 'marginal control' of SGEI claims but did not refer to the Commission's 2001 Communication. Paradoxically, in the three cases that he mentions in that footnote, the Court of Justice rejected arguments in favour of various SGEIs.[84] Those judgments give no indication of any special deference justifying supervision on the basis of marginal control.

[80] COM (2000) 580 final.

[81] C-155/73 *Sacchi* [1974] ECR 409.

[82] ibid, §15.

[83] See the reservations expressed in Bellamy and Child, *Common Market Law of Competition*, 4th edn (Sweet & Maxwell, 1993) 816, fn 86: 'It is submitted that whether an undertaking is operating a service of general economic interest is to be determined by Community law'.

[84] C-126/01 *GEMO* [2003] ECR I-13769, Opinion of 30 April 2002, where he says at footnote 75: 'It is clear that control is in principle a marginal control. None the less in Case C-18/88 *GB-INNO-BM* [1991] § 22, the Court did not accept that the production and sale of telephones constituted a service of general interest; see as regards dock work, Case C-179/90 *Porto di Genova*, paragraph 27, and as regards the transfers by banks of funds from one Member State to another, Case 172/80 *Züchner* [1981] ECR 2021, paragraph 7'.

In *Fred Olsen* the General Court held for the first time that, given the breadth of Member State discretion, the standard of control would be for 'manifest error' only.[85] As authority for that conclusion, the General Court cited a much earlier decision of the Court in *FFSA*, while also referring to the 2001 Communication. The paragraph relied upon from *FFSA* is only loose authority for the proposition that control should be for manifest error.[86] In 2007, in its judgment in *BUPA*, the General Court again approved the manifest error test, relying on the Commission Communication from 2001 and again, the less than conclusive *FFSA* judgment.[87] The manifest error standard was also expressly endorsed by the General Court in *Colt* in 2013.[88] Considering the wider constitutional backdrop, it is almost inconceivable that the Court of Justice will ever take a different stance.

(b) An Open Standard

The concept of marginal control based on manifest error has been adopted by the Commission considering the standard of review that it faces before the European Courts in the competition arena, although it has a general application extending across many forms of judicial review by the European Courts, including the supervision of the exercise of legislative and executive power. In *Alrosa*, Advocate General Kokott framed the manifest error standard as follows:

> If the factual and evidential position reasonably allows different assessments, there can be no legal objection if the Commission adopts one of them, even if it is not the one which the Court considers to be preferable. A manifest error of assessment exists only where the conclusions drawn by the Commission are no longer justifiable in the light of the factual and evidential position, that is to say if no reasonable basis can be discerned.[89]

The implication of such an approach in the context of Article 106(2) will be apparent by substituting 'Member State' for 'Commission' and 'Commission' for 'Court'. The position seems even clearer considering the socio-economic considerations that are often implicated in SGEIs. Chief among those choices are those relating to whether and to what extent a given policy pursues distributional objectives, whether it should be progressive from a wealth perspective, or instead, should have an overriding cohesion component that trumps equity concerns. It is very difficult to see, given the current state of the Union, how the Commission has the legitimacy to engage in a full-blown assessment of those choices. Despite that, and as will be considered next, occasionally the Commission intervenes very invasively in the formulation of distributional choices by the Member States.

[85] T-17/02 *Fred Olsen* [2005] ECR II-2031, §216.

[86] T-106/95 *FFSA* [1997] ECR II-229. The paragraph relied on in *FFSA* is 99. It says that 'the authorities of the Member States may in some cases have a sufficient degree of latitude in regulating certain matters, such as, in the present case, the organisation of public services in the postal sector'.

[87] T-289/03 *BUPA* [2008] ECR II-81, §§220–21.

[88] T-79/10 *Colt* ECLI:EU:T:2013:463, §92.

[89] C-441/07 *Alrosa* [2010] ECR I-5949, Opinion of AG Kokott of 17 September 2009.

C. Accounts of Article 106(2)

The following is a synthesis of certain conceptual accounts of aspects of Article 106(2). While it is true that the operation of Article 106(2) is not ad hoc, the very diversity of the subject matter of cases and the underlying political sensitivities present considerable challenges for the purposes of developing conceptual accounts of Article 106(2). This section is limited to those accounts of Article 106(2) that seek to give an overarching conceptual explanation of SGEI verification or disapplication review. As a result, with respect to SGEI identification, it considers the claims of Prosser, Ross, and Ølykke & Møllgaard, and with respect to proportionality specifically, it explores the pre-emption account of proportionality pioneered by Sauter and Schepel.

1. Prosser's Solidarity-based Account of SGEIs

The most distinctive conceptual account of SGEIs is the solidarity-based explanation advanced by Prosser.[90] This critique explains SGEIs as being intended to meet certain fundamental needs of a communal nature. As such, it is goal-based. Prosser regards the continental tradition of 'service public' as exemplifying solidarity through its emphasis on universalism and service provision on both mandatory and uniform terms. According to Prosser, the principal focus of a solidarity-based account of SGEIs is to 'prevent or limit the socially fragmenting role of markets'.[91] Solidarity is proffered as socially unifying, based in particular on a concern for satisfaction of needs that are capable of collective fulfilment.[92] Prosser traces his approach to solidarity to the early twentieth-century sociology of Emile Durkheim and his collaborator and public lawyer, Léon Duguit. He regards social solidarity as unrealisable through regular market provision.[93] According to Prosser, the social solidarity understanding of SGEIs is most coherent in the regulation of public services, and in particular utility regulation, where uniform pricing and obligations to serve frequently apply.[94]

[90] Prosser, T, 'Public Service Law: Privatisation's Unexpected Offspring' (2000) 63(4) *Law and Contemporary Problems* 63–82, 70–72. See also, Ross, M, 'Promoting Solidarity: From Public Services to a European Model of Competition' (2007) 44 *CML Rev* 1057–1080.

[91] Prosser, T, *The Regulatory Enterprise: Government Regulation and Legitimacy* (Oxford University Press, 2010) 16.

[92] This concept of solidarity is distinct from that deployed by the Court of Justice for the purpose of limiting the concept of 'undertaking' under the competition rules as considered in Chapter 4.

[93] There appears to be, at least to some degree, a general dismissal of the potential for markets to meet collective preferences without being dehumanising. That view may be as much borne of assumption as demonstration. See, Block, 'The Roles of the State in the Economy' in Smelser and Swedberg (eds), *The Handbook of Economic Sociology* (Princeton University Press, 1994) 696.

[94] Prosser, T, 'EU Competition Law and Public Services' in Mossialos et al (eds), *Health Systems Governance in Europe* (Cambridge University Press, 2010).

Prosser regards the position of economic analysis in the public policy sphere as hegemonic and accordingly objectionable, while taking issue with market failure-derived regulation as simultaneously too wide and too narrow.[95] The narrowness, he argues, is derived from the implicit assumption that 'in principle market solutions are always the first-best outcomes to decisions on the allocation of goods and services'.[96] The wideness he attributes to the treatment of other bases of intervention as arbitrary. Prosser advances a more general argument critically questioning whether much of the activity of the modern regulatory state can be categorised as being concerned with the correction of market failures only. Despite that, his opposition to a market failure account of SGEIs is in essence an argument for a wider moral dimension in economic organisation.[97]

The social solidarity critique has the advantage of identifying certain services as SGEIs on the basis that they meet a common basic need that is capable of being satisfied on a collective basis. In addition, solidarity seeks to objectivise a basis for regulatory intervention that appears to be more specific than generalised distributional claims. Despite that, there is no doubting its inherent subjectivity, or at the very least, the need for society to reach a consensus on basic needs.[98] That in turn focuses attention on which of those needs are solidarity derived, whether 'solidarity' can be objectivised, or instead is simply a question of social consensus or majority support.[99] Prosser's solidarity-based account is essentially concerned with the qualification of SGEIs based on the extraction of a single unifying purpose.[100] That very purpose may be regarded as inherent in the pursuit of any conceivable distributional goal. As a result, Prosser's account might be understood as a claim for an open-ended (and not market failure-constrained) approach to what is capable of qualifying as a general interest under Article 106(2). That, it is submitted, is largely unobjectionable.

2. Ross's Communautaire Core Reading of *BUPA*

While Prosser's approach to SGEI definition might be seen as a reaction to the possible limitation of general interests, by contrast, Ross's is derived from the

95 Prosser, T, 'Regulation and Social Solidarity' (2006) 33(3) *Journal of Law and Society* 364–87.

96 ibid, 369.

97 ibid, 378.

98 There are obvious parallels with Rawls's concept of social primary goods. See Rawls, J, *A Theory of Justice* (Belknap, 1971) 62.

99 For an ambivalent account of the justiciability of solidarity, see Davies, G, 'The Price of Letting the Courts Value Solidarity: The Judicial Role in Liberalising Welfare' in Ross and Borgmann-Probel (eds), *Promoting Solidarity in the European Union* (Oxford University Press, 2010.

100 See in this regard Commission Decision 2003/521/EC, *Bolzano Cableways*, §§46–47, where in the context of State aid, the Commission rejected the operation of cableways mainly used for skiing as meeting a 'basic need'. While the conclusion looks sensible, on slightly different facts, and in particular against another social context, the Commission's approach might have been harder to defend. More fundamentally, this raises the question of the legitimacy of the Commission taking a view on what amounts to basic needs.

stylised delivery characteristics approach to SGEI verification. Ross has argued that a 'communautaire core' must underpin a service in order to qualify as an SGEI.[101] The contention is that although the concept of SGEI is not communautaire in the conventional sense, there is nevertheless a minimum content that the European Courts insist on being present in order to qualify a particular activity as an SGEI. The nub of Ross's argument is based on the judgment of the General Court in *BUPA*.

In summary, *BUPA* concerned the operation of an inter-insurer levy that Ireland sought to justify on the basis that it was necessary to sustain the regulated terms on which private medical insurance was provided. Those included rules on open enrolment, lifetime cover, minimum benefits and community rating. The effect of those rules was to require insurers not to refuse cover to particular individuals, to renew cover annually where cover continued to be on general offer, to include cover at predetermined levels for particular conditions, and not to engage in price discrimination for the same level of cover. The General Court emphasised that while the concept of SGEI was not communautaire, nevertheless in every case it was essential that the SGEI mission was universal and compulsory.[102]

Although Ross' dissection of the General Court's approach in *BUPA* is revealing, it is not clear that *BUPA* establishes a general principle that a particular stylised delivery characteristic, namely universality, is a *sine qua non* of SGEI qualification, and even if it does, that is a questionable proposition. While the General Court emphasised that the obligation to contract with all consumers (subject to limited exceptions) meant that the service was 'compulsory', each of the other regulatory requirements was also mandatory. As such, the emphasis on compulsion serves to obscure the actual focus on the obligation to contract. Why the General Court sought to emphasise this particular feature of the system (itself brought about by the open enrolment and lifetime cover rules) to the exclusion of the other regulatory obligations is not entirely clear. The obligation to contract may have presented itself as the clearest mandated departure from typical commercial freedom. As a result, to the extent that *BUPA* does establish a *communautaire* core for SGEIs, its significance is in focusing on how obligations produce material departures from autonomous commercial conduct. That was first recognised by the Court of Justice as far back as in the *Electricity and Gas Cases*.[103] Stated otherwise, the litmus test for SGEIs is more about mandated departures from market-based outcomes than any one descriptor or an overall objective to be attained by a particular measure.

101 Ross (n 72) 136.

102 T-289/03 *BUPA*. [2008] ECR II-81, §163, §172.

103 See in particular, C-159/94 *Commission v France*, §81, where the Court concluded that a claimed obligation to set tariffs as low as possible was considered by the Court not to actually operate in that way.

3. Ølykke and Møllgard's Network Component Theory of SGEIs

Among the various accounts of SGEIs, this is the hypothesis that up to now is most closely based on a form of market failure analysis. The backdrop to its developments is Ølykke and Møllgaard's concern that the manifest error test for SGEI verification is not, of itself, a sufficiently clear or certain mechanism.[104] They argue that although market failure is part of that assessment, so too is the existence of relevant legislation and the universal and compulsory nature of the mandate. In the face of the uncertainty surrounding those elements they suggest that the concept of SGEI must be objectivised, and to that end they advocate an economic approach focusing on the concept of market failure. While considering various forms of market failure, they conclude that network effects are critical, before suggesting as an SGEI definition 'The strengthening of a component of a network that under provides services to a significant share of the population of a Member State'.[105] Subsequently, Ølykke and Møllgaard engage in a statistical analysis of the case law of the Court to argue that 'most SGEI cases determined by the European Courts indeed relate to industries with clear network aspects'.[106] In that regard, they rely on cases from transport, telecommunications, postal services, energy and waste collection. As a subsidiary line of argument, they maintain that other prominent sectors, such as pension and insurance schemes, health care and public employment agencies 'have network aspects that are linked to network effects'.[107]

Ølykke and Møllgard's analysis is significant because it takes forward the concept of market failure to try to develop a systematic account of the concept of SGEI. What is not entirely clear is why market failure is then effectively compressed in its entirety into a related phenomenon, namely network effects.[108] Furthermore, although the authors acknowledge very fairly that an activity may have network characteristics without exhibiting network effects, the implications of that distinction do not appear to have fully impacted on the findings. For example, Ølykke and Møllgaard specifically acknowledge that electricity, gas and water networks do not exhibit network externalities, yet they rely on cases from those sectors where SGEI claims have been accepted as demonstrating their hypothesis.[109] While they do instead refer to those activities as being public goods, they do not broaden their overall claim accordingly. It remains focused on networks or network effects only. In any event, in many of the cases from those sectors, the explicit basis of the Court of Justice's acceptance of the SGEI

[104] Ølykke, G and Møllgaard, P, 'What is a Service of General Economic Interest' 1–3, section 2.1.2.

[105] ibid, section 2.4.

[106] The statistical analysis identifies various sectors where SGEI claims have been considered. Those sectors are the subject of general claims as to the existence of networks or network effect and on that basis the acceptance of an SGEI claim is taken to confirm the broader hypothesis. See ibid, section 3.2.

[107] ibid, section 3.2.

[108] Specifically, they focus on the positive externality characteristics of certain networks, whereby the addition of a new user benefits all other users, ibid.

[109] ibid, section 2.5.

is by reason of apparent distributional or cohesional goals, and not any network element, be that in general terms or by reason of network externalities.

Separately, Ølykke and Møllgaard's subsidiary line of argument concerning the other activities identified, namely pension and insurance schemes, health care and public employment agencies exhibiting externalities is not fully substantiated with respect to the existence of networks, or network externalities for that matter. Instead, for some of them, respect for the principle of significant population coverage is highlighted. Again, that might be expected to lead to Ølykke and Møllgaard's overall claim being qualified, but nevertheless it remains the case that an SGEI strengthens a component of a network that provides services to a significant share of the population. In the end, it is not entirely clear whether the existence of a network externality or some generalised connection to networks is dispositive. More generally, the shoehorning of all SGEI claims into underpinning network externalities (if that is the actual claim) is not comprehensively justified.[110] That is not to say that network externalities are not relevant in SGEI cases, but why other recognised forms of market failure should be discounted is not apparent.

4. Sauter and Schepel's Pre-emption-based Account of Proportionality Review Under Article 106(2)

The pre-emption based approach to explaining the operation of proportionality under Article 106(2) was first advanced by Sauter and Schepel in a 2007 monograph.[111] It remains the most prominent conceptual treatment of this issue. Sauter and Schepel make their claim in the light of the outcome of the *Electricity and Gas Cases* and subsequent judgments, where the lack of EU sectoral legislation appears to have made a decisive difference to the nature of the proportionality review under Article 106(2). Accordingly, the fact of pre-emption, which they frame as the occupation of a field through legislative intervention, is said to be the critical driver.[112] Sauter and Schepel derive the variants of proportionality review from the Court of Justice's ruling in *Fedesa* concerning the Common Agricultural Policy.[113] There, the Court distinguished between judicial review based on 'manifest error' and on 'least restrictive means'.[114] Sauter and Schepel argue that the logic of *Fedesa* applies, but in reverse, in respect of proportionality

[110] ibid. In any event, Ølykke and Møllgaard suggest at the end of section 2.5 that the source of under-provisioning of an SGEI might be non-excludability, network effects or asymmetric information. As was explored in Chapter 2, non-excludability and information asymmetries are distinct drivers of market failure. It is not clear how they can in all (or many) cases be equated with network effects.

[111] Sauter, W and Schepel, H, '"State" and "Market" in the Competition and Free Movement Case Law of the EU Courts' (2007) 024 *TILEC Discussion Paper* 124.

[112] Sauter has his own slightly more detailed version of the claim in 'Services of General Economic Interest and Universal Service in EU Law' (n 71).

[113] C-331/88 *Fedesa* [1990] ECR I-4023.

[114] ibid, §§13, 14.

under Article 106(2). The subtext is that in political and legal terms the Member States are pre-eminent when it comes to SGEIs.[115]

The *Electricity and Gas Cases* provide the foundation stone for Sauter and Schepel's pre-emption claim.[116] There, the Court grappled with proportionality-related concerns in disposing of Commission arguments that the incumbent operators could continue to discharge their SGEI obligations without exclusive import and export rights. The Court held that in the absence of a Community framework in the field, and based on what it regarded as generalised claims made to it by the Commission as to possible alternatives, it was not in a position to condemn the operation by several Member States of import and export restrictions. In particular, the Court emphasised its inability 'to undertake an assessment, necessarily extending to economic, financial and social matters concerned with adopting the most efficacious means of delivering the SGEI'.[117] While acknowledging that the *Electricity and Gas Cases* could be read as meaning that a least restrictive means test applied, at least in principle, taken as a whole, Sauter and Schepel maintain that they stand for the proposition that there are two distinct proportionality standards, with the test of manifest error having been applied.[118]

Sauter and Schepel's theory raises the issue of whether it is possible to characterise a dispute as concerning a particular field or activity only. *BUPA*, which concerned insurance regulation, is a good example of that challenge, since on the one hand it was health related (as emphasised by the General Court) but on the other it concerned regulation of a financial product in a sector where EU legislation was very significant and touched on the general interest implicated (ignored by the General Court). That in turn raises the question whether in order to give rise to pre-emption the legislation must deal with the specific intervention that is at issue under Article 106(2), or whether comprehensive legislation, albeit not addressing that intervention, suffices to result in pre-emption. In that regard, the Court of Justice has held that a Member State is prevented from residual reliance on Article 106(2) in the presence of relevant legislation only when the general interest in question has been considered in the legislative process and is reflected in a specific legal provision.[119]

Obviously, a difficulty may arise for the pre-emption theory if there is in fact a single proportionality standard under Article 106(2). Sauter and Schepel acknowledge that this is a contentious point.[120] In *Deutsche Post* Advocate General La Pergola asserted the existence of a single proportionality standard based on

[115] Sauter and Schepel (n 111) 164.

[116] *Fedesa* was concerned with the legality of EU legislation where the Union had significant (if not pre-eminent) legislative competence at that time, leading the Court to consider that Community legislation should only be set aside if it was 'manifestly inappropriate' for its intended purpose.

[117] ibid, §106.

[118] C-147/97 *Deutsche Post* [2000] ECR I-825 and C-148/97 *Citicorp Kartenservice* [2000] ECRI-825, Opinion of 1 June 1999.

[119] C-206/98 *Commission v Belgium* [2000] ECR I-3509, §45.

[120] Sauter and Schepel (n 111) 165.

a consideration of less restrictive means under Article 106(2).[121] Perhaps of greater moment is Advocate General La Pergola's characterisation of the nature of proportionality review in the *Electricity and Gas Cases* as turning on the procedural distinctiveness of enforcement proceedings and the Commission's apparent failure to adduce the necessary proof.[122] As such, the result in the *Electricity and Gas Cases* does not necessarily vitiate the existence of a single strict proportionality standard.

Finally, the overall position considering the various cases relied upon by Sauter and Schepel is mixed. They include *Corbeau*, *Almelo*, *Ambulanz Glöckner*, *Albany*, *Brentjens* and *Drijvende Bokken*.[123] In neither *Corbeau* nor *Ambulanz Glöckner* was the Court of Justice confronted with any significant evidence or debate as to the potential for less restrictive means.[124] *Almelo* bears out Sauter and Schepel's pre-emption hypothesis, given that there was no sectoral legislation in place and the Court appears to apply a 'not manifestly disproportionate' standard to the choice of means, albeit when considering private conduct.[125] By contrast, *Albany*, *Brentjens* and *Drijvende Bokken* (which in effect comprise one judgment) are clearer authority in favour of the pre-emption-driven account of proportionality review. The cases concerned de facto exclusive rights over the provision of supplementary pension cover. In summary, having accepted the relevant pension funds as SGEIs, the Court of Justice refused to impugn the means deployed by the Netherlands, despite prima facie evidence concerning the viability of less restrictive alternatives. There was no relevant EU sectoral legislation in place.

While a more general testing of the case law that has been decided since Sauter and Schepel first published their claim is outside the scope of this work, and leaving aside the issue of what precisely is necessary by way of field occupation, Sauter and Schepel's hypothesis appears to explain much that is obscure. In particular, it is revealing by focusing attention on the nature of the evidential record before the European Courts. The existence of detailed legislation, in particular, may help to inform the judges, while also possibly offering reassurance as to likely outcomes in those situations where the denial of protection under Article 106(2) is being contemplated. More fundamentally, it may assist with the political legitimation of intensive proportionality review.[126]

[121] Opinion of AG La Pergola of 1 June 1999 in C-147/97 *Deutsche Post* and C-148/97 *Citicorp Kartenservice*, 853.

[122] ibid, fn 63.

[123] C 266/96 *Corbeau* [1993] ECR I-2533; C-393/92 *Almelo* [1994] ECR I-1477; C-475/99 *Ambulanz Glöckner* [2001] ECR I-8089; C-67/96 *Albany* [1999] ECR I-5751; C-115/97 *Brentjens* [1999] ECR I-6025; and, C-219/97 *Drijvende Bokken* [1999] ECR I-6121.

[124] That issue is considered in greater detail in Chapter 6 with respect to both of these cases.

[125] C-393/92 *Almelo* [1994] ECR 147.

[126] That concern might be regarded as central to Sauter and Schepel's contribution, given its grounding in a division of powers that recognises the right of initiative of the Member States with respect to SGEIs.

D. Conclusions

Without wishing to overstate its significance, the very framing of Article 106(2) within Article 106 immediately conveys its awkwardness. Simultaneously, it is both less and more than an exception to Article 106(1), while its enforcement as part of Article 106 takes the form of an exceptional implementing mechanism in the form of Article 106(3). Underscoring the idiosyncrasy of Article 106(2), the concept of SGEI has oscillated between objective and subjective renderings. The Court of Justice's own effort to build a generalised account of SGEIs never got beyond the tantalising *Porto di Genova* formula of 'special characteristics'. In seeking to head off constitutional change while attempting to objectivise the concept of SGEI, the Commission has tended to emphasise formalism based on stylised delivery characteristics. Separately, and most likely precipitated by the introduction of Article 16 TEC, the Commission was prompted to announce the manifest error supervision standard. While superficially attractive, that test requires a substantive underpinning standard. In systematic terms, its operation remains unexplained, for the moment.

Emerging from this analysis the indeterminate nature of Article 106(2) will be apparent. While many other Treaty provisions, including other rules contained in the competition chapter, are the focus of debate, the political contestation of Article 106(2) is probably unique. Certainly, the level of constitutional adjustment is unparalleled, even if the effects of those changes only operate at the margins. That constitutional stalemate is probably the reason for lamentable judicial claims that the concept of an SGEI is effectively unprincipled and a perpetually debated proportionality standard.[127] While offering very valuable insights, relevant academic accounts have not solved those fundamental indeterminacies. Sauter and Schepel have, very helpfully, focused attention on the wider legislative context as a determinant of the intensity of proportionality review.

It is not apparent how a mechanism that is so contested and uncertain as Article 106(2) can function as a central mediating mechanism for SGEI claims. In the face of such indeterminacy, it would not be surprising if the Court of Justice, in particular, looked to other ways of resolving the controversies that Article 106(2) appears intended to resolve. This is the case, and it is manifest in the form of the contingency of Article 106(2), which is explored in detail in the next chapter.

[127] As to the former, see T-289/03 *BUPA* [2008] ECR II-81, fn 15.

4

A Most Contingent Exemption

A. Introduction

In this chapter Article 106(2) is considered within the wider scheme of the Treaty and in particular other derogation mechanisms. It is a consideration of phenomena that are largely external to Article 106(2) that have a significant impact on whether and how it is applied. It follows from the internal exploration of Article 106(2) in the preceding chapter. A number of factors affecting the deployment and relevance of Article 106(2) are considered. They range from the contestation of Article 106(2) *ratione materiae*, through to impediments to the deployment of Article 106(2) and, ultimately, a seeming preference for reliance on other Treaty derogation mechanisms ahead of Article 106(2). In short, Article 106(2) is shown to be a most contingent Treaty exemption. That has significant implications for its potential to act as a brake on government failure.

The elements of this chapter are as follows. In the next section I consider the ways in which the territory capable of being occupied by Article 106(2) is contested. The focus is on how the Court of Justice has taken particular types of activity entirely outside the scope of the competition rules and in turn made Article 106(2) irrelevant. Following that, I consider the implications of the existence of derogation mechanisms under the free movement rules. A comparison is made between their availability and scope and those of Article 106(2). I then explore another competing derogation framework, namely the State aid regime. Given the rough equivalence of general interests under Article 106(2) and what may fall under Article 107(3)(c), the potential for overlap and worse for 106(2) will be apparent.

B. Contestation—The Scope of Article 106(2) *Ratione Materiae*

1. Introduction

In this section I demonstrate how the potential area of application of Article 106(2) is contested, specifically in the competition arena, through the development of two exceptions that shrink the scope of the competition rules. They are based on the concepts of solidarity and public authority. While the Court of Justice may not have developed those exceptions for the purpose of relegating Article 106(2) to a more marginal role, that has been one of their principal effects. As a result, significant incidents of government failure are left uncontrolled, a fact made all the worse by the clear suitability and fitness for purpose of Article 106(2) as a remedial tool.

2. The Public Authority Exception

The public authority exception concerns those instances where the characteristics of activity are sufficiently bound up with the exercise of sovereignty that it is not treated as economic for the purposes of the competition rules. The public authority exception is a specific aspect of the Court's more general approach to the interpretation of the term 'undertaking'. It is clearly related to, but is distinct from, the express Treaty exemption with respect to the exercise of 'official authority'. The nub of the exception concerning public authority is that in certain situations the state or its agents exercise essential or traditional state prerogatives, which result in the entity in question not being regarded as an 'undertaking'.

The origins of the public authority exception are to be found in Article 55 EEC through its inclusion of an exception based on the concept of 'official authority'. It appeared in Chapter II of the Treaty of Rome dealing with the right of establishment and stipulated that its provisions did not apply to activities that were 'concerned, even occasionally, with the exercise of official authority'. Article 66 EEC of Chapter III provided that the terms of Article 55 EEC applied with respect to services. Currently, Article 51 TFEU deals with the exercise of official authority in respect of freedom of establishment and Article 62 TFEU in respect of the provision and receipt of services. The classic instances of the exercise of official authority are the police and the judicial functions of the state, although functions with only incidental reliance on powers that are inherent in those activities are not accepted as falling within the exception.[1] Significantly, the official authority exemption only operates with respect to the specified free movement rules.

The first extended consideration of the official authority exception was in *Reyners*, which concerned a nationality requirement in connection with Bar admission.[2] That necessitated a consideration of the function of the legal profession in Belgium. There, Advocate General Mayras provided the elaborate but ethereal formula that:

> Official authority is that which arises from the sovereignty and majesty of the State; for him who exercises it, it implies the power of enjoying the prerogatives outside the general law, privileges of official power and powers of coercion over citizens.[3]

[1] See C-283/99 *Commission v Italy* [2001] ECR 4363, §15, dismissing a power of arrest for minor offences as peripheral to the main functions of private security guards.

[2] C-2/74 *Reyners* [1974] ECR 631.

[3] There are significant constitutional objections that could be made to this formula, not least the largely missing position of the rule of law. That omission is referred to by AG Cruz Villalón in *Belgian Notaries*, who cites but jettisons the Mayras approach in *Reyners*. See C-47/08 *Belgian Notaries* [2011] ECR I-4105, Opinion of 14 September 2010, §95.

Prominent considerations in the verification of the exercise of official authority include the nature of the interests to be advanced by the underlying activity (as between private and public) and the source of adherence to the arrangement or function in question (private agreement or state coercion).

The public authority exception was instigated and applied for the first time in connection with the competition rules in *Eurocontrol I*.[4] It concerned a dispute over the payment of charges for air traffic control (ATC) services, which led to the examination of Eurocontrol, a specialist regional ATC agency established by convention. Eurocontrol had three principal functions. Those were the provision of training to national ATC services, direct management of ATC on behalf of requesting signatory states, and the charge collection responsibility. A threshold issue was whether Eurocontrol was an undertaking. The claim was that the charges that it was imposing were abusive by reason of its pricing model.

In his opinion, Advocate General Tesauro expressly relied on *Reyners* and in particular Advocate General Mayras's extravagant exposition of the official authority exception to exclude the application of the competition rules. In emphasising the strategic nature of control over air space as an incident of sovereignty, Advocate General Tesauro highlighted the coercive nature of ATC and the legal obligation on persons in control of aircraft to obey ATC commands.[5] In addition, Advocate General Tesauro considered that ATC was a natural monopoly and that the operation of competing services might not be feasible or desirable in practice.[6] While Advocate General Tesauro did not justify that claim by reference to the cost function of the activity (the usual explanation for natural monopoly), he touched on the presence of insuperable co-ordination challenges.[7] Advocate General Tesauro also mentioned another market failure, namely non-excludability, a characteristic of public goods.[8] In practical terms, any aircraft in controlled air space is an inevitable recipient of ATC services. Separately, and although not mentioned by Advocate General Tesauro, the charge collection function undertaken by Eurocontrol tackled a different type of potential market failure. That was the co-ordination challenge presented by the need to collect charges in respect of aircraft traversing the airspace of signatory states where the operator might not have a place of establishment in several of them, thereby potentially frustrating the collection of fees.[9]

In respect of Eurocontrol's management of ATC services, the Court of Justice emphasised the 'powers of coercion' point, the link to the discharge of international

[4] C-364/92 *Eurocontrol I* [1994] ECR I-43.

[5] The need to apply coercion in an ATC system is surely overstated given the essential nature and purpose of the service.

[6] Opinion of 10 November 1993, section 13.

[7] ibid.

[8] ibid, section 15 of his opinion.

[9] In C-29/76 *LTU* [1976] ECR 1541 the Court had decided that the Brussels Convention did not apply to the recovery of Eurocontrol charges, a result that was only mitigated in part by Joined Cases 9 and 10/77 *Germanair* [1977] ECR 1517, which left open the possibility of recovery based on bilateral arrangements between signatory states.

legal obligations and the maintenance of territorial security.[10] Echoing its Advocate General, the Court also drew attention to the problem of non-excludability that is inherent in ATC services. Overall, the Court determined that the activities of Eurocontrol, which were derived from Member States' sovereignty over their airspace, was a public interest task aimed at safeguarding safety. These it treated as non-economic in nature, and instead as amounting to activities that were typically those of a public authority.[11] In grafting the 'official authority' exception on to the competition rules, the Court was no doubt alive to textual limitations. This probably explains its reference to the exercise of 'public' as opposed to 'official' authority.[12]

The Court of Justice's reliance on the coercion point may have been overstated since compliance might be taken to be implicit in the nature of the service, and not as such based on any public authority power of compulsion. Separately, the Court's reliance on the problem of excludability served to highlight the public goods nature of ATC and as a market failure, that might have been used to treat its provision of ATC services as a pan-European SGEI.[13] In that regard, Eurocontrol was the subject of an absolute duty to supply, even in the event of non-payment. Instead, the Court preferred to treat the underlying activity as 'non-economic' even though it was clearly an aggregation of paid services provided by a combination of public entities and Eurocontrol.

The judgment in *Eurocontrol I* left open the possibility that Eurocontrol might be regarded as an undertaking in respect of certain of its activities. That underpinned a subsequent complaint made to the Commission by an Italian ATC equipment supplier, SELEX. It was alleged that Eurocontrol's selection of prototypes in connection with research and development led to a significant advantage for successful suppliers by reason of the impact on the standard ultimately adopted by Eurocontrol and in turn its assistance to national ATC providers making procurement decisions. The Commission rejected the complaint, inter alia, on the basis that Eurocontrol was not an undertaking and for each of its functions, including the preparation and adoption of standards, it was engaged in the exercise of public authority. In a challenge to this rejection in *Eurocontrol II*, the General Court found that Eurocontrol was an undertaking when engaged in consulting because of its participation in a market.[14] In reversing the General Court, the Court of Justice held that to fall within the public authority exclusion, the nexus with a given Eurocontrol activity did not need to be essential or indispensable for ensuring the safety of air navigation.[15] It held that once the exercise of public authority

[10] C-364/92 *Eurocontrol I* [1994] ECR I-43, §24.
[11] §30.
[12] ibid.
[13] Despite the usual national focus of SGEIs, unsurprisingly the Commission has confirmed that the scope of SGEIs may be cross-border. See, for example, Commission Decision 2011/3/EU, *Danske Statsbaner*, §265.
[14] T-155/04 *Eurocontrol II* [2006] ECR II-4797, §§91–92.
[15] C-113/07 P *Eurocontrol III* [2009] ECR I-2207, §79.

exception arose, any activity that was even plausibly related to it was also covered by the public authority exception.[16] That meant that in respect of the development and adoption of standards, contracting, and prototype purchasing, Eurocontrol was not an undertaking.[17] Again, an approach based on the identification of SGEIs informed by market failure might have been more meaningful than the Court's category exclusion approach. Standardisation is a typical response to market failures, the severity of which is variable, depending in large measure on the potential for commercialisation.[18] At the very least, an Article 106(2) inquiry would have considered the objective necessity of the impugned practices if they were regarded as abusive.[19]

The hollowness of the public authority exception is more apparent in the Court of Justice's subsequent ruling in *Calì*.[20] In that case, a dispute arose about the levying of charges in respect of port anti-pollution surveillance activity. The plaintiff was resisting a claim for charges for this service, which were levied by a private corporation given an exclusive right to provide a surveillance service around the Genoa oil port. The applicants argued that since the ships that they used were equipped with their own surveillance equipment, to require them to pay for duplicative services was an Article 102 abuse. An issue arose as to whether or not the provider of the port's surveillance service was an undertaking. The Court confirmed that the activities of the Member State in the exercise of public authority had to be distinguished from those activities of an industrial or commercial character. Ultimately, the Court held that anti-pollution surveillance of this type formed part of 'the essential functions of the State' and was not economic.[21]

The possibility of deciding *Calì* by reference to Article 106(2) was partially dealt with by Advocate General Cosmas in the alternative. He argued that the surveillance service was not capable of being provided under competitive conditions. Advocate General Cosmas considered that the provider, SEPG, was entrusted with an SGEI mainly predicated on his view of the importance of environmental protection, as reflected in the legal order of the Communities as existing then.[22] Separately, he reasoned that since the intended beneficiaries of environmental surveillance

[16] ibid, §76.

[17] The judgment of the Court of Justice in *Eurocontrol III* is the subject of comprehensive and convincing criticism by Sánchez Graells on the basis of its abandonment of functionalism as deployed by the General Court in a very forensic way. See Sánchez Graells, A, 'Distortions of Competition Generated by Public Buyer Power' (2009) University of Oxford, Centre for Competition Law and Policy, Working Paper CCLP (L) 23.

[18] See generally, Swann, G, 'The Economics of Standardization; An Update, Report for UK Department of Innovation and Skills', 27 May 2010.

[19] Internal Commission documents disclosed during the procedure demonstrated significant concerns about possible anti-competitive effects of Eurocontrol's behaviour.

[20] C-343/95 *Calì* [1997] ECR I-1547.

[21] ibid, Opinion of AG Cosmas of 10 December 1996, §22.

[22] ibid, §§55–60. At §3 of his opinion, AG Cosmas refers to the case as important because it afforded the Court 'an opportunity to clarify to what extent protection of the environment is or is not a core public authority activity'.

services were ultimately the public at large, the universality element of Article 106(2) was satisfied.[23] While Advocate General Cosmas argued for the treatment of environmental surveillance activity as an SGEI on the basis of the public benefits, a more convincing approach may have been to treat the activity as economic and consider the potential for market failure.[24] The crucial issue in the proceedings was the obligation on all port users to pay for the surveillance services. Such an obligation could stem from two particular causes of market failure that appear to have been unavoidable once a system of general surveillance was decided upon, namely that such a service is non-excludable and non-rivalrous in consumption.[25] It appears to be a public good in the technical economic sense, although issues of geography also need to be considered. This conceptualisation, rather than the police powers argument partly underpinning the Advocate General's view (and accepted by the Court), would have been a much more compelling justification for the system of charging and could have been sustained under Article 106(2) on the basis of necessity review.[26]

Overall, the nature and extent of the public authority exception has important implications for the relevance and application of Article 106(2). Although cases applying this exception are few in number, conceivably they could have been determined on the basis of underlying SGEIs. Market failures and consequential government failures in tackling the underlying problems feature very prominently in the four judgments in which the exception for the exercise of public authority has been applied to oust the competition rules.[27] To the extent that greater reliance on the concept of market failure could be incorporated within Article 106(2), there is reason to doubt whether the public authority exception should exist in its current form.[28] That would still leave the Court free to have applied an exclusion based on the exercise of regulatory power in line with some of its older precedent.[29] In its current form, the public authority exception is static and appears to disregard

[23] Again, we see a stylised delivery characteristic as key to SGEI treatment.

[24] C-343/95 *Calì* [1997] ECR I-1547, §96.

[25] In line with *Porto di Genova*, AG Cosmas distinguishes prior surveillance from subsequent clean-up activity and treats the latter as 'ordinary' economic activity. Although his market failure analysis is inchoate, he treats the surveillance activity as having special characteristics. See §97. Separately, his analysis of diffuse public benefits is compelling and shows the advancement of the general interest other than through stylised direct service provision to the public.

[26] Buendía Sierra has observed that in some cases, including *Calì*, a number of the factors relied upon to conclude whether an activity is 'non-economic' are more relevant to the qualification of an activity as an SGEI under Art 106(2). See Buendía Sierra, JL, *Exclusive Rights and State Monopolies under EC Law* (Oxford University Press, 2000) 276.

[27] For another instance of the activity not being treated as performed by an undertaking and being justified by the General Court on the basis that it was inherently social in nature, see T-347/09 *Germany v Commission* ECLI:EU:T:2013:418, §31.

[28] Sánchez Graells (n 17). Writing in the context of public procurement specifically, he argues for a more limited application of the public authority exception as opposed to greater reliance on Art 106(2).

[29] See, in particular, C-82/01 *Aéroports de Paris* [2002] ECR I-9297, §§76–77, upholding the General Court's distinction in the same proceedings between supervisory and entrepreneurial functions.

the rise of the modern regulatory state. The difficulties of applying its progenitor, the official authority exemption, were well summarised by Advocate General Cruz Villalón in the *Belgian Notaries Case*, where he stated that

> For all those reasons, reliance on the criterion of purpose (general interest/individual interest) or the criterion of the manner of imposition of the obligation secured by (unilateral/bilateral) force is an approach, which inevitably leads to shaky ground. For the concepts involved are extraordinarily imprecise, subject as they are to the vagaries of relative proportions, and, therefore, inaccessible to the slightest degree of objectivity.[30]

In short, the official authority exemption is backward looking in nature yet its derivative, the concept of the exercise of public authority, has successfully ousted Article 106(2).

3. The Solidarity-based Exception and Undertakings

The essential features of the Court's approach to the concept of undertaking in the application of Articles 101 and 102 are by now very well established. The Court's expansionary approach to the definition of undertaking reached its apotheosis in its ruling in *Höfner*, where a federal employment agency was found to be engaging in economic activity in the provision of job placement services on a universal basis.[31] Given that historically the provision of universal employment services was a classic welfare function engaged in by many Member States, *Höfner* signalled the potential for broad areas of state provision to be subject to the competition rules.[32] The result in *Höfner*, which saw the invalidation of the employment placement monopoly, at least in so far as it extended to executive recruitment, came about despite the Court's acceptance of the activity of the German public employment agency as an SGEI.[33] In many respects *Höfner* is an exemplar of government failure in public service provision and its condemnation came using Article 106(2). While commentators such as Giubboni argue that *Höfner* was an instance of a complete failure to apply Article 106(2) that is hardly the case. As will be explored in Chapter 6, while the Court ultimately relied on a manifest failure to meet demand, the underlying problem was the mismatch between the market failures and the scope of the exclusive rights. Article 106(2) is capable of being used both to identify and censure such mismatches.

Within two years of the judgment in *Höfner*, in 1991, the Court began to develop a very significant exception to the concept of undertaking. This focused on activities of a social nature exhibiting strong solidarity and related features.

[30] C-47/08 *Belgian Notaries* [2011] ECR I-4105, §99.

[31] C-41/90 *Höfner* [1991] ECR-1979, §21.

[32] The 'solidaristic' nature of the activities of the Federal Employment office is emphasised by Giubboni, S, *Social Rights and Market Freedom in the European Constitution* (Cambridge University Press, 2009) 198–99.

[33] §24. Giubboni regards *Höfner* as an instance of a failure to apply Art 106(2) at all. Ibid, 198.

Its development was to have very significant implications for Article 106(2) as a result of the competition rules being found not to apply *ratione materiae*. The solidarity exception was first deployed in the *Poucet and Pistre* cases concerning the operation of compulsory sickness funds in France.[34] In both cases the applicants sought to avoid their obligations to make the requisite contributions to the schemes by claiming that the funds to which they were affiliated held dominant positions.[35] They also raised the possibility of buying cover from an insurer in another Member State. The critical issue was whether or not the funds were undertakings. Advocate General Tesauro emphasised three critical features demonstrating the social solidarity characteristics of the funds before concluding that they were not undertakings.[36] First, contributions were determined by reference to the income (whether salary or pension) of the person insured. Second, the benefits provided and the method of calculating premia were established by the French state. Third, the schemes were operated on a 'not-for profit' basis and there was a system of internal subsidies for funds in deficit. The Court characterised the activities of the funds as 'social' by reference to the same features emphasised by Advocate General Tesauro, and it concluded that the funds were not undertakings.[37] Overall, the Court appears to have proceeded on the assumption that where redistributive elements were sufficiently strong, then in principle competition could not be sustained.

While no Article 106(2) argument was advanced in *Poucet and Pistre*, an SGEI approach may have been viable. Advocate General Tesauro referred to the fund as a 'public service' as a way of emphasising their pursuit of significant redistributionist policies.[38] The funds were constituted in a manner that clearly satisfied the entrustment requirement under Article 106(2).[39] If they had been treated as such, then the essential issue would have been the justification for the grant of special rights given the requirement of compulsory affiliation for specified funds by sector. That, in essence, is a consideration of possible less restrictive alternatives. It would have entailed the Court deciding whether a system of authorisation (under conditions of free entry and regulated exit) that respected the features of the French system would have been equally efficacious in terms of advancing the general interest. By contrast with *Höfner*, in *Poucet and Pistre*, and this may have been crucial, there was no evidence before the Court of any market operating,

[34] C-159/91 and C-160/91 *Poucet & Pistre* [1993] ECR I-637.

[35] Obviously the holding of a dominant position is not per se abusive, so as such, the precise Art 102 abuse being relied upon is not very clear.

[36] Opinion of AG Tesauro of 29 September 1992.

[37] See C-159/91 and C-160/91 *Poucet & Pistre* [1993] ECR I-637, §18. For a clearer example of that tendency, see the Opinion of 14 November 2002 of AG Stix-Hackl in C-355/00 *Freskot* [2003] ECR I-5263, §71. The provision of compulsory agricultural insurance on terms that supported smaller producers is framed as social rather than economic by reference to its aims.

[38] Opinion of AG Tesauro of 29 September 1992, section 4.

[39] ibid, section 4. The referring Court refers to them as being 'charged with the management of a special social security scheme' under national legislation. See §§16, 20.

apart from a claim that the applicants wished to have the opportunity to buy cover elsewhere.[40]

A prominent feature of the Court of Justice's rendering of the solidarity concept is its emphasis on the 'capitalisation' principle. That appears to refer to the practice of generating returns through investment, which is frequently engaged in by insurers. Capitalisation is to be contrasted with systems that are based on 'pay as you go' models, such as classic social welfare-based tax-funded schemes of insurance. In *Société d'Assurance* the Court relied in part on the scheme's capitalisation to justify the finding that it was an undertaking.[41] The Court also emphasised the voluntary nature of the cover as important for the purpose of that finding.[42] As with reliance on capitalisation, this claim is problematic. Compulsion is frequently the means of preventing free riding and far from negating the existence of a market, it is often essential in order to prevent consequential market failures. That is especially so if the regulatory design builds in the achievement of certain distributional goals.[43]

The solidarity exception was also applied in *Cisal*.[44] The applicant resisted making payments to INAIL, a not-for-profit public law entity that was established to handle contributions and make payments in the form of short-term sickness assistance and long-term disability pensions.[45] The applicant argued that he had procured adequate cover on the private insurance market. Advocate General Jacobs emphasised two facts in particular, having reiterated a view he expressed in *Poucet and Pistre*, namely that the critical question was whether the activity in question, subject to the applicable obligations, could be undertaken for profit.[46] The first factor he relied on was that pension payments involved an element of redistribution, breaking what he saw as a more direct link between contributions and benefits, which he regarded as characteristic of market-provided insurance. The second was that benefits were set by law and could be determined ultimately by the state.[47] Advocate General Jacobs regarded the facts that INAIL was not for profit and that it pursued social objectives as irrelevant for the purpose of determining whether it was an undertaking. He considered that its social function might be relevant for the application of Article 106(2), although he ultimately concluded that this should be a matter for the referring court. For its part, the

[40] It may be that the existence of the impugned regulation precluded that possibility.

[41] C-244/94 *Société d'Assurance* [1995] ECR I-4013, §17,22.

[42] ibid.

[43] A recent notable example is compulsory cover mechanisms included in the Patient Protection and Affordable Care Act in the United States.

[44] C-218/00 *Cisal* [2002] ECR I-691.

[45] The system had its origins in dissatisfaction with nineteenth-century tort-based liability and offered employees engaged in manual labour greater security in return for waiving their rights to seek court compensation.

[46] Opinion of 13 September 2001, §38. AG Jacobs appears to use this as a shorthand way of asking whether the social objective in question could be fulfilled under market conditions.

[47] Italy was astute in bringing evidence of the solitary occasion when the terms of cover were rejected by the authorities. The relevant Minister had used powers to refuse approval for INAIL of a proposal for the price of cover for craft workers.

Court of Justice treated the activities of INAIL as an aspect of the operation of the Italian system of social insurance. It emphasised the importance of Member State autonomy in the organisation of their social security systems.[48] The Court then focused on the aspects of the system identified by Advocate General Jacobs, namely the system of internal redistribution and the degree of state supervision. It found that the rate of contribution was not systematically proportionate to the risk insured.[49] To that end, it emphasised the setting of contributions in part by reference to income, which meant that it was not a standard insurance system of risk-based pricing.[50]

In *Cisal* the Court considered that neither the method of calculating contributions nor the payment of benefits displayed sufficient proportionality to make the activity economic. That overlooks the pooling mechanism that is inherent in the operation of insurance markets.[51] While an element of risk pricing will be contract specific, it is highly unlikely that private insurance markets will price using a system of direct proportionality.[52] Separately, the Court's reliance on the degree of state supervision as resulting in certain activity no longer being economic is unconvincing. Although Advocate General Jacobs also relied on supervision as negating the existence of economic activity, that was undermined by his candid acknowledgment that there were many situations where 'the rules of the game', including price and minimum benefits, were determined by the state but where entities engaged in such activities were treated as undertakings.[53] With respect to Article 106(2) and the issue of entrustment, it will also be recalled that the Court has emphasised the intrusiveness of Member State supervision going beyond mere regulation.[54]

Conceivably, Article 106(2) could have been applied in *Cisal* as an alternative to the solidarity exclusion, although unlike *Poucet and Pistre*, that may have resulted in a different outcome. The applicant had argued that it would be possible to rely on regular insurance markets but with provision for a loss compensation fund of some sort in place so as to guard against the possibility of INAIL (or other

[48] C-218/00 *Cisal* [2002] ECR I-691, §31.

[49] ibid, §39.

[50] In addition, pensions were calculated by reference to a band using a national average salary with a 30% fluctuation meaning that there was a significant element of internal redistribution. Lower-paid workers received higher payments while higher-paid employees received less than their previous income.

[51] It also ignores the possibility that pricing with reference to salaries was a viable proxy for risk, given that workers exposed to the greatest risk may have earned some element of a premium. See Thaler and Rosen, 'The Value of Saving a Life: Evidence from Labour Markets' in Terleckyj (ed), *Household Production and Consumption* (National Bureau of Economic Research, 1976), who, drawing on an insight of Adam Smith, quantify a risk premium for various occupations so as to provide a meaningful input for cost-benefit analyses of contemplated safety interventions.

[52] The existence of price discrimination alone calls into question whether strict proportionality is to be observed in insurance pricing.

[53] C-218/00 *Cisal* [2002] ECR I-691, §73, Opinion of AG Jacobs of 13 September 2001.

[54] C-7/82 *GVL* [1983] ECR 483, §41.

providers) having a disproportionate number of riskier employees on its books.[55] Framed in those terms, it appears to be a classic Article 106(2) question, and one that might possibly have led to the invalidation of the exclusive rights, depending on the applicable proportionality test. As a result, a significant potential government failure went uncorrected.

A later case, *AOK*, reveals the 'all-or-nothing' nature of the solidarity-based exception, which allows conduct having significant competitive consequences to escape the competition rules entirely.[56] *AOK* concerned the system whereby representatives of German sickness funds determined the maximum amounts of reimbursement to be paid by individual funds to pharmaceutical suppliers. Under German law, a two-stage process operated whereby a representative association was obliged to decide which drugs were subject to price regulation, and in turn, was required to make a decision about the applicable maximum rate of reimbursement, subject to annulment by the relevant ministry. The representative association set the maximum reimbursement rates for drugs supplied by the two applicants. They claimed that these prices were excessively low. The pharmaceutical suppliers sought to rely on Article 101 by arguing that the association of sickness funds was a purchasing cartel.

Again, the characterisation of the sickness funds was critical to the applicability of Article 101. Significantly, the national Court also referred a number of questions in the alternative, including two in relation to the possible application of Article 106(2). Under the German system, funds were required to respect certain fundamental principles such as the obligation to provide a set of minimum benefits established by law. According to Advocate General Jacobs, certain features of the German system suggested that the funds were engaged in economic activity.[57] In particular, the various funds competed with each other in that employees (who were obliged to buy cover from at least one fund) were free to choose from among several. The funds also competed with each other in relation to supplementary benefits and their efficiency in claims management. As against that, the Court of Justice emphasised that there was no direct relationship between prices charged for cover and the level of benefits. In addition, a system of cost equalisation operated between the different funds. In making reference to competition between funds, the Court emphasised that ultimately there was none between them in respect of mandatory benefits.[58] Although acknowledging that Germany had introduced a limited amount of competition between providers, the Court emphasised that this was solely with a view to supporting the social objectives of the funds, in particular by helping to ensure that the funds operated in accordance with the principles of

[55] The principle of a loss compensation scheme was not just a speculative suggestion. Provision for such a mechanism was included in the Third Non-Life Directive liberalising the provision of general insurance. See Council Directive 92/49/EEC, at recital 24.

[56] C- 264/01 *AOK* [2004] ECR I-2493.

[57] Opinion of AG Jacobs of 22 May 2003, §§37–42.

[58] The funds competed on price with evidence of differentials of up to 30%.

sound management.[59] For these reasons, the Court concluded that the funds were not undertakings and on that basis the representative body engaged in maximum rate setting was not an association of undertakings.

The Court's dismissal of the economic nature of the activities of the funds is unconvincing. It sought to emphasise the lack of competition around minimum benefits.[60] While it was true that minimum cover was specified, the various funds were entitled to charge different prices for the mandatory offering and they competed on top-up cover. Separately, the Court's claim that limited competition had been introduced in order to improve the realisation of social objectives did not mean that the underlying activity was not economic, at least in exhibiting rivalry and having the potential for anti-competitive consequences. In referring to the provision of encouragement for principles of sound management, in reality the Court was referring to productive efficiency through managed competition. Since Germany was deploying constrained market-based mechanisms to achieve social goals, the competition rules could have been applied, subject to Article 106(2), given the plausible treatment of the funds as SGEIs.[61] There would then, on that approach, have been some underlying inquiry as to whether the German system resulted in government failure. In particular, there would have been an inquiry as to whether horizontal price fixing on the purchasing side was strictly necessary.[62]

Subsequently, *FENIN* brings about the expansion of the solidarity exemption.[63] It concerned complaints of violations of Article 106(2) to the Commission concerning the activities of constituent elements of the Spanish public health system in their dealings with suppliers, where waiting periods of up to 300 days for payment were alleged. The Commission rejected the complaints in part because it did not consider that the Spanish public health system was an undertaking given the social function that it performed. This result was confirmed by the General Court, which accepted that while the making of those purchases by the Spanish public system of supplies was a distinct activity, this could not be dissociated from their subsequent use in order to pursue social goals.[64] The General Court emphasised that it was the activity of selling as opposed to purchasing that characterised economic activity, a distinction that is at odds with the typically symmetrical nature of markets.[65] The Court of Justice upheld this finding, emphasising the nature of the subsequent use of goods or services as decisive.[66] Separately, in *Eurocontrol II*

[59] C- 264/01 *AOK* [2004] ECR I-2493, §56.

[60] ibid, §54.

[61] This is how AG Jacobs provisionally treated the funds, while noting that the necessity test would not inevitably have led to the condemnation of the price-setting mechanism, in respect of which he argued that a test of manifest disproportionality applied. See §§95ff.

[62] The underlying policy may have been to use collective buying power to curb monopoly-selling power. Whether that concern arose across the board is unclear. An independently determined ceiling price on a case-by-case may have sufficed for that purpose.

[63] T-319/99 *FENIN v Commission* [2003] ECR II-357.

[64] ibid, §36.

[65] ibid, §37.

[66] C-205/03 P *FENIN* [2006] ECR I-6295, §26.

the classification of purchasing activity as non-economic when carried out for the purpose of solidarity-related reasons was extended to purchasing for the purpose of exercising powers of public authority. Both the General Court and the Court of Justice confirmed that the Commission was entitled to consider that the exemption for related purchasing activity was not just limited to the solidarity-based exception, the decisive consideration being that the underlying activity is not economic in nature.[67]

FENIN demonstrates the 'all-or-nothing' nature of the solidarity exemption. Activities of the public health system that may have been abusive escaped any potential censure under EU competition law. There was no assessment of whether there was any causal link between the functions of the entity and the abuse as alleged. Conceivably, the Court could have found that elements of the Spanish public system were undertakings in relation to their purchasing activities, not least because it entailed direct participation in a market. Extended credit periods can generate anti-competitive effects by creating significant business dependencies.[68] The Court could then have gone on to consider the application of Article 106(2), given that system pursued obvious redistributive goals. It is difficult to see how (if it was the case) delays in payment for suppliers of the public health system were necessary for its operation. Even if it was argued that a reduction in credit periods would impact on the overall operation of the system, it is not clear that this would compromise the operation of the Spanish system or its overall capacity to serve.

Subsequent case law illustrates that even in the presence of strong solidarity this does not guarantee that an insurance provider will not be treated as an undertaking. This is evident in *AG2R Prévoyance*, where, despite finding that there was a high degree of redistribution in the scheme, the Court of Justice decided that it was probably an undertaking, having regard to the degree of state supervision.[69] The designation of the funds was initiated in a collaborative process between employers and unions, which occurred against a backdrop of other entities competing with respect to the supplemental cover provided under the scheme.[70] In addition, the fund enjoyed a degree of autonomy over the nature of supplementary benefits characteristic of economic activity.[71] *AG2R Prévoyance* is also significant in that the Court applied Article 106(2) even though it appeared to accept the analysis of Advocate General Mengozzi to the effect that no abuse was established. This may signal greater potential recourse to Article 106(2) in these situations,

[67] T-319/99 *FENIN v Commission* [2003] ECR II-357, §65; C-205/03 P *FENIN* [2006] ECR I-6295, §102.

[68] It is possible that the funding arms of the Spanish state operated a policy of staggered payments to the purchasing entities within the public system in Spain, which in turn led them to seek to impose extended credit terms. It is noteworthy that under Art 4(4) of Directive 2011/7/EU on Combating Late Payments in Commercial Transactions, entities providing healthcare are now limited to an additional 60 days beyond the general 30-day default rule. See also recital 25.

[69] C-437/09 *AG2R Prévoyance* [2011] ECR I-973. This part of the ruling, §53–§65, is not a model of clarity. It appears to be largely influenced by the opinion of AG Mengozzi of 11 November 2010.

[70] ibid, §63.

[71] ibid, §54.

even if, as will be explored in Chapter 6, the necessity and proportionality review in *AG2R Prévoyance* was very shallow.[72] As such, the probability of obviating government failures may be slim, but at least it may be a possibility.

C. Competition—The Free Movement Derogations

1. Introduction

This section is principally concerned with a number of factors affecting the choice between the free movement derogation mechanism and Article 106(2) as a means of excusing compliance with fundamental Treaty provisions. Initially, I consider the comparative direct effect and scope of the free movement derogation mechanisms and Article 106(2). I do so by identifying the largely untrammelled nature of mandatory and imperative requirements in the public interest and compare them with a perception of significant limitations on the nature of general interests that may be accommodated under Article 106(2). That is followed by a consideration of the doubts that Article 106(2) is actually capable of doing what it says, namely permitting the disapplication of any other Treaty provision. The analysis then turns to how a preference for recourse to the free movement derogation mechanisms has become manifest and suggests that this is unsurprising given both the modalities of litigation before the European Courts as well as the likelihood of a preference given the more embedded nature of the free movement derogation mechanisms. Although the evolution of the overall position is understandable, I argue that Article 106(2) has been relegated to a peripheral and contingent position. Accordingly, its utility as a safeguard against government failure is significantly compromised.

2. Direct Effect and Scope

(a) The Free Movement Derogations

The requirements for direct effect dating back to *van Gend en Loos* have been stable for some time under EU law and in essence require clarity, precision and unconditionality.[73] More specifically, provisions should not require any implementing

[72] As Kersting notes: 'Balancing the Member States' interest in the functioning of their social security systems with the Union's interest in the protection of competition by applying Article 106(2) TFEU is a far more differentiated approach than the previous all-or-nothing approach according to which the applicability of the competition rules depended on whether the entity was an undertaking'. Kersting, C, 'Social Security and Competition Law—ECJ Focuses on Article 106(2)' (2011) 2(5) *Journal of Competition Law and Practice* 475.

[73] C-26/62 *van Gend en Loos* [1963] ECR 3.

measures or the exercise of discretion on the part of the Member States or any EU institutions. The direct effect of Treaty derogation mechanisms is a function of the direct effect of the related primary right or prohibition. The Court's 1978 judgment in *Cassis* introduced the concept of mandatory requirements in the public interest justifying restrictions on the free movement of goods. That was in response to the unqualified condemnation in *Dassonville* of any trading rules that directly or indirectly, actually or potentially might hinder trade.[74] While it may not be accurate to refer to those mandatory requirements as directly effective on a stand-alone basis, it is clear that those exceptions could be relied upon as a function of the direct effect of the free movement rules since, at least in the Court's conception, they are inherent in them.

It is instructive to note for comparative purposes the timing and ease with which direct effect was accorded to those free movement provisions that tend to feature in SGEI cases, namely Article 49 on the right of establishment and Article 56 on the freedom to provide services. Article 49 TFEU was first found to be directly effective in the *Reyners* judgment of the Court in 1974.[75] That was followed at the end of the same year by the ruling in *Van Binsbergen* on the direct effect of Article 56 on freedom to provide services.[76] Article 56 was found to be directly effective at least in so far as it was intended to end discrimination specifically by reason of nationality.[77]

The corollary of an all-embracing approach to what might constitute a restriction on free movement was the development of a variety of inbuilt justifications giving the Court of Justice the ability to avoid a finding of a violation of the relevant free movement provision. In that way, it also avoided being constrained by the limited number of general interest derogation grounds included in the Treaty of Rome.[78] In *Thieffry* the Court indicated that the availability of mandatory requirements in the public interest was capable of justifying restrictions on the right of establishment.[79] Two years later, in *Van Wesemael*, the Court confirmed the potential availability of imperative requirements in relation to the public interest to justify restrictions on the freedom to provide services.[80]

The only seeming limitation placed by the Court on mandatory and imperative requirements in the public interest concern attempts to justify restrictions on free movement by reference to what the Court has characterised as 'solely economic' reasons.[81] That proposition was formally endorsed in *Gouda*, which interpreted

[74] C-120/78 *Cassis de Dijon* [1979] ECR 649, C-8/74 *Dassonville* [1974] ECR 837.

[75] C-2/74 *Reyners* [1974] ECR 631.

[76] C-33/74 *Van Binsbergen* [1974] ECR 1299.

[77] Subsequently, the Court moved beyond limiting direct effect based on discrimination and even began to insist on equivalence assessments ahead of legislation. See C-340/89 *Vlassopoulou* [1991] ECR I-2357.

[78] Art 36 of the Treaty of Rome had a number of notable omissions, including the protection of health.

[79] C-71/76 *Thieffry* [1977] ECR 765, §§12, 15.

[80] C-110/78 *van Wesemael* [1979] ECR 35, §28.

[81] The Court has also taken a similar approach under Art 36, see C-251/78 *Denkavit* [1979] ECR 3369.

an earlier ruling in *Bond van Adverteerders* as suggesting that economic considerations could not be taken into account to justify restrictions on freedom to provide services.[82] Despite that, the Court has accepted that reasons of a fiscal nature linked to the possible destabilisation of social security systems are in principle capable of justifying restrictions on certain Treaty freedoms.[83] The Court, however, will not accept as justifications the protection or enhancement of the tax base independently of a specific funding requirement.[84] In overall terms, there are very few meaningful constraints on the scope of imperative requirements in the general interest.[85]

The Court's adoption of exceptions to the free movement rules in the form of mandatory and imperative requirements relating to the public interest was probably unavoidable considering the expansive interpretations given by the Court to the free movement protections set against a relatively narrow set of express Treaty exceptions.[86] In particular, the Court's desire to extend the scope of the free movement provisions to prohibit not just direct or indirectly discriminatory measures, but also those tending to impede or render less advantageous cross-border provision, meant that a high hurdle was raised, even if there had been some adjustments.[87] A loose equilibrium was achieved though a system of expansive prohibitions matched by an unlimited set of possible exceptions.[88] The availability of those exceptions is tempered by the overlay of a proportionality test and a general refusal to countenance measures that are directly or indirectly discriminatory. Nevertheless, the open-ended nature of the imperative requirements case law means that they are capable of being applied to a myriad of situations, including cases involving SGEIs.

The potential application of the free movement rules was also to be further enhanced by the gradual weakening of the rule concerning purely internal situations. That had operated so that where there was no cross-border dimension, the free movement provisions, and in turn the associated derogation mechanisms, were not applicable.[89] By way of example, in *Höfner*, which concerned the employment of a German national by a German company, the Court faced a question on the potential applicability of Article 56 TFEU as part of the reference questions.[90]

[82] C-288/89 *Gouda* [1991] ECR I-4007, §11 and C-352/85 *Bond van Adverteerders* [1988] ECR 2085. That is a generous reading of the *Bond van Adverteerders* judgment.

[83] C-372/04 *Watts* [2006] ECR I-4325, §103.

[84] For example, see C-243/01 *Gambelli* [2003] ECR I-13031.

[85] They range from protection of the environment, workers and health, through to the advancement of important constitutional values.

[86] See to that effect, Scott, J, 'Mandatory or Imperative Requirements in the EU and the WTO' in Barnard and Scott (eds), *The Law of the Single European Market* (Hart Publishing, 2002).

[87] That began with C-267/91 *Mithouard* [1993] ECR I-6097, and in respect of services is applied in cases such as C-544/03 *Mobistar* [2005] ECR I-7723.

[88] See in this regard, Scharpf, F, 'The Asymmetry of European Integration, or Why the EU Cannot Be a "Social Market Economy"' (2010) 8 *Socio-Economic Review* 211–50, 219.

[89] See C-175/78 *Saunders* [1979] ECR 1129, §11.

[90] C-41/90 *Höfner* [1991] ECR-1979, §§37–39.

It avoided the free movement of services issue by holding that it had no application to an entirely domestic situation. That was so even though the German monopoly on employment services may have hampered the recruitment of workers from other Member States.[91] As anomalies emerged, the purely internal situations rule soon began to be qualified. In particular, that occurred in respect of residence rights for third-country nationals where, on the immediate facts, no cross-border movement had occurred.[92] The Court of Justice softened the purely internal situations rule to exclude scenarios where there had been a prior exercise of some free movement right.[93] That in turn broadened the potential for the application of the free movement derogation mechanisms. A similar phenomenon is observable with respect to goods where the Court on occasion has held that even if the facts as presented are wholly referable to a purely internal situation by applying to domestic production only, nevertheless Article 34 may still be engaged because of the potential hindrance to trade.[94]

Separately, the Court began a collateral undermining of the purely internal situation rule based on the possibility that certain national legal systems might afford their citizens the same rights and protections as would apply as a result of the application of EU law.[95] More importantly for present purposes, since it allows the Court to answer preliminary reference requests concerning the free movement rules even when they are not directly engaged, it also means that the Court is free to apply the associated free movement derogation mechanisms so as to provide a complete answer to a preliminary reference. Where previously the application of free movement rules would have been barred, they may now be capable of being applied.[96] As a result of these changes, far from supplementing the Court's analysis under Article 106(2), and as will be considered below, recourse to the free movement derogation has led to Article 106(2) being bypassed entirely.

(b) Article 106(2)

The initial approach of the Court was to deny direct effect to Article 106(2), thereby preventing litigants from relying upon it before national courts.[97] The view that

[91] The Court went on to decide the case by reference to Art 106(2), albeit incoherently.

[92] See generally, Foster, N, *Foster on EU Law*, 2nd edn (Oxford University Press, 2009) ch10.

[93] See C-370/94 *Vigel* [1995] ECR II-487.

[94] C-321/94 *Pistre* [1997] ECR I-2343, §44–45. For a comprehensive criticism of this approach, see Oliver, P (ed), *Oliver on Free Movement of Goods in the European Union*, 5th edn (Hart Publishing, 2010) §§6.121–6.129.

[95] See C-448/98 *Guimont* [2000] ECR I-10663, §23; C-451/03 *Calafiori* [2006] ECR I-2941, §29; and, C-245/09 *Omalet* [2010] ECR I-3771, §15. In addition, the transposition by some Member States of certain EU rights takes place in such a way as to extend them to purely internal situations. In those situations, the Court will answer preliminary reference questions in part because of the scope of Art 267 of the Treaty and out of concern to ensure consistency. See C-297/88 *Dzodzi* [1990] ECR I-3763, §§32–38. See, however, the Opinion of AG Jacobs in C-321/94 *Pistre* [1997] ECR I-2346, §40 for a criticism of this approach.

[96] See also C-84/2011 *Susisalo* ECLI:EU:C:2012:374.

[97] For a detailed treatment of the complex evolution of the position on direct effect, see Buendía Sierra (n 26) 341–52.

Article 106(2) was not directly effective was in part based on the view that as Treaty guardian only the Commission could apply the development of trade criterion included in the second sentence of Article 106(2). In *Port de Mertert* the Court held that Article 106(2) was too conditional for direct effect since it required an appraisal of the tasks entrusted to the undertaking in question and of the interests of the Community.[98] That appeared to suggest that the difficulty arose from the requirement to apply the second sentence of Article 106(2) on the effect on the development of trade. In *BRT v SABAM II*, Advocate General Mayras foresaw the possibility that Article 106(2) might become directly effective, but predicated on the Commission's exercise of its powers under Article 106(3).[99]

In *Fabricants Raffiniere d'Huile* from 1983 the Court, again citing *Port de Mertert*, ruled that 'at this stage' Article 106(2) was not capable of creating individual rights that a national Court was obliged to protect.[100] It was not until 1989 that the direct effect of Article 106(2) was effectively confirmed, at least in part, in *Ahmed Saeed*.[101] There the Court ruled that inaction by the European Commission under Article 106(3) did not mean that Article 106(1) or Article 106(2) could not be invoked before national courts.[102] The judgment also contemplated national authorities taking a view on SGEI entrustment and the question of obstruction.[103] Later judgments in *ERT* and *Almelo* also appeared to confirm the ability of Member State courts to determine the issues of SGEI entrustment and the application of the obstruction test.[104] Subsequently, in his opinion in *Porto di Genova*, Advocate General Van Gerven suggested that in earlier cases the Court was receptive to the direct effect of the first sentence of Article 106(2).[105] This meant that a national Court could make a determination on whether or not any SGEI had been entrusted. Presumably, his point was that if the conclusion of that analysis was negative, then Article 106(2) was not available, irrespective of the outcome of the application of the second sentence of Article 106(2).[106] By the time of the Court's judgment in *Corbeau* in 1993, the direct effect of Article 106(2) was not doubted.[107] In cases such as *Corbeau*, the Court was confronted with

[98] C-10/71 *Port de Mertert* [1971] ECR 723, §14.

[99] C-127/73 *BRT v SABAM II* [1973] ECR 313, 740.

[100] C-172/82 *Inter-Huiles* [1983] ECR 555, §15.

[101] C-66/86 *Ahmed Saeed* [1989] ECR 803. In C-393/92 *Almelo* [1994] ECR I-1147, AG Darmon in his opinion of 8 February 1994 identified *Ahmed Saeed* as the crucial turning point on direct effect.

[102] C-66/86 *Ahmed Saeed* [1989] ECR 803, §53.

[103] See generally, Hancher, L and Slot, PJ, 'Article 90' (1990) 11(1) *ECL Rev*, who refer to the holding that national authorities could apply the obstruction test as 'remarkable' considering the general assumption following *Sacchi* that only the Commission could apply it.

[104] C-260/89 *ERT v Dimotiki* [1991] ECR I-2925, §§33–34; C-393/92 *Almelo* [1994] ECR I-1477, §§49–51(c).

[105] C-179/90 *Porto di Genova* [1991] ECR I-5889, Opinion of AG Van Gerven of 19 September 1991, §28.

[106] This meant that if a national court finds that an SGEI has been entrusted it is stuck and can go no further, except possibly to consult the Commission.

[107] Earlier Art 106(2) precedent such as *Port de Mertert* suggested that the basic tests for direct effect were not satisfied, but the subsequent abandonment of that position in *Ahmed Saeed* and *Corbeau* was not on the basis of any elaborate argument. It was simply asserted.

questions concerning whether Article 106(1) was being violated in conjunction with Article 102, with only Article 106(2) available to rescue the situation.[108] Necessity may have been the mother of invention in that case.

Turning to the issue of scope, a basic question arises as to the nature of the general interests that are capable of qualification under Article 106(2). This is analogous to the issue of what reasons are capable of constituting an imperative requirement in the public interest under the free movement rules.[109] The perception of Article 106(2) as being limited in terms of the general interest that may qualify under its terms is probably attributable to two reasons. The first arises from the clumsy formulation of the provision and, in particular, the use of the formula 'general economic interest'. Read literally, Article 106(2) might be taken to refer only to services that implicate interests that are economic in nature.[110] Instead, it refers to the nature of the underlying activities as opposed to limiting the nature of the general interest basis for the intervention.[111] Reflecting that interpretation, an enabling approach to the definition of SGEI was advanced by the Commission in the Green Paper on Services of General Interest.[112] After noting that the concept was not defined in the Treaty, the Commission indicated that 'there is broad agreement that the term refers to services of an economic nature which the Member States or the Community subject to specific obligations by virtue of a general interest criterion'.[113] The Commission's approach to the concept is also consistent with various pronouncements (albeit negatively formulated) of the Court in cases such as *Albany* and *Federutility* to the effect that in formulating SGEIs, Member States may not be prevented from taking into account national policy objectives.[114]

The second, and perhaps more significant, reason for treating the general interests that are capable of accommodation under Article 106(2) as constrained stems from an argument based on its relationship to the scope of imperative requirements

[108] In *Corbeau* the Court was unforthcoming as to whether there was a violation of Art 106(1) in conjunction with Art 102. It noted that the mere granting of exclusive rights is not impermissible but then referred to the duty of the Member States not to impair the effectiveness of the competition rules before then turning to Art 106(2). See §§10–12.

[109] There are some differences in terms of what is recognised as an imperative requirement as between workers, goods, services, establishment and capital, with an understandably more restricted category of exceptions for goods. See Barnard, C and Deakin, S, 'Market Access and Regulatory Competition' in Barnard and Scott (eds), *The Law of the Single European Market* (Hart Publishing, 2002).

[110] As Bauby observes, 'Certainly the expression "service of general economic interest" is particularly improper, because the authors' main aim was the "economic" nature of the services rather than any particular "economic" category of general interest'. See, Bauby, P, 'From Rome to Lisbon: SGIs in Primary Law' in Szyszczak, Davies, Andenæs and Bekkedal (eds), *Developments in Services of General Interest* (Asser Press, 2011) 23.

[111] See Hancher, L and Sauter, W, *EU Competition and Internal Market Law in the Health Care Sector* (Oxford University Press, 2012) 284.

[112] Commission Green Paper on Services of General Interest, COM (2003) 270 final.

[113] ibid, §17.

[114] C-67/96 *Albany* [1999] ECR I-5751, §104, C-265/08 *Federutility* [2010] ECR I-3377, §29 and C-121/15 *ANODE* ECLI:EU:C:2016:638, §§50–52.

in the general interest. The basic contention is as follows. By its terms, Article 106(2) is concerned with economic interests. Yet, the Court has consistently indicated that imperative requirements in the public interest can never be based solely on economic concerns. Completing the argument, Article 106(2) can only be used to justify economically motivated restrictions on the free movement rights. As will be shown, there is no substance to this assignment of mutually exclusive roles, not least considering what has already been considered concerning the proper interpretation of the word 'economic' in Article 106(2). Nevertheless, given the plausibility of the dichotomy, it may have a limiting impact in practice.[115]

While the scope of 'economic' would probably extend to a restriction for reasons of efficiency or equity and those of a macro-economic or fiscal nature, there may be many others that would be excluded. There is little reason to assume that the general interest to be pursued under Article 106(2) should be confined to narrow economic motivations, whether the term 'economic' is given a technical meaning or is taken to pertain to part or all of the national economy. There is therefore a broad potential equivalence between what might constitute an imperative requirement in the public interest under implied free movement derogation mechanisms and the scope of general interests capable of being pursued under Article 106(2). This is so even though the Court has on occasion identified profit considerations as falling outside the purview of the free movement derogations, with the implication that they are to be analysed under Article 106(2).[116]

3. Hard Limits on Article 106(2)?

The express terms of Article 106(2) provide that entities entrusted with SGEIs are subject to 'the rules contained in the Treaties, in particular the rules on competition' except where its provisions are satisfied. It does not say that those entities are subject to the 'prohibitions' contained in the Treaties, but instead refers to 'rules' that must be taken to import the rules and any derogation mechanisms. Despite the apparently unqualified nature of the powers of exemption under Article 106(2), the question of which Treaty provisions it can qualify and whether the Member States themselves can rely on it has been beset by doubt. The first indication of possible limitations as to the scope of Article 106(2) was provided by the *Campus Oil* judgment of the Court.[117] The context was a challenge to Ireland's operation of a national oil refinery from which all distributors were obliged to source a fixed proportion of their requirements. According to the Court, this

[115] A limiting view has been challenged, most prominently by Judge Koen Lenaerts, now President of the Court of Justice, in 'Defining the Concept of "Services of General Economic Interest" in Light of the "Checks and Balances" Set Out in the EU Treaties' (2012) 19(4) *Jurisprudencija* 1247, 1255–56.

[116] See C-203/96 *Dusseldorp* [1998] ECR I-4075, §44.

[117] C-72/83 *Campus Oil* [1984] ECR 2727.

requirement operated as a quantitative restriction on imports in violation of Article 34 TFEU. The Court ruled that

> Article [106(2)] does not, however, exempt a Member State which has entrusted such an operation to an undertaking from the prohibition on adopting, in favour of that undertaking and with a view to protecting its activity, measures that restrict imports from other Member States contrary to Article [34] of the Treaty.[118]

Separately, although stipulating that Article 106(2) was not available to cure a breach of Article 34, the Court left open the possibility of allowing the Irish measures to be justified under Article 36.[119] *Campus Oil* thus provides an early example of the Court's preference for resolving disputes under the free movement derogations, in this instance relying on an express Treaty derogation concerning public order. Ultimately, the *Campus Oil* position was not sustainable. The Court's ruling in *Corbeau* implicitly called into doubt the *Campus Oil* approach. That was reinforced by the judgment in the *Electricity and Gas Cases*. There, in rejecting the Commission's challenge to the national electricity monopolies, the Court found a violation of Article 37 on the basis that an import and export ban amounted to discrimination.[120] Prior to holding that Article 106(2) could cure that violation of Article 37, the Court made a more general statement to similar effect with respect to the Treaty rules generally. Logically, this meant that, contra the judgment in *Campus Oil*, Article 106(2) could be used to justify import restrictions operated by the Member States.

Despite the apparent unshackling of Article 106(2) in the *Electricity and Gas Cases*, where it was used to justify restrictions on free movement provisions, fresh doubts have emerged. Those are as a result of *Hanner*, a 2005 judgment of the Court concerning the operation of the Swedish monopoly in relation to medical and related products. Sweden operated a public monopoly over prescription and non-prescription drugs.[121] The Court of Justice held that Article 37 of the Treaty prohibited a procurement system operated by a monopolist that was liable to place trade in goods from other Member States at a disadvantage.[122] It also found that Article 106(2) could not be relied upon in the absence of a system that prevented discrimination against products from other Member States.[123] As a result, it is

[118] ibid, §19. Buendía Sierra interprets this judgment, not as an indication of limits as to which Treaty provision may be disapplied under Art 106(2), but instead, as to whether the Member State (as opposed to the entrusted undertaking) may rely on Art 106(2). Buendía Sierra (n 26) 292–93. As against that, Johnston treats the *Campus Oil* judgment as referring to limits on the provision that may be disapplied under Art 106(2). See Johnston, A, 'Other Exception Clauses' in Oliver (ed) (n 94) §10.15.

[119] The Court of Justice proceeded to do so having regard to the public security imperative of ensuring availability of minimum quantities of oil.

[120] C-157/94 *Commission v Kingdom of the Netherlands* [1997] ECR I-5699; C-158/94 *Commission v Italian Republic* [1997] ECR I-5789; C-159/94 *Commission v French Republic* [1997] ECR I-5815; Case C-160/94 *Commission v Kingdom of Spain* [1997] ECR I-5851.

[121] C-438/02 *Hanner* [2005] ECR I-4551. This is a judgment of the Grand Chamber.

[122] It must be acknowledged that Art 37 has itself presented significant difficulties in terms of its interpretation and consistency. See Oliver (ed) (n 94) ch 12.

[123] ibid, §48.

possible that there are hard limits on the potential of Article 106(2) to be used to disapply other Treaty rules.

4. A Preference Revealed

On its face, the Treaty presents a national court confronted with a restriction on economic activity with a significant dilemma. Under which Treaty rules, and in particular which derogation mechanism, should such a restriction be analysed, assuming that it gives rise to a prima facie violation of a directly effective Treaty provision? When faced with reference questions, the Court of Justice must address the issues as formulated by the national court although it enjoys significant discretion as to the order in which it replies to questions and as to the perfection of the questions that it has been asked.[124] The national courts can be forgiven for preferring to seek the resolution of a case by reference to the most straightforward principles of EU law. In that regard, Article 106(2) is not always an attractive option. Where a particular restriction obviously implicates trade within the EU, and a question can be framed in terms of a restriction on one or more of the free movement provisions, then arguably it may be easier to rely on those provisions and their associated derogations, even when the provisions of Article 106(2) also appear to be satisfied. Understandably, the Court of Justice is also likely to prioritise answering questions that will resolve a case with the least effort.[125] Nevertheless, where a measure is found not to be capable of being saved under the free movement rules, there is a marked disinclination to rescue it under Article 106(2).[126]

There are also signs of judicial aversion to Article 106(2). A 2009 judgment of the Court on a reference from the Netherlands in *Sint Servatius* is instructive.[127] It concerned a challenge to a decision of the Dutch authorities to refuse a social housing association a permit to participate in the financing and construction of a housing project in Liège, Belgium, close to the border with the Netherlands. Under Article 22(2) of the Constitution of the Kingdom of the Netherlands, the provision of sufficient living accommodation is described as a concern of the public authorities.[128] In the Netherlands there is significant regulation of the provision of social housing, including a requirement that any regulated association obtain prior consent before engaging in cross-border investments. The Dutch Council of

[124] See C-365/02 *Lindfors* [2004] ECR I-7183, §43.

[125] This point is made by Hatzopoulos, V, 'The Economic Constitution of the EU Treaty and the Limits between Economic and Non-economic Activities' (2012) 23 *European Business Law Review* 973, 985, although he suggests that the Court prioritises questions likely 'offering the most credible solutions'. That is not always apparent.

[126] In some cases that will be justified, especially where there is no obvious connection between the nature or performance of the SGEI and the restriction in question. See, for example, C-271/09 *Commission v Poland* [2011] ECR I-13613.

[127] C-567/07 *Sint Servatius* [2009] ECR I-9021.

[128] It would appear though that this does not translate into a legally enforceable right to housing.

State asked a series of questions roughly divided between those concerned with free movement of capital under Article 63 TFEU and the associated Article 65 exemption on the one hand, and Article 106(2) on the other. It had been argued that the activities of Dutch housing associations constituted an SGEI. The Court found that the requirement of prior consent was a restriction on the free movement of capital in violation of Article 63. Given the connection to the provision of public housing, it was in principle capable of constituting an imperative requirement. That, however, would only be the case if the basis on which a request for exemption would be appraised was sufficiently clear. This the Court found not to be the case.[129]

Bizarrely, in *Sint Servatius* the Court refused to answer the reference questions concerning Article 106(2) on the basis that it was obvious that the provisions of Article 106(2) did not apply to the dispute. It did so without calling into question the claim that the housing association was entrusted with an SGEI. Instead, the Court maintained that since the proceedings were concerned with neither the grant of special or exclusive rights, nor the classification of the association's activities as an SGEI, Article 106(2) was not relevant.[130] This reasoning makes no sense since the permissibility of the prior authorisation system was at issue in circumstances where the national court justifiably regarded it as having been entrusted with an SGEI in the context of a grant of special rights.[131]

The Court of Justice was exacting in that while it admitted that a system of prior authorisation might be necessary, it only did so after concluding that a system of *ex post* notification might be ineffectual considering the irreversible nature of building projects.[132] Furthermore, it recast the prior authorisation system by condemning the standard on which it operated as not being based on objective criteria, known in advance and applied in a non-discriminatory manner.[133] It is difficult to see, on the current law, how Article 106(2) could have been applied to similarly invalidate the prior authorisation requirement as applied under Dutch law. The lack of EU competence may have led to the application of relatively weak necessity

[129] There is an air of surrealism about this case considering that the delivery of social housing is presumably predicated on it being furnished within the Netherlands. It is not apparent how Member State efforts to do that should be diluted by having to consider cross-border investments by housing foundations. Ironically, the Dutch authorities were concerned about State aid aspects of the project, given the ability of the social housing entity to borrow on preferential terms.

[130] C-567/07 *Sint Servatius* [2009] ECR I-9021, §46.

[131] Van de Gronden observes with reference to this case and social services of general interest (SSGI), 'applying the well-known Treaty provisions on free movement to SSGI providers without paying attention to solidarity (by, for example, explaining the role Article 106 TFEU may play in the present case) comes down to ignoring the problems that Member States encounter in organising the provision of SSGI in a market setting'. See van de Gronden, J, 'Free Movement of Services and the Right of Establishment' in Neergaard (ed), *Social Services of General Interest in the EU* (Asser Press, 2013) 150.

[132] C-567/07 *Sint Servatius* [2009] ECR I-9021, §34. Separately, the Court rejected any reliance on the public policy exemption provided for in Art 65 in respect of restrictions on capital on the basis that a sufficiently fundamental interest was not at stake despite claims by the Dutch authorities about a lack of social housing.

[133] The test used appears to be a 'tight rationality' test of the kind contemplated by Bermann, G, 'Proportionality and Subsidiarity' in Barnard and Scott (eds), *The Law of the Single European Market* (Hart Publishing, 2002) 81.

and proportionality tests under Article 106(2). Even if a particular project need not contribute to the stock of public housing in the Netherlands, an assessment would be necessary of what if any opportunity was foregone by participating in cross-border investment.[134] Article 106(2), which is sometimes presented as a *bête noire* of public services, may have saved the Dutch mechanism without amendment, while the application of the free movement provisions necessitated the recasting of the system of prior authorisation. In effect, proportionality review under the free movement rules appears stricter than under Article 106(2).[135] While *Sint Servatius* is not an extreme intervention (in terms of what is required of the Netherlands), it appears that Article 106(2) was bypassed intentionally.

In *Sint Servatius* the application of Article 106(2) might have left the Dutch permit system unscathed. There are, however, other instances where Article 106(2) might have invalidated a restriction that the Court has found to fall within one of the exemptions to the free movement rules. The 2012 judgment of the Court in *Susisalo* is a striking example. It concerned a system of restrictive licensing for pharmacies in Finland.[136] The Finnish rules provided that the University of Helsinki (UoH) had the right to open up to 16 pharmacies, while private entities were limited to three. Certain training, documentation and specialist medicine production responsibilities that had been conferred on the UoH were relied on, at least in part, to justify the differential regime. Although the Court was asked questions under Article 49 and Article 106(2), it determined the case exclusively by reference to Article 49. Consistent with precedent, it decided that Article 49 applied on the basis that national law required a Member State to grant the same rights to its nationals as those that a national of another Member State in the same situations would derive from European law.[137] The Court found that the licensing system was a restriction on freedom of establishment secured under Article 49 of the Treaty, since although it was not discriminatory it was likely to hinder the exercise of the right of establishment. Before doing so, it referred to the general autonomy of the Member States in the design of their social security systems.[138]

[134] It is not entirely clear that the Belgian project would also have been social housing.

[135] As an example of the Commission claiming the broad equivalence of necessity and proportionality review under Art 106(2) and the free movement derogations, see Commission Decision of 10 May 2007, C(2007)2110 final, *Livret A et Livret Bleu*, §146, fn. 17.

[136] C-84/2011 *Susisalo* ECLI:EU:C:2012:374.

[137] The Court did not even insist on the national court suggesting that a reverse discrimination rule under Finnish law operated so as to necessitate the application of Art 49. Instead, the Court proceeded on a suggestion to that effect by the applicant during the oral hearing. See ibid, §21, where the Court said it could not conclude that an answer under Art 49 would be irrelevant. The judgment in C-268/15 *Ullens de Schooten v Belgium* of the Grand Chamber of 15 November 2016 (§§50–56) suggests that in future a more demanding approach will be taken, requiring confirmation from the national court in the order for reference. More generally, in that judgment the Court moved to a more structured connection approach. In a situation confined in all respects to a single Member State, one or more of the specified plus factors must be present before a preliminary reference concerning the free-movement rules will be answered.

[138] This is an odd characterisation of the nature of this case. More generally, reference to the competence of the Member States to organise their social security systems usually signals significant deference towards them by the Court. See, for example, C-70/95 *Sodemare* [1997] ECR I-3395, §§27, 32.

The Court then noted that Article 52(1) of the Treaty potentially justified restrictions on freedom of establishment to ensure the quality of medical products and separately, the lack of European harmonisation on the opening of pharmacies. In doing so, it provides an interesting contrast with *Sint Servatius* where the EU's general lack of competence concerning social housing is ignored.

In *Susisalo* the Court found that the tasks assigned to UoH fell within the protection of public health, and subject to the national court establishing that UoH was in fact engaged in these three activities across its branch network, concluded that there would be no violation of Article 49 TFEU. This is more than lax considering that the weakest form of necessity inquiry under Article 106(2) would have involved verifying at least a plausible connection between the means chosen and the particular end sought to be achieved.[139] It is interesting to consider how Article 106(2) might have been applied whether to avoid a violation of either Article 49 or Article 106(1) in conjunction with Article 102.[140] The UoH may have been entrusted with an SGEI (the referring Court thought so) in that it was charged with responsibilities that a pharmacy chain operating in the normal course of business was unlikely to undertake. As the Court noted, there was no EU legislation on the opening of pharmacies, so a weaker version of the proportionality test may have applied to the restriction imposed on other pharmacies. What is remarkable about the Court's ruling under Article 49 is that it did not require any causal connection between the special privileges accorded to UoH and the exceptional responsibilities entrusted to it. It therefore overlooked the decisive question as to whether the performance of those tasks necessitated the restriction in question at all.

5. Explaining the Court's Preference

The difficulty in establishing the true position as to the scope for using Article 106(2) to cure a violation of any Treaty provision is exacerbated by the Court of Justice's frequently minimalist reasoning. Apart from fleeting references to the final sentence of Article 106(2), it is not entirely clear what really motivates the approach taken by the Court in choosing between free movement derogations and Article 106(2). Given that deficit, the argument advanced by Bekkedal in support of Article 106(2) not being available to cure any violation of a free movement provision is notable. It seeks to differentiate the essential interests that are advanced by fundamental Treaty freedoms on the one hand and the competition rules on

[139] See Berman (n 133) 80, for a consideration of the variants of proportionality, including its weakest form, namely the rational connection test.

[140] The privileges accorded to UoH appear to be in the nature of a special right. That would bring the case under Art 106(1), which might then have made Art 106(2) unavoidable. Furthermore, a finding of inevitable abuse would have been probable given the suggestion that the range of available products on offer was restricted.

the other.[141] Bekkedal argues that Article 106(2) should not be used to exempt violations of free movement provisions. His principal concern appears to be that the weaker proportionality test deployed by the Court in Article 106(2) cases should not be deployed when a fundamental Treaty freedom is at stake. At the heart of Bekkedal's thesis is a value judgement that places the freedom protected by the free movement provisions on a higher constitutional plane than those protected by the competition rules. It is true that much of the rhetoric of the Court, and in particular its tendency to exalt the free movement provisions, might be regarded as justification for this distinction. Nevertheless, it is difficult to distinguish the essential nature of free movement and competition law principles, given that arguably both exist for instrumental purposes connected with the creation of the internal market.[142]

D. Subordination—The State Aid Rules

1. Introduction

Although the contingency of Article 106(2) is fairly apparent with respect to the free movement derogation mechanism, that phenomenon is even clearer with respect to the State aid rules. This is not just because of the effective equivalence of the mechanics, but also because of the procedural distinctiveness of Article 107, based on largely centralised control by the Commission. As a result, this issue warrants separate consideration. From a government failure perspective it might be regarded as irrelevant whether curbing that phenomenon takes place under Article 106(2) or Article 107. There is, however, a fundamental complication in that if Article 107 is applied with particular strictness then Article 106(2) may be applied with greater laxity. The problem then becomes one of spill-over effects into the wider Article 106(2) jurisprudence. In this section I explore both those effects and the multifaceted implications of the *Altmark* ruling for Article 106(2).

2. Procedural Relationship Between Article 106(2) and State Aid Enforcement

While the preceding subsection has tracked the eventual confirmation of the direct effect of Article 106(2), Lynskey argues that ultimately this is limited to 'private

[141] Bekkedal, T, 'Article 106 TFEU is Dead. Long Live Article 106 TFEU!' in Szyszczak, Davies, Andenas and Bekkedal (eds), *Developments of Services of General Interest* (Asser Press, 2011).

[142] As far back as 1974, the Court in finding that Arts 101 and 102 were directly effective, categorised those prohibitions as conferring important rights on individuals. See C-127/73 *BRT v SABAM II* [1973] ECR 313, §16.

sector competition rules' and that, in particular, it has never been accorded direct effect in the context of State aid procedure.[143] In this regard, it is important to bear in mind that the direct effect of Article 107(1) is itself limited, given the curtailment of the role of Member State courts to verifying the existence of aid, with matters of compatibility being the preserve of the Commission.[144] As such, in procedural terms, the question of the impact of Article 106(2) is in large measure about whether its applicability could serve to obviate the need for State aid notification and the suspension of newly proposed aid.

The issue of the procedural relationship between Article 106(2) and Article 108(3) was first subject to extended debate before the Court of Justice in *Banco Exterior*.[145] There, Advocate General Lenz relied on earlier precedent effectively equating the substance of Article 106(3) enforcement with State aid procedure.[146] He saw no prejudice accruing to the Member State through the assessment of Article 106(2) claims in the context of State aid review.[147] That approach was followed by the Court, which may have been concerned that to conclude otherwise could lead to a coach and four being driven through State aid procedure.[148] Subsequently, in *CELF*, France attempted to distinguish between the notification and standstill obligations, arguing that the latter might justifiably be suspended for SGEIs.[149] That was rejected by the Court on the basis that these obligations were two sides of the same coin and essential to overall control to safeguard the operation of the then common market.[150] Separately, Advocate General La Pergola had advised that while Article 106(2) could be used to declare aid compatible, in the event of non-notification, it could not cure the illegality of unlawful implementation.[151] In *Ferring*, Advocate General Tizzano took a different view, considering that qualification under Article 106(2) removed any possible illegality by reason of non-notification.[152]

The direct effect of Article 106(2) in the context of State aid procedure was not directly at issue in *Altmark*, which, as will be considered in the next subsection, was concerned with the prior issue of whether there was aid to begin with. As a result, *Banco Exterior* appears to continue to be good law. In practice, the application

[143] Lynskey, O, 'The Application of Article 86(2) to Measures Which do Not Fulfil the Altmark Criteria; Institutionalising Incoherence in the Legal Framework Governing State Compensation of Public Service Obligations' (2007) 30(1) *World Competition* 153, 163–164.

[144] C-354/90 *FNCEPA* [1991] ECR I-495, §14.

[145] C-387/92 *Banco Exterior* [1994] ECR I-877.

[146] Opinion of 11 January 1994, §§68–69.

[147] ibid, §70.

[148] C-387/92 *Banco Exterior* [1994] ECR I-877, §17. Arguably, the proportionality standard built into Art 106(2) justifies this approach. Other Treaty rules are only disapplied to the extent that it is necessary. With respect to new aid, it seems hard to see how the non-observance of either the notification or standstill requirement could be justified, even for an SGEI, except in response to a catastrophic event.

[149] C-332/98 *CELF* [2000] ECR I-4833.

[150] ibid, §32.

[151] ibid, Opinion of 14 December 1999, §19.

[152] C-53/00 *Ferring* [2001] ECR I-9067, Opinion of 8 May 2001, §§76–80.

of Article 106(2) in conjunction with Article 107 is now largely policed within the State aid procedure. This leaves the Commission with a significant amount of discretion as to whether to deploy specific State aid guidelines or a more generic Article 106(2) approach to aid for SGEIs. In effect, the procedural assimilation of Article 106(2) under the State aid machinery has resulted in more substantive subordination. That has been brought about in large measure through the *Altmark* judgment, which is now considered.

3. *Altmark* as a Proxy for Article 106(2)

In *Altmark*, the Court of Justice was confronted by the issue of whether funding for public service bus routes in a small German city was State aid, but exemptible under Article 107 ('the State aid approach').[153] Alternatively, the funding was capable of not amounting to State aid provided that it was necessary and proportionate ('the compensation approach').[154] The challenge confronting the Court of Justice in *Altmark* was to find a way to avoid an across-the-board carve-out for financing of public services, while at the same time preserving some measure of control over the Member States. In doing so, the Court faced conflicting advice of various Advocates General in other cases, who were divided as between the State aid and compensation approaches.[155] An important feature of *Altmark* is that Article 106(2) was not applied, nor could it have been. Instead, Article 93 TFEU was in principle relevant as a *lex specialis* for transport-related aid, but was not invoked on the basis that a sectoral regulation was in place.[156]

The Court stipulated four tests which, if satisfied, meant that there was no advantage accruing to the recipient of public service compensation, guaranteeing that funding would not amount to State aid to begin with.[157] First, there must be a public service obligation (PSO), with such obligation being well defined. Second, the parameters of compensation must be established in advance in an objective and transparent manner. Third, compensation must not exceed the costs incurred in discharging those PSOs, taking account of revenues and a reasonable profit. Finally, where the selection of the provider had not been made on the basis

[153] In T-106/95 *FFSA* [1997] ECR II-229 the General Court had endorsed this approach.

[154] In C-53/00 *Ferring* [2001] ECR I-9067, the Court held that compensation to cover additional costs associated with a PSO would not be treated as an advantage, thereby taking it outside of the State aid rules. This view has its origins in an earlier judgment in C-240/83 *ABDHU* [1985] ECR 531. The compensation approach was subsequently reflected in the Community Guidelines on the Application of Articles 92 and 93 of the EC Treaty to State Aids in the Aviation Sector, 10.12.1994, OJ C350/07, p 5, and in the Guidelines on State Aid to Maritime Transport, 05.07.1997, OJ C205, p 5.

[155] AG Jacobs proposed a compromise third way in his opinion in *GEMO*, which was based on 'quick look' review of the compensation, such that if the necessary connection between the assistance and the public service were not immediately apparent, then the State aid approach would apply. See C-126/01 *GEMO* [2003] ECR I-13769, Opinion of AG Jacobs of 30 April 2002, §§117–19.

[156] Regulation (EEC) 1191/69 as amended by Regulation (EEC) No. 1893/91.

[157] C-280/00 *Altmark* [2003] ECR I-7747, §§89–93.

of a public procurement process securing the lowest-cost provision for the community, then the costs should be based on the costs of a well-run operator adequately resourced for its purposes.

The co-incidence between the *Altmark* criteria and the essentials of Article 106(2), at least in its stricter incarnations, is striking but also essential, considering what the Court of Justice was attempting to do.[158] The first test incorporates the concept of an SGEI in the form of a PSO and mirrors the mandatory dimension to 'entrusted' under Article 106(2).[159] The second and third tests are focused on the necessity and proportionality of the compensation. The second test has echoes of *Ahmed Saeed*, where the Court emphasised that in the absence of sufficient cost information and transparency, it would be difficult to justify the conclusion that without compensation, the performance of the SGEI would be imperilled.[160] Finally, the last test is efficiency oriented and is the kind of approach that one would have expected to apply to the calculation of allowable costs if a strict proportionality test applied under Article 106(2). As I explore in Chapter 6, despite some tentative suggestions in that regard, ultimately efficiency was disclaimed as a core Article 106(2) requirement.

Although conceived as a filter for the exclusion of advantage for the purposes of State aid verification, the *Altmark* criteria are an elaborate variant of several of Article 106(2)'s core elements, but with some significant innovations. Hancher and Larouche have summarised the overall effect of *Altmark* as internalising the problem of PSO compensation within Article 107 through the concept of SGEI being 'evacuated' in favour of the possibly more pliable PSO concept, but at the price for the Member States of greater strictness and transparency as to the compensation parameters.[161]

While the Court of Justice must have been concerned about the high-profile schism in the case law, the implications of the *Altmark* solution have been profound for Article 106(2). In voicing his opposition to the *Ferring* approach in his first opinion in *Altmark*, Advocate General Léger argued that Article 106(2) was the central Treaty provision for reconciling Community objectives.[162] In the immediate wake of the judgment the Commission confirmed that Article 106(2) was still applicable to measures failing the *Altmark* criteria.[163] The relative severity

[158] See, Biondi, A and Rubini, L, 'Aims, Effects and Justifications: EC State Aid Law and its Impact on National Social Policies' in Spaventa and Dougan (eds), *Social Welfare and EU Law* (Hart Publishing, 2005) referring to *Altmark* as a 'rather successful transplant, after the necessary adjustments, of the main requirements of Article [106(2)]', 95.

[159] The interchangeability of the terms 'PSO' and 'SGEI' is confirmed in cases such as *BUPA*, although it that case that proposition was effectively agreed by the parties in argument and accepted by the Court. See T-289/03 *BUPA* [2008] ECR II-81, §162.

[160] C-66/86 *Ahmed Saeed* [1989] ECR 803, §§56–57.

[161] Hancher, L and Larouche, P, 'The Coming of Age of EU Regulation of Network Industries and Services of General Economic Interest' in Craig and de Búrca (eds), *The Evolution of EU Law* (Oxford University Press, 2011) 761.

[162] Opinion of AG Léger of 19 March 2002 in C-280/00 *Altmark* [2003] ECR I-7747, §80.

[163] *Redevance Radiodiffusion*, C(2005) 1166 fin, §37.

of the *Altmark* tests had the potential to result in an actual or perceived weakening in Article 106(2). After all, if compensation was adequate or less than adequate then there would be no State aid, but if it was excessive, then it is difficult to see how it could be regarded as necessary under Article 106(2).[164] Despite that, and as will be explored in greater detail in Chapter 6, the proportionality requirement exhibits significant variability.[165] This is reflected to a degree in the Commission's decision in *BBC Digital Curriculum*, coming only months after *Altmark*.[166] There, despite the absence of any demonstration that the BBC's costs were those of a typical well-run operator, the Commission approved the funding as proportionate, largely on the basis that since the BBC was not going to be allowed to recover all of its estimate of the costs of the service, there would be no over-funding.[167]

Altmark was an innovative solution to a problem created by divergent case law, but at the price of Article 106(2)'s relevance. If, instead, the Court had accepted the State aid classification then, leaving aside its inapplicability on the facts of *Altmark*, Article 106(2) would have been generally available in these situations. Moreover, although that would have confirmed the necessity of State aid filings, there would almost certainly have been a political response. In particular, the Commission may have wished to bring forward a proposal so as to have allowed the Council to act under Article 107(3)(e) TFEU.[168] Alternatively, the Commission may have done precisely what it did in response to *Altmark* by adopting a decision under Article 106(3) so as to relieve Member States of the obligation to notify a wide category of supports for public services that were SGEIs.[169] In the process, Article 106(2) may have gained greater prominence. Instead, Article 106(2) is now contingent on the prior application of the *Altmark* principles. The position has, however, become more complicated in the light of the post-*Altmark* SGEI packages, the implications of which are also considered in detail in Chapter 6.

E. Conclusions

In this chapter I have charted the overall contingency of Article 106(2). Article 106(2) cannot be properly understood based solely on internal analysis. An essential

[164] See Buendía Sierra, JL, 'Finding the Right Balance: State Aid and Services of General Economic Interest' in *EC State Aid Law, Liber Amicorum Francisco Santaolalla Gadea* (2008) 215.

[165] See the argument to that effect in Biondi and Rubini (n 158) 73, 100.

[166] State Aid No. N 37/2003, *BBC Digital Curriculum*, C(2003)3371.

[167] ibid, §152.

[168] The Commission may not have been able to cope with all of the State aid notifications that this could have generated.

[169] See Commission Decision 2005/842 on the application of Article 86(2) of the EC Treaty to State aid in the form of public service compensation to certain undertakings entrusted with the operation of services of general economic interest.

element of such an exercise is an exploration of its operation as against possible alternatives. While it might appear facile to characterise the operation of Article 106(2) and the free movement derogations in competitive terms, I consider that it captures the underlying dynamics. The free movement derogation mechanisms enjoyed 'first mover advantage' on direct effect and expanded in direct proportion to the reach of the free movement provisions. Their application has in turn been boosted by the effective abandonment of the purely internal situation rule. By contrast, Article 106(2) played 'catch-up' on direct effect, while the range of general interests capable of accommodation under Article 106(2) appeared to be limited. Separately, when Article 106(2) comes up against imperative requirements, it is hardly a contest, since invariably they will be first applied, in the process determining not just the outcome but, in some instances, the very applicability of Article 106(2).

My demonstration of contingency has been undertaken by investigating its interaction with other Treaty provisions and constructs capable of producing similar outcomes. Even where SGEIs are centrally implicated in cases, with national courts raising Article 106(2) questions, and in some cases Advocates General providing clear answers, in some instances the Court of Justice has avoided recourse to Article 106(2). It has created exceptions to the undertaking concept in respect of solidarity and the exercise of public authority. Yet, the solidarity-based exemption appears not to extend to any concern that is not capable of accommodation as a distributional general interest under Article 106(2). Separately, the public authority exception is a problematic extension of the official authority exception and one based on a highly elusive justification. In the process, obvious market failures susceptible to Article 106(2) analysis are not interrogated and patent government failures go uncorrected.[170] What is common to both the solidarity and public authority exceptions is their binary character, leading to an 'all-or-nothing' application of the competition rules. This is to be contrasted with the potential for their calibrated application under Article 106(2).

Despite the variety of phenomena that I have considered in this chapter, the overall position might be summarised by understanding Article 106(2)'s contingency in terms of its failure to emerge as the *über* exemption for the resolution of SGEI-related claims. Perhaps that is most apparent in the area of State aid, where *Altmark* appears to confirm both the procedural and substantive emasculation of Article 106(2) by the State aid regime. Although having the appearances of such an ultimate rule, Article 106(2) has never really been accorded that role. The suitability of Article 106(2) to operate as the *über* exemption for SGEIs is in serious

[170] The official authority exemption is clearly applied with greater rigour to the free movement rules than the public authority exception is applied to the competition rules. See the comments of AG Cruz Villarón in C-47/08 *Belgian Notaries* [2011] ECR I-4105 that in the 15 cases that had by then resulted in Court judgments on the official authority exemption, in no instance were its terms found to be satisfied. See §87.

doubt. Accordingly, Advocate General Léger's description of Article 106(2) in *Altmark* as a crucial mediating provision under the Treaty is at best a normative aspiration and not a reflection of the underlying reality.[171] Far from being central, Article 106(2) is contingent and it continues to struggle for relevance. It is not even master of its own domain. As a result, it is significantly compromised as a tool in mitigation of government failure.

[171] Opinion of AG Léger of 19 March 2002 in C-280/00 *Altmark*, §80.

5

Government Failure in Assessing Market Feasibility

A. Introduction

This chapter is a critique of the extent of government failure in disapplication review under Article 106(2). I undertake this exposition of Article 106(2) case law using the concept of market feasibility. That entails a consideration of how markets are performing and the nature of any impediments to them delivering on general interest objectives. The concept of market failure is a critical component of market feasibility. While several commentators have suggested that the concept of market failure may provide a natural starting point for the assessment and verification of SGEI claims, so far these have not been empirically tested.[1] A particular focus of this chapter is on the extent to which Article 106(2) is used to verify not just the existence or otherwise of market failures, but also the extent to which their existence is considered in the context of achieving distributional objectives.

This demonstration of government failure in SGEI verification is carried out with respect to telecommunications, environmental protection, and broadcasting. Although allowing for the obvious variations between them, the broad approach is to identify relevant market failures in the light of Chapter 2, to consider the nature of SGEI claims and to pay particular attention to the issue of market feasibility. In principle, a concern for market feasibility should extend to an assessment of how markets are performing in practice and whether political goals might be achieved, perhaps through the identification of disabling market failures. That is what a determination of market feasibility entails. Part of the relevant context for each of the sectors considered includes the constitutional underpinning, some of which is already reflected in my treatment of the political, constitutional and administrative battles to which Article 106 generally and Article 106(2) in particular have been central.[2]

[1] See Schwintowski, H, 'The Common Good, Public Subsistence and the Functions of Public Undertakings in the European Internal Market' (2003) 4 *European Business Organization Law Review* 353–82; van de Gronden, J, 'The Internal Market, the State and Private Initiative: A Legal Assessment of National Mixed Public-Private Arrangements in the Light of European Law' (2006) 33(2) *Legal Issues of European Integration* 105–37 and Sauter, W, 'Services of General Economic Interest and Universal Service in EU Law' (2008) 33(2) *European Law Review* 167–93.

[2] See Chapter 3.

The position that I go on to describe across the sectors should be a source of concern. Government failure is all too common with respect to SGEI verification under Article 106(2). While the concept of market failure is having some impact, provider-centric political forces still appear to be in the ascendancy by blocking recourse to an objective assessment of market feasibility. Apart from the field of environmental protection, where the deployment of market failure has mitigated the potential for government failure under Article 106(2), government failure is frequent and positively abounds in the field of public service broadcasting. There is, however, some reason for hope, not least in the first sector to be considered, telecommunications, where provider interests were long in the ascendancy before a technological revolution rewrote the underlying economics, released the political grip and led to a more rational (albeit, still imperfect) approach to SGEI verification. Government failure is by no means eliminated but at least that target is in better sight in that sector.

The elements of this chapter are as follows. I first consider the position of telecommunications, long considered the provider of the exemplary SGEI, namely a Universal Service Obligation. Technological developments have changed things in that sector dramatically. That is followed by a consideration of environmental protection where the importation of a market failure critique has changed the nature of SGEI verification from declaratory to probing. The final section concerns broadcasting, and in particular public service broadcasting, where constitutional change has been a significant determinant of the position concerning SGEI verification. That has had very significant adverse implications from a government failure perspective.

B. Telecommunications

For many, the textbook example of an SGEI is a Universal Service Obligation (USO) in the telecommunications sector. At one point, that typically entailed the delivery of a Plain Only Telephone Service (POTS) to the home but also included the provision of public pay phones, almost now a technological relic. The story of how SGEIs were originally conceived in this sector is instructive both in and of itself, but also because telecommunications has provided not just the terminology, but also the analytical framework within which the entire SGEI verification debate takes place. Very valuably, despite profound change, it still engages distributional concerns that beget intervention. Tellingly, the Commission's desire to prevent and mitigate government failure through support for pan-national broadband networks has led to an artificially deflated role for SGEIs. The mitigation of government failure comes at a price, at least for Article 106(2)'s relevance.

1. The Economics of the Telecommunications Sector

Traditionally, analogue telecommunications networks were regarded as exhibiting strong natural monopoly characteristics, driven by the cost function of local distribution infrastructure.[3] Given that single supplier provision was less costly than that pertaining under competitive provision, the granting of exclusive rights was common.[4] In many countries, that led to formalised arrangements whereby in return for exclusivity, a sole provider was obliged to meet reasonable requests for connection onto the network.[5] The suppression of competition in turn led to the likelihood of monopoly pricing without further regulatory intervention. Complicating matters, typically distributional and cohesion objectives were also pursued through tariff structures that kept the cost of local services low at the expense of high long-distance and international tariffs. Underpinning this in many jurisdictions was price regulation of varying degrees of sophistication, ranging from rate of return regulation to price caps.[6] To differing degrees, each is concerned with correction of market failures through curbing the exercise of market power, the achievement of productive efficiency and the implementation of distributional goals.[7]

Analogue telecommunications also exhibit both positive and negative externalities. Positive externalities are associated with the addition of new customers onto a network. The benefit that existing users receive from an additional user is uniform even though their individual valuations of that addition may diverge very widely.[8] Optimal pricing should operate to expand the network on the basis of the marginal cost being equal to the sum of the marginal benefits to all users of the network. In practice, both because of distributionally motivated regulatory interventions, and by reason of the likely impracticability of this form of pricing, charges are usually calculated on the basis of uniform or geographically averaged rates. The positive externality issue has instead been addressed through wholesale pricing arrangements between providers. In addition to the positive externality problem just described, and perhaps counter-intuitively, telecommunications also

[3] See generally, Sharkey, W, *The Theory of Natural Monopoly* (Cambridge University Press, 1989) ch 9.

[4] See generally Kerf, M and Geradin, D, 'Controlling Market Power in Telecommunications: Antitrust v Sector Specific Regulation—An Assessment of the United States, New Zealand and Australian Experiences' (1999) 14(3) *Berkeley Technology Law Journal* 919.

[5] For an account of the rise of universal service as the quid pro quo for the suppression of competition in telecommunications in the US in the early twentieth century, see Thierer, A, 'Unnatural Monopoly: Critical Moments in the Development of the Bell System Monopoly' (1994) 14(2) *Cato Journal* 267.

[6] See Littlechild, S, 'Privatisation, Competition and Regulation' (2000) *Institute of Economic Affairs*, Occasional Paper 110.

[7] Price caps, in particular, combine both the achievement of productive efficiency through setting of an appropriate X rate, albeit often by means of the construction of 'baskets' of tariffs often constructed by reference to underlying competitive conditions, but also the delivery of a PANS on affordable terms.

[8] See generally, Shy, O, 'The Economics of Network Industries' in *Introduction to Network Economics* (Cambridge University Press, 2001).

exhibit negative externalities due to traditional charging principles. That arises from the fact that although communications are two way, typically the cost is borne by the call originator, even though both sides are effectively consuming the same telecommunications services.[9] Given that the positive externality problem can be dealt with through wholesale arrangements and the negative externality problem through social conventions, the result is that up to the 1980s, natural monopoly was the pre-eminent market failure problem impacting on the competitive structure of the analogue telecommunications world.

2. Universal Service Obligations as the Exemplary SGEI

Despite the presence of several actual and potential sources of market failure, the treatment of telecommunications under Article 106(2) has been characterised by much greater emphasis on the pursuit of distributional and cohesion goals as justification for the qualification of ubiquitous network provision as an SGEI. The very first instance of a telecommunications service being recognised as an SGEI occurred in the European Commission's 1982 enforcement Decision in *BT-Telespeed*.[10] The Commission accepted the qualification of the activities of the British Post Office, which had just been superseded by the establishment of British Telecommunications (BT), as the provision of an SGEI under Article 106(2). It did so on the basis of legislation that required that BT meet only reasonable requests for service.[11]

Following *BT-Telespeed*, USOs came onto the political agenda as part of the adoption in 1987 of a Green Paper on Telecommunications Policy ('the Telecommunications Green Paper').[12] Despite its detail, the Telecommunications Green Paper does not even mention the natural monopoly characteristics of telecommunications and is equally light on references to other market failures.[13] Instead it focused on the impediments to the introduction of competition presented by ITU-influenced tariff setting, which tended to keep international rates extremely high so as to fund lower domestic rates.[14] Although digitalisation was only beginning across Europe, in pushing for liberalisation, the Commission

[9] That problem is usually solved by the social convention of alternating the origination of calls. The alternative is to part charge both the originator and the receiver, although this is not very common in practice.

[10] Commission Decision 82/861/EEC of 10 October 1982, *BT-Telespeed*.

[11] Under s 3(1) of the British Telecommunications Act 1981, BT was placed under a general duty to serve subject to reasonable practicality.

[12] Towards a Dynamic European Economy, Commission Green Paper, COM 87/290.

[13] The Telecommunications Green Paper emphasised other market failures such as the risk presented by digitalisation and the uncertainty about prospective demand for new services, ibid, 50.

[14] In the initial stages of EU telecommunications liberalisation, the rules of the International Telecommunications Union (ITU), as a specialist agency of the United Nations, were a major stumbling block to progress and were the indirect target of the Commission's very first enforcement decision using the competition rules in *BT-Telespeed*.

did not signal any concerns in relation to the possible existence of natural monopoly as justification for the retention of exclusive rights. Instead, the focus of the Telecommunications Green Paper was on how tariffs could be adjusted through 'rebalancing' so as eventually to allow for unrestricted competition.[15] The then existing distributional regulatory overlay was the biggest impediment to the introduction of competition. Stating that otherwise, the nature of the SGEI needed to be redefined to make space for competition but with the Member States given significant time and discretion in terms of how that was accomplished.

As EU liberalisation of telecommunications progressed, the basic characteristics of USOs were harmonised through secondary legislation. This built on a political consensus reflected in a 1994 Council Resolution identifying universality, continuity and equality as comprising its essentials.[16] USOs combined elements of universal network provision and the formalisation of pricing obligations, typically based on uniform (geographically averaged) charging principles. Under the first Universal Service Directive, USO took the form of voice telephony and basic data functionality, subject to uniform pricing principles that could be imposed at the discretion of the Member States.[17] In addition it covered access to emergency services and public payphone provision. For the incumbents, the core voice telephony obligation could be discharged by continuing provision of services over pre-existing copper technology.[18] The original USO in telecommunications came to signify the essence of an SGEI, while also providing the lexicon for the stylised delivery characteristics approach to SGEI qualification explored in Chapter 3.

3. The Digital Revolution

(a) Technological Transformation

The effects of digitalisation on the telecommunications industry are difficult to overstate.[19] From the 1980s, every element of underlying network provision from switching and transmission, through to local distribution, was overhauled. Underpinned by exponential increases in computer processing power, advances in

[15] In introducing the Telecommunications Green Paper, the Commission proposed accepting continuing exclusivity on the basis that it was considered 'essential at this stage for safeguarding public service goals'. See Proposed Positions, 16.

[16] Council Resolution of 7 February 1994 on Universal Service Principles in the Telecommunications Sector [1994] OJ C48/01. Demonstrating the pliability of these concepts, universality was equated with affordability, equality with territorial access, and continuity with quality.

[17] Directive 98/10 of the European Parliament and of the Council of 26 February 1998 on the Application of Open Network Provision to Voice Telephony and on Universal Service for Telecommunications in a Competitive Environment. See Arts 3 and 5. The preceding Directive 95/62 did not detail any specific obligations.

[18] Although it is not prescriptive, Directive 98/10 appears to assume operator levies as the likely source of USO funding.

[19] For a comprehensive and generally prescient account before digitalisation took hold, see Negroponte, N, *Being Digital* (Alfred A. Knopf Inc., 1995).

optical electronics and new technology capable of digitalising copper connections, the basic functionality of telecommunications networks was transformed.[20] In parallel, electronic devices underwent a revolution, with improvements in performance in turn driving demand for increased capacity, necessitating the deployment of broadband networks. As a result, underlying service provision shifted from voice and basic data services to the provision of undifferentiated high-capacity bi-directional connections, with voice being just one of a myriad of overlaid services. Over a period of 20 years the telecommunications industry was transformed into the electronic communications sector.

(b) Economic Reordering

While traditionally the notion of natural monopoly was understood to be driven by the presence of economies of scale, extensive research in the 1960s and 1970s revealed that they were not a necessary or sufficient condition for a natural monopoly.[21] Instead, the focus turned to 'subadditivity' of costs, with a very important distinction emerging between single-product and multi-product firms.[22] As a result of this new understanding, the possibility of a natural monopoly in a multi-product setting (as the telecommunications industry was then becoming) was considerably reduced. Around the time that the subadditivity concept began to emerge in the economic analysis of natural monopoly, digitalisation began to be implemented in telecommunications. Its advent and changes to the modes of deployments of networks, together with additions to traditional services, began to undermine the economics of the standard natural monopoly claim. With the sector being transformed in the space of two decades, the view of telecommunications as a natural monopoly was no longer inhibiting.

4. Broadband and Hybrid-Market Failure

From 2002 the Commission and the Council began endorsing ambitious goals for the availability of high-speed (broadband) communications networks. This culminated in the Digital Agenda Europe Strategy (DAE 2020) adopted in 2010 as part of the Europe 2020 Strategy in response to the global financial crisis.[23] As a result, in the context of realising national and EU-level broadband targets, it was always likely that the Member States would turn to direct financial assistance to fulfil those ambitions, with that becoming a certainty once EU funding became

[20] See Laffont, JJ and Tirole, J, *Competition in Telecommunications* (MIT, 2001) ch 1.

[21] See generally, Sharkey (n 3) ch 9.

[22] This is a situation where the cost of total output is less than the sum of the costs of a range of products separately produced.

[23] Europe 2020, A European Strategy for Smart, Sustainable and Inclusive Growth, COM (2010) 2020 final, p 14. Earlier documents such as eEurope 2005: An Information Society for All, COM (2002) 263, sets basic targets directed at government.

available for the purpose.[24] That has resulted in 149 individual State aid decisions, concerning the broadband, mobile and submarine capacity since 2003, and the adoption of two sets of guidelines in 2009 and 2013.[25] Both sets of guidelines largely codified the accumulating case law on State aid for broadband funding.[26] The Commission has exercised control using the State aid rule, and to that end deployed market failure-oriented guidelines as foreshadowed by the SAAP.[27] In the process, and as will be explored, Article 106(2) has been largely sidelined.

The Commission's 2009 Broadband Guidelines prioritise market failure as the Commission's analytical framework for the determination of the compatibility with the internal market. The only efficiency-related market failure that is identified is positive externalities in terms of spillover effects.[28] That said, the precise justification is very thin. A myriad of economic activities are characterised by positive externalities but are not considered instances of market failure justifying intervention. Surprisingly, the Commission's 2013 Broadband Guidelines on this specific issue are even looser that the 2009 version. They specify the problem as related to the inability of prospective investors to internalise the 'whole benefits' of a prospective investment.[29] Although acknowledging wider knock-on benefits from broadband investment, basing the justification on the inability to capture all the positive externalities of an activity is surely too broad. The crucial issue is whether a prospective investor is capable of capturing a sufficient part of the overall economic benefits so as to have the requisite incentive to proceed.[30]

It is clear that the Commission's 2009 Broadband Guidelines extend beyond inefficiency causing market failures of the type emphasised in the SAAP. The Commission acknowledged that even where market outcomes are efficient, Member States might still wish to pursue 'cohesion' goals, especially with a view to bridging the 'digital divide'.[31] The Commission also flagged a concern in relation to the crowding out of private investment, and in line with the 2005 SAAP, expressed particular concerns about the incentive effects of public support for competing

[24] On this problem generally, in relation to telecommunications, see Gomez Barroso, JL and Perez Martinez, P, 'Assessing Market Failures in Advanced Telecommunications Services: Universal Service Categories', paper presented at ITS 14th European Regional Conference, Helsinki, 23–24 August 2003.

[25] This number is that presented by the Commission as being the position as of 10 April 2017.

[26] Community Guidelines for the Application of State Aid Rules in Relation to Rapid Deployment of Broadband Networks (2009/C235/04) ('the 2009 Broadband Guidelines'), and EU Guidelines for the Application of State Aid Rules in Relation to the Rapid Deployment of Broadband Networks (2013/C25/01) ('the 2013 Broadband Guidelines').

[27] State Aid Action Plan, Less and Better Targeted State Aid: a Roadmap for State Aid Reform 2005–2009, 07.06.2005, COM (2005) 107 final.

[28] (2009/C235/04), §39.

[29] (2013/C25/01), §37.

[30] For a demonstration of a rather loose approach to this problem of positive externalities, see State aid SA. 36918 (2014/N) Finland Baltic Sea Backbone Cable, §96. In that case there were no estimates relied upon of wider effects and it was assumed that a more cyber-secure cable (seemingly on the basis that it would bypass Russia) offering redundancy was 'arguably' not going to be valued sufficiently to induce investment.

[31] (2009/C235/04), §4.

private investment.[32] Separately, the 2009 Broadband Guidelines demonstrated the difficulties that arise in separating interventions on the basis of equity and cohesion as opposed to efficiency, not least considering that particular measures may be directed at all three. It is, therefore, crucial that the position with respect to market failures first be established.

As a result of the need to take a pragmatic approach that fuses efficiency (ie, market failure) and cohesion objectives, the Commission has relied on the mapping of broadband roll-out using a three-colour system in order to reveal the existence of current and planned networks. Mapping exercises can suffer from gaming by existing players (who could exaggerate or accelerate their plans, so called 'crowding-in') and do not model the crowding-out effects of direct intervention. Nevertheless, they establish parameters for supervising distributional and cohesion objectives in a structured way that is known in advance by the Member States.

Under the Commission's 2009 Broadband Guidelines, a white area is one that has no broadband networks, and a grey area has at least one such network, while a black area has two or more broadband networks. The Commission refers to intervention in white areas (normally rural areas) as correcting market failures and contributing to territorial cohesion, reflecting the intermingling of efficiency and cohesion objectives.[33] Despite that, it is clear that cohesion objectives predominate and will be deferred to by the Commission even if there are no market failures, strictly speaking. For grey areas, the Commission prescribes more detailed inquiry, focusing in particular on the efficacy of national regulatory interventions. Since most of those measures are directed at the control of market power as a form of market failure, this suggests that the efficiency paradigm predominates in the consideration of aid for grey areas. By contrast, in black areas, the Commission usually treats the presence of two or more networks as ruling out the need for public intervention 'in the absence of a clearly demonstrated market failure'.[34] That implicitly reveals that intervention for cohesion purposes is in general not likely to be permitted in those areas. This approach is maintained in the 2013 Broadband Guidelines, subject to a new possibility of authorising funding even in black areas in order to deliver a 'step change' in available capacity.[35] This concern is qualitatively different from the usual cohesion objective and is a reflection of industrial policy in State aid enforcement.[36]

While the role of market failure under Article 107 has become increasingly prominent since the adoption of the SAAP in 2005, up until 2013 there had been no explicit pronouncements by either the Commission or the EU Courts concerning the role of market failure under Article 106(2). That would appear to

[32] ibid, §43.
[33] ibid, §42.
[34] ibid, §43.
[35] (2013/C25/01), §84.
[36] On this issue generally, see Sauter, W, 'Squaring EU Law and Competition Policy: The Case of Broadband' (2013) *TILEC Discussion Paper* No. 2013-021.

have changed considering the judgment of the General Court in *Colt* in 2013.[37] In that case, the Court indicated that the verification of a market failure 'is a prerequisite for qualification of an activity as an SGEI'.[38] For the first time, there appeared to have been explicit judicial support for the concept of market failure as central to the operation of Article 106(2). Nevertheless, there is good reason for considerable caution.

The question that arises in respect of *Colt* is whether in referring to 'market failure', the General Court was referring to an efficiency-derived market failure of the kind considered in Chapter 2, or a more wide-ranging category capable of including distributional and cohesion goals.[39] Given that the Court's claim was made in the context of the Commission's application of Article 107, and specifically the verification of the existence of an SGEI for the purposes of considering the first *Altmark* criterion, the General Court's claim is problematic. The Commission's assessment of that issue was made in the light of the 2009 Broadband Guidelines, which as already considered—although grounded in the language of market failures—are not limited to the inefficiency-derived kind.[40] Instead, and unsurprisingly, they subsume the pursuit of cohesion goals in particular.[41] As a result, the judgment in *Colt* on this point needs to be approached with caution.

5. The Curtailment of Permissible SGEIs

The Commission's approach to the recognition of SGEIs for broadband can be traced back to a 2004 Decision in *Pyrénées-Atlantiques*.[42] Before considering the evolution of the issue since then, it bears emphasising that the relevant point in that Decision was whether there was a PSO for the purposes of the first *Altmark* criterion, which was equated with verification of the existence of an SGEI.[43]

[37] T-79/10 *Colt* ECLI:EU:T:2013:463.

[38] 'Il ressort de ces dispositions que l'appréciation de l'existence d'une défaillance du marché constitue un préalable à la qualification d'une activité de SIEG et ainsi à la constatation de l'absence d'aide d'État'. T-79/10 *Colt* ECLI:EU:T:2013:463, §154. See also the largely identical judgments in T-258/10 *Orange* ECLI:EU:T:2013:471 and T-325/10 *Illiad* [2010] OJ C288/82. Both were unsuccessfully appealed in C-621/13 P (Order, ECLI:EU:C:2015:114) and C-624/13 P (Order, ECLI:EU:C:2015:112), respectively.

[39] As Sauter notes, 'In the context of SGEI the relevance of the concept of market failure is increasing, but it is not always clear if this includes only efficiency (market failure narrowly defined) considerations or also equity (market failure broadly defined) considerations'. Sauter, W, *Public Services in EU Law* (Cambridge University Press, 2015) 221.

[40] In 2012 the Commission approved €6.5 billion of broadband State aid. See Kliemann, A and Stehmann, O, 'EU State Aid Control in the Broadband Sector—the 2013 Broadband Guidelines and Recent Case Practice' (2013) 3 *European State Aid Law Quarterly* 493, 494.

[41] Community Guidelines for the Application of State Aid Rules to the Rapid Deployment of Broadband Networks (2009/C 235/04).

[42] N 381/2004 *Pyrénées-Atlantiques*. See also a similar decision in N 382/2004 *Limousin (DORSAL)*.

[43] As such, it is not the residual application of Art 106(2) in circumstances where one or more of the *Altmark* criteria are not satisfied. The same approach was taken in C 35/2005 (ex N 59/2005) *Appingedam*, which is discussed below.

Pyrénées-Atlantiques concerned the provision of a wholesale passive network by a concessionaire and recipient of public funding, which was to be used to offer facilities and services to enable downstream providers of retail communications services to deliver broadband services throughout the region. Pre-existing network roll-out was very patchy, accounted for mainly by the presence of France Telecom, and a smaller mainly urban provider. As a result, the Pyrénées-Atlantiques authorities issued a tender for a ubiquitous network on the basis of minimising the contribution from public funds, while constraining the concessionaire's business model and profitability. Retail providers of telecommunications services were to be offered access on non-discriminatory terms to network elements, with the concessionaire prohibited from serving final consumers.

Although the state-funded wholesale network was intended to facilitate the provision of broadband services to the territory as a whole, the intervention relied on the regulated provision of services to providers of telecommunications services, without any guarantee that they would be made available to end users.[44] As such, the measure enabled service provision through the commercial offerings of retail providers. It will be apparent that this type of intermediate provision of a service differs from the more usual final consumer-delivered offerings that tend to predominate with respect to SGEIs.[45] Heavily influenced by the lack of broadband services, the paucity of advanced networks, and with passing reference to the possibility of market power problems, the Commission accepted the measure as an SGEI.[46] According to the Commission, to qualify as an SGEI, the intervention needed to be motivated by public service reasons. To that end, it emphasised that since the network to be deployed was not likely to be duplicated, it would be necessary to ensure open non-discriminatory access to it. As a result, although the original problem was not necessarily directed at a market failure, the proposed intervention entailed a risk of market power, the regulation of which was decisive in terms of SGEI qualification.[47]

The result in *Pyrénées-Atlantiques* is significant given that the Commission's emphasis on the exclusion of the concession holder from retail provision was a method of minimising competitive distortions. Subsequently, it became clear that the type of structure deployed by the French authorities is the only acceptable form of SGEI for broadband. This was illustrated by the *MANS* Decision concerning broadband deployment in Ireland adopted in 2006. In it, the Commission denied SGEI status for the operation of metropolitan area networks in parts of the country that lacked broadband services.[48] Ireland proposed the granting of a concession to

[44] *Pyrénées-Atlantiques*, §11.

[45] Despite this and no doubt live to the potential SGEI implications, the Département still maintained that the network was universal: 'En ce qui concerne plus précisément la typologie du réseau, les autorités françaises ont précisé que le projet était relatif à un réseau universel pour tous les publics'. *Pyrénées-Atlantiques*, §12.

[46] The market failure problems concerned possible refusals to supply. *Pyrénées-Atlantiques*, §59.

[47] This might be regarded as a consequential market failure.

[48] N 284/05 *MANS*.

operate passive networks subject to non-discriminatory access to retail providers, and a prohibition on the provider competing in that segment. This was refused SGEI treatment, however, on the basis that since the service would principally be made available to business users, there would be nothing 'to enable broadband access to the general public, citizens and business in rural and remote areas'.[49] In *MANS*, the direct connectors were expected to be large business users on account of their likely bandwidth requirements. The Commission's approach suggests a reversion to the more orthodox direct public benefits requirement, seemingly relaxed in *Pyrénées-Atlantiques*, although there the concessionaire was subject to an absolute obligation to connect all customers, both business and residential, on behalf of the commercial providers.

In *MANS* the Commission concluded that the measure was not an SGEI and doubted that the market investor test was passed. The result was that the Irish plan was considered to be State aid. The Commission analysed the compatibility of the aid on cohesion and market failure grounds under Article 107(3)(c). The analysis tipped in favour of the compatibility of the aid on the basis that sectoral regulation had not brought wholesale prices to marginal costs levels and had only required a limited suite of mandatory offerings from the incumbent that did not include access to dark fibre.[50] In effect, the presence of market failures as a result of the imperfectly constrained exercise of market power was accepted as part of the overall justification for the intervention. Stated otherwise, there was government failure in the efficacy of the pre-existing economic regulation of the sector.[51]

Although in *MANS* the Commission accepted these market failure justifications (although not expressly labelled as such), it appears that it would not have done so if it had been satisfied with the efficacy of existing regulation. In that regard, the *Appingedam* Decision provides a useful contrast. There, the existence of sectoral remedies and voluntary wholesale offerings was treated as negating any possible market failure justification from intervention.[52] By contrast with *Appingedam*, which concerned an urban network, in *MANS* cohesional concerns loomed large in relation to Ireland's argument concerning the emergence of a digital divide disadvantaging rural areas.[53] The Commission's interrogation of the cohesion

[49] The Commission attached some significance to the Irish government's labelling of the initiative as a 'public-private partnership' as indicating that a sufficient 'public' dimension was somehow lacking. In the same paragraph (§38), the Commission also claimed that Ireland had never used the term 'public service' to describe its objective. Ireland appears not to have engaged in the elaborate 'service public' labelling exercise that typifies the approach of other Member States to setting up SGEI claims. Overall, this kind of formalism on the part of the Commission is unconvincing. It doe suggest that SGEI claims are as much to be formally asserted as established.

[50] *MANS*, §62. Dark fibre is optical cable that has not been connected to lasers.

[51] Ultimately, that might be laid at the door of the Commission, or more generally the EU, to the extent that Ireland may not have been permitted to impose that requirement.

[52] C(2006) 3226 final. That included a range of mandated offerings and the voluntary offer by the incumbent of wholesale broadband access in competition with a similar offering by the other existing operator. See §77.

[53] In *Appingedam* the Commission highlighted domestic research as revealing 'that existing market failures are limited and mainly related to market power and minor production externalities'. See §75.

argument was necessarily superficial. This is perhaps a very clear illustration of deference to such goals in circumstances where the Commission lacks an objective basis and perhaps the legitimacy to supervise the Member State's policy choices. The subsequent move to a formal mapping exercise as part of the 2009 Broadband Guidelines was an effort to build some objective constraints around the realisation of those goals.[54]

Through the 2009 Broadband Guidelines the Commission codified its treatment of SGEI claims in conformity with its approach in *Pyrénées-Atlantiques*. In them, the Commission was highly prescriptive and stipulated that

> the recognition of an SGEI mission for broadband deployment should be based on the provision of passive, neutral and open access infrastructure. Such a network should provide access seekers with all possible forms of network access and allow effective competition at the retail level, ensuring the provision of competitive and affordable services to end users.[55]

That approach is maintained in the 2013 Broadband Guidelines.[56] While as a result of *Altmark* it is the public service mission that is being tested, the Commission's approach is highly prescriptive by limiting assistance to wholesale provision only. The Commission ordains a single kind of business model for wholesale intervention. While this appears at odds with the usually open-ended potential for SGEI claims, it may be borne of a more fundamental perspective. Although acknowledging the case for intervention in part on efficiency grounds and more generally for cohesion purposes, the Commission is seeking to keep the locus of interventions as far away as possible from activities that are potentially competitive. Since the Commission must accommodate non-efficiency-related goals, it uses an elementary form of market counterfactual testing (based on the mapping exercise) to particularise the market inadequacy. It then seeks to minimise the consequent competitive distortions by targeting and circumscribing the nature of the intervention. With Article 107(3)(c) guidelines as the Commission's preferred analytical framework, Article 106(2)'s relevance is inevitably contingent.

C. Environmental Protection

Providing a useful contrast to the position concerning telecommunications, I now consider the issue of government failure in the deployment of Article 106(2) in the environmental arena. The consideration of market feasibility in this area is characterised by a considerably 'purer' approach to the consideration of market failure than in telecommunications. In the environmental realm, there

[54] Arguably, the objectivisation of the assessment and the expansive approach to market failure assists the Commission with the problem of legitimacy.

[55] (2009/C235/04), §27.

[56] (2013/C25/01), §23.

is an important distinction between market failures as the underlying causes of environmental problems, and separately, the issue of whether the remedial activities (either in total or in any of their elements) are themselves prone to disabling market failures. That distinction has not always been made in the context of SGEI qualification, but increasingly it is, through forensic recourse to the concept of market failure on the part of the Commission in particular. Separately, recent Decisions on ecological preservation point to the possibility of preservation activity giving rise to diffuse public benefits as SGEIs.

1. The Economics of Environmental Protection

The prominence of environmental concerns as a pre-eminent global political concern might be regarded as setting an ideal context for greater reliance on market failure analysis for their resolution.[57] In 2006 the report of the Stern Review on behalf of the UK government described climate change as the 'greatest and most wide-ranging market failure ever seen'.[58] Several of the most pressing environmental problems are regarded as classic market failures. Prominent among them is pollution, which can be controlled, inter alia, through greater equalisation of social costs and benefits.[59] Separately, many environmental amenities, such as clean air, access to forests, wetlands etc., may be treated as public goods exhibiting various degrees of congestion depending on the nature of the underlying ecosystem. In parallel, the problem of the tragedy of the commons has been explained on the basis of the perverse incentives that arise from unrestricted collective access to resources.[60]

Despite the obvious relevance of economic techniques and in particular of market failure in the environmental sphere, in some quarters there is suspicion of any form of market-based solution to environmental problems.[61] This most likely stems from the role of unconstrained market forces as the root cause of many very serious environmental problems.[62] Accordingly, it is unsurprising that positing the

[57] See generally, Sagoff, M, *The Economy of the Earth*, 2nd edn (Cambridge University Press, 2008) chs 2 and 3.

[58] Stern Review: The Economics of Climate Change, Executive Summary (2006) 2. The Report identifies negative externalities, public goods characteristics and information problems with the transition to new technologies as critical market failures contributing to climate change.

[59] See generally Mankiw, G, *Principles of Economics*, 4th edn (South-Western College Publishers, 2006) ch 10.

[60] Hardin, G, 'The Tragedy of the Commons' (1968) 162 *Science* 1243. Hardin suggested 'either socialism or the privatism of free enterprise'. For a consideration of a third way, based on formal and informal cooperative arrangements for shared access, see Ostrom, E, Burger, J, Field, CB, Norgaard, RB and Policansky, D, 'Revisiting the Commons: Local Lessons, Global Challenges' (1999) 284(5412) *Science* 278–282.

[61] For an early example of the argument for determining levels of pollution having regard to overall resource allocation, see Baxter, W, *People or Penguins: The Case for Optimal Pollution* (Columbia University Press, 1974).

[62] Leaving aside the issues of failure to regulate and enforce.

solution to an environmental problem as requiring no more than the correction of a market failure through recourse to another market mechanism is frequently viewed with suspicion.[63] That is exemplified by criticism of regulatory constructs such as tradable pollution permits effectively conferring a 'right' to pollute without any moral opprobrium.[64]

While the actual manifestation of environmental problems can frequently be attributed to underlying market failures, Article 106(2) is more likely to be directly engaged in the analysis of a service or intervention that is directed at resolving an underlying environmental difficulty. As a result, under Article 106(2) one would expect the focus to shift to whether remedial activity has 'special characteristics' that would qualify it as an SGEI as well as on determining the precise locus of the market failure. The intervention necessary to resolve or mitigate an environmental problem may involve several interconnected activities, with the possibility of a variety of market failures. They can range from classic natural monopoly characteristics (perhaps justifying exclusive rights), through to public good-type problems, most especially concerning non-excludability, in particular where a service generates diffuse benefits. There is also the possibility of pricing leading to the sub-optimal provision of certain kinds of infrastructure.[65]

2. The Constitutional Treatment of Environmental Issues

Unlike other fields such as transport, it has taken environmental protection some time to acquire both free-standing and cross-cutting constitutional significance within the EU legal order.[66] In 1983 in *ABDHU* the Court declared environmental protection to be one of the Community's essential objectives.[67] It was not until the entry into force of the Single European Act (SEA) in 1987 that it achieved overt constitutional prominence, even though the 1970s and 1980s had seen the adoption of copious amounts of legislation relating to environmental issues.[68] As a qualifier to the new Article 100a legislative mechanism, the SEA introduced

[63] There is also a fundamental debate in the literature as to the relative superiority of markets or governments in overcoming information asymmetries as a fundamental source of market failure impacting on the environment. See generally, O'Neill, J, 'Ecological Economics and the Politics of Knowledge: the Debate between Hayek and Neurath' (2004) 28 *Cambridge Journal of Economics* 431–447.

[64] Dryzek, J, 'Foundations for Environmental Political Economy: The Search for Homo Ecologicus' (1996) 1(1) *New Political Economy* 27, 36.

[65] See in that regard, albeit with reference to energy infrastructure of common interest, Guidelines on State Aid for Environmental Protection and Energy 2014–2020 (2014/C 200/01) §207.

[66] As AG Rozès explains in C-172/82 *Inter-Huiles* [1983] ECR 555 'A Community policy for the environment was only considered necessary in order to achieve the objectives of the Community only after the signature of the Treaty in 1957'. Seep 578.

[67] C-240/83 *ABDHU* [1985] ECR 531, §13.

[68] In 91/79 and 92/79 *Commission v Italy* [1980] ECR 1099 and [1980] ECR 1115, the Court of Justice ruled that recourse to Art 100 for legislation dealing with the environment could not be precluded provided that a lack of harmonisation led to a distortion of competition within the internal market.

a requirement that this power was to be exercised with the attainment of high levels of environmental protection as a base.[69] Equally important, the SEA included a distinct chapter on the environment, which in Article 130r(2) included two very significant stipulations. The first was that environmental problems should be rectified at source, while the second required the observation of the 'polluter pays' principle.[70] The implications of the former for free movement of goods will be apparent, not least considering that remedial environmental action such as waste disposal is frequently undertaken on a cross-border basis. The consequences of the latter would prove to be equally profound in that it constitutionalised the internalisation of the costs of pollution so as to correct the underlying market failure.[71]

The adoption of the Maastricht Treaty saw environmental protection become a clearer aim of the EC through its inclusion in the description of the fundamental tasks of the then Community.[72] In addition, the requirement for unanimity was relaxed with respect to certain kinds of environmental legislation.[73] Under the Amsterdam Treaty the replacement of the co-operation with the co-decision procedure significantly increased the powers of the European Parliament with respect to the adoption of environmental legislation. In addition, the Member States were also to be allowed to proceed with implementing more stringent national requirements despite the overall harmonisation dynamic.[74] Article TFEU requires that environmental protection must be integrated into the definition and implementation of Union activities. Nevertheless, Article 4 TFEU identifies the environment as an area of shared competence between the EU and the Member States. Unsurprisingly, and as will be considered below, that has already been the basis of an argument (albeit unsuccessful) regarding the nature of control for manifest error for SGEIs with respect to the resolution of environmental problems.[75]

3. Environmental Arguments and SGEIs

Consistent with the lower prominence accorded to environmental issues in the early days of the EU, initially the Court was not especially receptive to SGEI claims in an environmental context. This makes the Court's eventual conversion on these issues all

[69] Art 100a(3).

[70] The 'polluter pays' principle was first reflected through legislation in Directive 75/439/EEC on Waste Oils. See Art 14.

[71] In his opinion in *GEMO*, AG Jacobs, stated that 'The polluter pays principle has its origins in economic theory and was conceived to deal with a market failure: pollution is perhaps the most important example of what economists refer to as a negative externality, that is a loss (normally to society) which is not priced' C-126/01 *GEMO* [2003] ECR I-13769, §66.

[72] Art 2 EC.

[73] For an overview of the evolution in the constitutional standing of the environment, see Sadeleer, N, *EU Environmental Law and the Single European Market* (Oxford University Press, 2014) 10–13.

[74] Art 95 EC.

[75] T-295/12 *Germany v Commission* ECLI:EU:T:2014:675 and T-309/12 *Zweckverband Tierkörperbeseitigung* ECLI:EU:T:2014:676.

the more striking. One of the earliest claims for SGEI qualification on environmental grounds was the 1983 judgment of the Court in *Inter Huiles*.[76] That case principally concerned a dispute over the export for recovery of waste oil, and, in particular, efforts to prevent non-authorised operators from exporting waste oil for recovery. Under Directive 75/439/EEC, France had implemented a system of regional exclusive rights, the holders of which took action to prevent third-party exports of waste oil. France claimed that the activity was an SGEI. The Court of Justice interpreted the Directive as permitting exclusive rights but not export restrictions. This then left it with the issue of applying Article 106(2), which by its terms was capable of justifying an outright ban on exports. The Court avoided Article 106(2) by relying on *Port de Mertert* for the proposition that Article 106(2) was not directly effective.[77] Consistent with the seeming ascendancy of the free movement rules over Article 106(2) as described in Chapter 4, the environmental context was not dispositive.[78]

In *Almelo*, in confirming that obligations of security of supply, non-discrimination and uniform pricing comprised an SGEI for electricity, the Court also indicated that compliance with environmental legislation should form part of the necessity review.[79] In the subsequent *Electricity and Gas Cases*, and in defence of exclusive rights over the import and export of electricity and gas, France argued that environmental and regional policy considerations under concessions constituted acts of entrustment of SGEIs under Article 106(2).[80] While ostensibly standing over *Almelo*, the Court of Justice rejected the French argument on the basis that adhering to generally applicable environmental legislation could not be regarded as a specific act of entrustment of an SGEI.[81] That approach is reflected even more emphatically in a 2009 Decision of the Commission concerning long-term power purchasing agreements in the electricity sector in Poland.[82] There the Commission held that mere compliance with generally applicable environmental standards could not be treated as SGEI entrustment and would also contravene the 'polluter pays' principle.[83]

4. The Presumptive Environmental SGEI

On a number of occasions, the Commission and the Court of Justice have treated interventions connected with the remedying of environmental problems as SGEIs. The mere linkage to remedying an environmental problem appears to have been

[76] C-172/82 *Inter-Huiles* [1983] ECR 555.

[77] ibid, §15. In his opinion in *Inter-Huiles*, AG Rozès considered that the existence of an SGEI was highly possible. See p 581.

[78] Although rejecting the SGEI argument, the Court also dealt with the claim under the Directive that exclusive rights might entail an export ban. It rejected this on the basis that it was necessary considering the provision made for indemnities. See C-172/82 *Inter-Huiles* [1983] ECR 555, §14.

[79] C-393/93 *Almelo* [1994] ECR I-1477, §49.

[80] Specifically, see C-159/94 *Commission v France*, §62.

[81] ibid, §69. The Court muddies the position subsequently in §71, but it appears that this should be read in the light of §69. It also accords with the Court's rejection of France's argument in §70. It is also worth emphasising that the issue was what fell within the scope of entrustment.

[82] Commission Decision 2009/287/EC, *Polish Power Purchase Agreements*.

[83] ibid, §230.

dispositive. The most prominent example is the 2000 judgment of the Court in *Københavns Kommune* concerning the grant of exclusive rights for the recovery of non-hazardous waste from the construction industry arising from a shortage of capacity for handling of this waste in the Copenhagen area.[84] A handler of building waste had been authorised to construct and operate a facility within the Copenhagen municipality but when it sought to source and process waste from within the municipality, it was refused authorisation. The municipal authorities had decided that in principle the waste from Copenhagen should be processed at a designated site, which was operated by a consortium that had been selected through tendering.[85]

The refusal was challenged in part on the basis that this was an impermissible grant of exclusive rights contrary to Article 106(1) read in conjunction with Article 102. The Danish authorities sought to justify the restriction, arguing that the processing of such waste was a task of general economic interest and that the arrangements were essential to ensure sufficient capacity. Advocate General Léger doubted that any particular tasks had been allocated to the members of the consortium by way of entrustment.[86] The Court accepted the SGEI claim holding that 'the management of particular waste may properly be considered to be capable of forming the subject of a service of general economic interest, particularly where the service is designed to deal with an environmental problem'.[87] The Court's seeming focus was on the purpose for which the service was rendered as opposed to the inherent or stylised delivery obligations of the service.[88] This is in contrast to the approach of the Court only a year earlier in *Dusseldorp*, when it was agnostic about whether the incineration of dangerous waste in the Netherlands was an SGEI.[89]

An equally lax approach to an SGEI claim was taken in the 2006 Decision of the Commission in *AVR* concerning the provision of aid to a single operator of incinerator services in respect of certain categories of hazardous waste in the Netherlands.[90] The Decision is significant because of the reasons accepted by the Commission for qualifying the incineration services provided by AVR as an SGEI.[91] In summary, they were: (i) there was an obvious public interest in the appropriate treatment of hazardous waste; (ii) that without the aid, the relevant facility would have closed; (iii) that the public interest was real in that even though the need for

[84] C-209/98 *Københavns Kommune* [2000] ECR I-3743.

[85] In practice it gave permission to other operators in respect of occasional activities.

[86] C-209/98 *Københavns Kommune* [2000] ECR I-3743, Opinion of 21 October 1999, §104.

[87] C-209/98 *Københavns Kommune*, §75. It will be recalled that a similar approach to the treatment of an activity as an SGEI because it is related to environmental protection featured in the opinion of AG Cosmas in C-343/95 *Calì* [1997] ECR I-1547 considered in Chapter 4 with respect to the exercise of public authority exception.

[88] Although the service entailed some general benefits to the public, it was clearly directed at the construction industry, once more revealing inconsistency in the public benefit requirement under Art 106(2).

[89] C-203/96 *Dusseldorp* [1998] ECR I-4075, §67.

[90] Commission Decision 2006/237/EC, *Netherlands Hazardous Waste.*

[91] All of the reasons are set out at section 6.2 of the Commission decision.

the facility was predicated on a miscalculation of the required capacity, there was no demonstration by any of the objectors that without it exports would not have been necessary; (iv) that there was no infringement of the 'polluter pays' principle; (v) that the Environmental Aid Guidelines would still apply notwithstanding the treatment of the activity as an SGEI; and (vi) that the aid was of a general character since some of the waste came from households. It is notable that the obligations imposed on AVR are not highlighted as constituting the SGEI.[92]

With the exception of point (iii), none of these explanations makes sense or, worse, is directly contradicted either by the Commission's own analysis elsewhere in the Decision or by its usual practice elsewhere in the field of State aid. Point (i) is a *Københavns Kommune*-type generalisation on the importance of the task on environmental grounds.[93] It is unclear why the fact that an activity is directed at an environmental problem should mean that it is treated as a presumptive SGEI.[94] Point (ii) concerning the risk of closure goes to the necessity of the intervention, but that is quite distinct from qualification as an SGEI. Point (iii) in relation to capacity may have been valid although it goes to the proportionality of the contested measures. Point (iv) is contradicted by the Commission's analysis that charges were suppressed to some degree, hence the full cost of pollution was not internalised.[95] Point (v) does not appear to be relevant to whether the activity was an SGEI, which in principle should be considered independently of the potential application of sectoral guidelines. Finally, point (vi) as to the take-up of the service appears to ignore the fact that the service was overwhelmingly directed at commercial and industrial users, a point that the Commission has used in other sectors to deny SGEI status to particular activities.[96]

The General Court approved an accommodating approach to environmental protection measures in its 2013 judgment in *Germany v Commission*.[97] That concerned a challenge by Germany to a Decision of the Commission concerning the transfer of land to an ecological conservation organisation.[98] At issue, among other things, was the distinction between conservation and related economic activities such as land leasing, wood sales and tourism. The underlying Decision is considered in greater detail in the following section, but it is noteworthy that the General Court, in referring to the position of the parties, explained the underlying Decision of the Commission (and adopting the submissions of the parties to that end) as having held that the environmental protection measures were social and

[92] With respect to entrustment, the decision refers to the 'public service' obligations being sufficiently clear. See §86. These appear to be requirements in relation to non-discrimination, transparency and the offering of 'socially acceptable' tariffs. See §17.

[93] C-209/98 *Københavns Kommune* [2000] ECR I-3743 is expressly relied upon and quoted from at §77of the Commission decision.

[94] That is not affected by the fact that certain environmental problems can be regarded as market failures.

[95] *Netherlands Hazardous Waste*, §29.

[96] For example in N/284 05 *MANS* in telecommunications. At the very least, the issue of consistency arises.

[97] T-347/09 *Germany v Commission* ECLI:EU:T:2013:418.

[98] State aid NN 8/2009 Germany of 2 July 2009, C(2009) 5080 final, *German Ecological Reserves*.

not economic in nature.[99] This typifies an approach that is even more indulgent that the presumptive SGEI treatment of environmentally directed interventions given the complete denial of the main conservation activity as economic in nature.

5. Market Failure Deconstructing the Presumptive SGEI

Despite the *Københavns Kommune* approach, there are a small number of cases where the Commission has been much more discriminating about the identification of market failures in environmental cases and in turn much more robust about rejecting SGEI claims based on the pliable *Københavns Kommune* construct. In particular, while accepting that providers have formal obligations, the Commission has used market failure analysis to vitiate the general interest claim. This is exemplified by two Decisions in particular. The first Decision, *WRAP Newsprint*, was adopted in 2003 and concerned aid for recycling of paper for the manufacture of newsprint paper. The second, *Tierkörperbeseitigung*, is a Commission Decision of 2012 concerning Germany's provision of operating assistance to the provider of reserve slaughtering capacity in the event of an epidemic. In both cases the manifest error test for SGEI qualification was deployed, and in neither case was any special deference extended to the assessments of the Member States as to either the relevance or existence of market failures. Similarly, the presence of stylised delivery obligations did not serve to qualify the activity as an SGEI given the lack of a relevant underlying market failure.

In *WRAP Newsprint* the UK provided aid for the establishment of a waste paper recovery system, which was to focus on the production of newsprint-quality paper.[100] There were two principal concerns behind the UK's intervention, the first being the low levels of domestic reprocessing of paper, and the second being the lack of any UK facility producing newsprint, which typically is made from waste paper. The proposed facility was required to use specified volumes of waste paper from the municipal waste system. Citing *Københavns Kommune*, the aid recipient argued that the activity in question was an SGEI given that it concerned a waste management service and could be expected to reduce the volume of waste going to landfill by diverting it to newsprint production. Significantly, the UK did not argue that the activity was an SGEI. Instead, it argued that as State aid, it could be justified under the Community Guidelines on State Aid for Environmental Protection ('the Environmental Aid Guidelines').[101]

[99] T-347/09 *Germany v Commission* ECLI:EU:T:2013:418, §31. It is noteworthy that in referring to the position of the parties, the General Court explained the underlying decision of the Commission (and adopting the submissions of the parties to that end) as having held that the environmental protection measures were social and not economic in nature.

[100] Commission Decision 2003/814/EC, *WRAP Newsprint*.

[101] Community Guidelines on State Aid for Environmental Protection, 03.02.2001 [2001] OJ C37/03). For a comprehensive account of the overall operation of the Environmental Aid Guidelines, as well as successor versions, see Haslinger, B, 'Part III' in Säcker and Montag (eds), *European State Aid Law—A Commentary* (CH Beck, Hart and Nomos, 2016) 835–64.

The Commission's treatment of the SGEI claims in *WRAP Newsprint* exhibits some of the formalism that often features in its approach under Article 106(2), but reinforced by more meaningful market failure analysis. First, the Commission claimed that to qualify as such an SGEI must be necessary for and available to all citizens.[102] To that end, the Commission relied on its 2001 Communication on Services of General Interest, even though it made no such assertion in that document.[103] The Commission added that if the activity had been paper collection, then that would have been of universal benefit, but since the aid was directed at ensuring the use of only certain amounts of waste for reprocessing, that was not the case.[104] Again referring to the 2001 Communication, the Commission maintained that to qualify as an SGEI, a service must be one 'that the State should normally provide to the public and is limited to the needs of this service, or if the market would never be able to realise the service in the same conditions'.[105] The Commission then argued that the production of newsprint from waste paper was not a service that a state should normally provide.[106]

Turning more forensically to the issue of market failures, the Commission found that if they existed, they arose on the paper collection as opposed to the paper processing side.[107] Although not expressly relying on this evidence, earlier in its analysis, the Commission had made reference to the likely under-pricing of landfill (owing to the UK not taxing this activity appropriately in line with some other Member States) as discouraging the collection and sorting of paper for reprocessing.[108] The Commission declined to accept the production of newsprint from waste paper as an SGEI. That was by reference to its inherent characteristics, namely the absence of significant market failures. Moreover, the denial of the SGEI claim was not overcome by the presence of a prominent stylised delivery characteristic, namely the compulsory use of fixed quantities of waste paper from the municipal system and ongoing obligations with respect to reductions in by-products.[109] Although it is difficult to speculate as to why the Commission was so rigorous in its approach, once Article 106(2) did not apply, that allowed the Commission to use the Environmental Aid Guidelines very precisely to determine an acceptable level of investment support.[110] While that might also have been feasible by way of proportionality review under Article 106(2), the prescriptiveness of those guidelines was probably a more attractive analytical framework, and in any event, was the basis on which the UK sought to justify the measure.

[102] *WRAP Newsprint*, §97.

[103] ibid.

[104] ibid, §97. This misses the point that the mandatory waste diversion from the municipal waste stream was to a significant extent comprised of public waste.

[105] ibid, §98.

[106] ibid, §99.

[107] That was in direct opposition to the stance taken by the UK in seeking to justify the measure under the Environmental Aid Guidelines.

[108] *WRAP Newsprint*, §190.

[109] The obligation to extract waste from the public stockpile is not emphasised as part of the SGEI analysis.

[110] The decision was handed down the day before judgment in *Altmark*.

Turning to the second Commission Decision, in *Tierkörperbeseitigung* the Commission objected to financing from a public authority provided to a slaughterhouse that was responsible for making available sufficient excess capacity to ensure that large numbers of cattle could be processed in the event of a mass cull affecting several of the German *Länder*.[111] In related domestic proceedings, the Bundesverwaltungsgericht appeared to accept that the provision of reserve capacity was simultaneously an SGEI and bound up with the exercise of public authority.[112] In response to complaints from competitors invoking the 'polluter pays' principle, the Commission argued that the cost of such capacity should be carried by the farming sector as a cost that was inherent in the activity. By relieving farmers of it, this principle was being ousted and in turn a separate advantage conferred on the provider of the capacity. The Commission also considered that the provider had sufficient excess capacity in the ordinary course of the operation of its business such as not to require any separate reserve capacity to meet emergency requirements, or in turn, direct support for its provision.[113] That was despite the measure having been put in place in the context of responding to the BSE crisis.

During the investigation, the German government argued that the activity was an SGEI, not least by reason of the need to protect human health. It relied on the legal obligation on public authorities to procure the proper disposal of certain types of animal waste.[114] Germany also argued that compliance with the 'polluter pays' principle would be impossible for this activity given that costs of disposal in a specific instance could not be attributed to a particular farmer. That was akin to a claim that the maintenance of reserve capacity was a public good, the use of which could not be attributed to a particular polluter. Germany elaborated on this argument by maintaining that under state law, the recipient of aid for reserve capacity was prohibited from using charges for ordinary rendering services to recover the costs of dedicated excess capacity.[115] In effect, Germany was arguing that the regulatory system led to a market failure in the sense of disabling the recovery of the cost of reserve capacity other than through direct public subsidy.[116]

The Commission rejected the broad SGEI claim on two grounds. The first was on the basis that public payment of the cost of excess capacity relieved users of a cost inherent in the underlying activity in which they were engaged and so violated the 'polluter pays' principle.[117] According to the Commission, that principle precluded the existence of an SGEI. In the alternative, the Commission asserted that in other parts of Germany, epidemic capacity was met within spare operating capacity.[118] In principle, the Commission considered that the cost of an epidemic

[111] Commission Decision 2012/485/EU, *Tierkörperbeseitigung*.
[112] This appears to mirror the approach of the Court of Justice in *Calì*.
[113] *Tierkörperbeseitigung*, §§25–28.
[114] ibid, §94.
[115] ibid, §114.
[116] ibid, §214.
[117] ibid, §114.
[118] ibid, §186.

reserve should be recovered through regular end user charging and on the facts it considered that this was possible.[119] There was no market failure inherent in the activity or (contrary to Germany's argument) one arising from regulatory design frustrating the operation of a regular price mechanism. As a result, according to the Commission, it did not matter that the provider was the subject of a formal obligation to provide excess capacity.[120] In effect, market failure analysis trumped the stylised delivery characteristics approach to SGEI verification.

By way of postscript to the *Tierkörperbeseitigung* Decision, Germany and the aid recipient subsequently sought the annulment of the Commission Decision before the General Court.[121] Germany did so in part by relying on the *Københavns Kommune* judgment together with a wider argument that this area of policy was at most the subject of shared competence, and in respect of which there had been no specific EU legislative intervention.[122] As a result, it argued that the Commission should have acceded to its SGEI claim. In dismissing this argument, the General Court recited the formula from the *Porto di Genova* judgment concerning the need for special characteristics, before going on to find that such characteristics were not present in the *Tierkörperbeseitigung* case.[123] While that may have been true, it is difficult to argue that they were any more or less apparent than in *Københavns Kommune*. The main difference in *Tierkörperbeseitigung* was that the economic analysis had exposed the lack of any underlying market failure, meaning that neither the obligation to process all carcasses on presentation nor the obligation to maintain reserve capacity (which the General Court regarded as closely linked) supported the existence of an SGEI.[124]

6. Environmental Public Goods as SGEIs

Finally, a relatively new phenomenon under Article 106(2) concerns the treatment of the restoration and conservation of lands for ecological purposes as SGEIs. This began with a 2009 Decision of the Commission in *German Ecological Reserves* concerning Germany's transfer of land to conservation organisations without charge and separately the funding of ecological restoration programmes.[125] In both instances, Germany argued that the underlying purpose was a Service of

[119] ibid, §220.
[120] ibid, §188.
[121] T-295/12 *Germany v Commission* ECLI:EU:T:2014:675 and T-309/12 *Zweckverband Tierkörperbeseitigung* ECLI:EU:T:2014:676.
[122] ibid, §44, 45.
[123] ibid, §64.
[124] The unsuccessful challenges to the *Tierkörperbeseitigung* Decision were appealed to the Court of Justice as C-446/14P and C-447/14P, respectively. C-447/14P was withdrawn following the entry into liquidation of the appellant. The appeal in C-446/14P was rejected by the Court but without shedding any light on the underlying reasons for rejecting the existence of an SGEI. See ECLI:EU:C:2016:97.
[125] NN 8/2009 *German Ecological Reserves*. This decision was the subject of an unsuccessful challenge in T-347/09 *Germany v Commission* ECLI:EU:T:2013:418.

General Interest (SGI) and that as a result, the recipients were not undertakings. The Commission rejected this on the basis that the recipients were undertakings by reason of engaging in economic activity and that there was State aid. Instead, it asserted that given the public benefits of ecological enhancement and diversity, but considering the economic context, ecological restoration and conservation, it was an SGEI.[126] Having decided that sectoral guidelines covering forestry only covered a small part of the potential economic activity, the Commission instead applied the Monti-Kroes SGEI Package, in the process revealing the somewhat arbitrary division of roles between Article 106(2) and Article 107(3)(c).[127] Ultimately, the Commission exempted the measure under the 2005 SGEI Framework on the basis that the conservation and development tasks were adequately specified and there was no over-compensation. A similar approach was taken in a notification from the Netherlands.[128] As in the German case, in *Netherlands Ecological Reserves I* the Commission noted that in its 2004 White Paper on Services of General Interest, it had referred to the possibility of recognising SGEIs in the environmental arena.[129]

What is striking about both of these cases is that no 'public service' as such was directly delivered or guaranteed by these projects. Furthermore, the focus of the acts of entrustment was not on the guarantee of access but rather on the specificities of how the land was to be managed and developed for ecological purposes. While public access was envisaged for several of the projects, including for fisheries- and forestry-related initiatives, those dividends were ancillary. In reality, the real public benefits were diffuse so the affirmative finding of an SGEI is significant. The Commission took a similar approach in *Netherlands Ecological Reserves II*.[130] It concerned a scheme that actually pre-dated that approved in *Netherlands Ecological Reserves I*. The Commission held that an SGEI arose by reason of the conservation activities being an SGI and secondary economic activities, which on the aggregate were treated as an SGEI.[131] That has led to criticism from Nicolaides that whatever the nature of the 'service' ultimately provided, it could not be 'consumed' by individuals.[132]

Equally significant in *Netherlands Ecological Reserves I* is the rejection of the SGI arguments in favour of SGEI designation.[133] Nicolaides takes issue with the way in

[126] ibid, §58.

[127] ibid, §59.

[128] NN.

[129] ibid, section 3.4.

[130] NN/2015, SA.27301, *Netherland Ecological Reserves II*.

[131] In Case T-146/16 the beneficiaries lodged an appeal against the Commission decision on the bases that nature conversation is a service of general interest only, is not economic and that as such they are not undertakings. See OJ C191 from 30.05.2016, p 41.

[132] See Nicolaides, P, *Critical Analysis of Developments in State Aid* (Lexxion, 2016) 257ff.

[133] See *Netherlands Ecological Reserves I*, §74. The decision in the Dutch notification (N308/2010) was appealed to the General Court in T-15/12 and T-16/12. Among the arguments was a claim that environmental protection is an SGI under Art 2 of Protocol 26 to the TFEU and that as such, competition law is inapplicable. The Fifth Chamber struck out both challenges as inadmissible on 19 February 2013.

which the Commission's seeming acceptance of the conservation as an SGI could morph into the global treatment of the entrusted entities as SGEI providers.[134] Perhaps an even better target for criticism is the General Court's judgment in *Germany v Commission*, which repeats the error in *Calì* of treating environmental protection as 'social' in nature.[135] If, instead, the underlying problems were treated as market failure, then conservatory acts directed at overcoming them could have constituted an SGEI. Ecosystems display public goods characteristics since they are non-rivalrous and non-excludable and also generate considerable positive externalities.[136] More explicit recourse to market failures would assist with avoiding a lapse into *Københavns Kommune* generalities or *Netherlands Ecological Reserves II* artifice. There would still be the issue of ancillary activities, but their identification would simply serve to identify a separate but related economic sphere likely affected by the intervention.

D. Broadcasting

The focus now switches to broadcasting, a sector where the pull of the political on the operation of Article 106(2) is much more apparent than in the telecommunications and environmental arenas. As with telecommunications, historically the sector was replete with market failures, but digitalisation has eroded many of the traditional justifications for intervention. The remaining economics-inspired justification for public service broadcasting (PSB), namely the public goods justification, is never deployed in a forensic manner. To some degree that would require a focus on what markets might be capable of producing. As will be considered, that has been outlawed by the General Court. As a result, market feasibility as the touchstone for intervention has been jettisoned. As against that, public funding of digital infrastructure for broadcasting has been the subject of quite rigorous market failure analysis but again under Article 107(3)(c) and not Article 106(2). Further underlining the latter's contingency, the Article 107 analysis, which tends to occur first, appears to determine the position under Article 106(2).

1. The Economics of Broadcasting

(a) Market Failures in Broadcasting

Traditionally, the field of broadcasting in its analogue form displayed several forms of market failure. Those have included natural monopoly characteristics

[134] Nicolaides (n 132) 260–61.

[135] Case C-343/95 *Calì* [1997] ECR I-1547.

[136] See, Eco Logic, The Use of Market Incentives to Preserve Bio-diversity, Final Report for the European Commission, July 2006, p 41.

in the operation of the underlying transmission network, strong public goods characteristics of outputs, and associated positive and negative externalities. With respect to transmission, given the single-product nature of the output and the associated cost structure, natural monopoly is likely. The public goods argument stems from the problem of non-rivalrous consumption considering that any single use of a widely propagated broadcast signal will not diminish or affect its availability to others. Linked to that, given that the marginal cost of incremental consumption is virtually non-existent, allocative efficiency may be violated through charging, even if that is essential in order to underwrite the costs of future production and for the purpose of rewarding innovation. With respect to the public goods characteristics, analogue broadcasting also displays non-excludability given that a free-to-air analogue signal is not easily encrypted, and so to the extent that provision must be underwritten by charging, there may be a significant excludability problem.[137]

Separately, the positive and negative externality characteristics, although hardly unique to broadcasting, appear to have elevated significance considering the nature of the output and its assumed importance in opinion forming. With respect to negative externalities, certain types of output may be regarded as harmful, making the case for prohibition or other forms of control. By contrast, the positive externality argument has been used to justify public support for certain types of output regarded as delivering wider societal benefits, such as education. This is an enduring argument in favour of PSB mandates and as will be considered, drives their presumptive treatment as SGEIs under Article 106(2). In this regard, there is the potential for a distinctly paternalistic subtext. That phenomenon was well reflected in the observation of Lord Reith, a former head of the BBC in the UK, to the effect that the corporation was concerned with delivering not so much what people wanted as what the BBC thought they should have.[138]

While frequently the problem of public goods—and in particular the problem of non-excludability—is tackled on the basis of government financing through either general taxation or a licence fee, the alternative has been to finance the activity through advertising. Common to both of these interventions is that they break the direct connection, through the price mechanism, between consumers and provider, with consumers only having indirect means for signalling preferences or

[137] Technically, it is unclear whether an analogue signal can be encrypted although it can be scrambled. Practically speaking digitalisation has facilitated encryption to a very significant extent.

[138] 'So the responsibility at the outset conceived, and despite all discouragements pursued, was to carry into the greatest number of homes everything that was best in every department of human knowledge, endeavour and achievement; and to avoid whatever was or might be hurtful. In the earliest years accused of setting out to give the public not what it wanted but what the BBC thought it should have, the answer was that few knew what they wanted, fewer what they needed'. Reith, JCW, *Into the Wind* (Hodden & Stoughton, 1949) 145.

their intensities.[139] As a result of this disconnect, and considering the usually finite number of channels that analogue broadcast technology can support, both the advertising and publicly funded models may lead to consequential deficiencies in terms of outputs, with respect to quality and diversity. By contrast, pay television models tend to perform better in relation to both of those parameters, but perhaps at the price of reduced accessibility.[140] Furthermore, given the channel restrictions in the analogue world, even if competition is technically viable, there is a risk of less programming diversity than under monopoly. That arises because a new provider has incentives to replicate the offering of the incumbent if its share of the existing market based on a replicated formula is more valuable than the profits that could be extracted from a differentiated format targeting niche audiences.[141]

(b) The Merit Goods Argument for PSB

As previously referred to and most prominently of all, traditional broadcasting has attracted the argument that its output is a merit good.[142] As noted in the discussion of merit goods as an adjunct to the causes of market failures contained in Chapter 2, this concept is highly problematic. That is both in terms of the underlying explanation of the phenomenon as well as in relation to the setting of parameters around public intervention with respect to merit goods. The degree of indeterminacy is considerable, as is the potential to possibly justify any form of intervention in markets. Nevertheless, the merit goods argument has intuitive appeal in the context of broadcasting, especially considering the reflexive equation of quality broadcasting with merit. Among the various possible justifications for public goods advanced by Musgrave, the 'community values' paradigm appears most relevant. It can be relied upon to justify collective determination of a favoured stock of information, which can be combined with a redistributive goal in order to justify mass access on egalitarian grounds. Similarly, by drawing on the assumed educational capacity of television, it is not difficult to connect that to empowering the individual to make 'better' choices. Despite that, as Armstrong and Weeds have pointed out, viewers are heterogeneous and so it is implausible

[139] On this and other economic shortcomings of the analogue broadcasting world, see Coase, R, 'The Economics of Broadcasting' (1966) 56(1/2) *The American Economic Review* 440–47.

[140] That will, to a significant degree, be affected by the extent to which the underlying markets are competitive.

[141] On this problem generally, see Steiner, P, 'Program Patterns and Preferences and the Workability of Competition in Broadcasting' (1952) 66 *Quarterly Journal of Economics* 194–223, and from a more empirical perspective, Brown, A, 'Economics, Public Service Broadcasting, and Social Values' (1996) 9(1) *The Journal of Media Economics* 3–15, 10–12.

[142] See, for example, Department of Culture Media and Sport (UK), The Future Funding of the BBC (Davies Report), July 1999, Annex 8, p 203.

that a broadcaster can make optimal decisions that 'improve' the preferences of such large numbers of people.[143] Separately, it is far from clear that there is much difference in substance between the merit goods argument and the more conventional positive externality dimension to broadcasting considered under market failures.[144]

2. The Informed Citizenry Justification for PSBs

Despite the prominence of several market failures in the field of broadcasting, and the frequent recourse to the merit goods argument, arguably the active citizenry justification for PSOs has assumed general ascendancy over the past 20 years. As summarised by Armstrong and Weeds, through television and in particular PSB, citizens are made aware of pressing social and economic issues and as a result are better prepared to engage in democratic debate and, as a result, are more capable of keeping governments and other political institutions under control and accountable.[145] The view of broadcasting as enabling democratic participation emerges very clearly from the terms of the Amsterdam Protocol, which also emphasises the need to preserve media pluralism.[146] The active citizenry justification for PSB mandates is even more apparent in the Commission's 2001 Communication on the Application of State Aid rules to Public Service Broadcasting, which is replete with references to democratic concerns but with no reliance at all on the concepts of market failures or merit goods.[147] That approach has been carried forward into the digital era by the 2009 Communication on the Application of State Aid rules to Public Service Broadcasting, which again makes no reference to market failures despite referring to the 2005 SAAP (where market failure analysis predominates) as setting part of the context for the revision of the 2001 Guidelines.[148] Instead, in specifying the 'manifest error' standard for SGEIs in broadcasting, invoking the Amsterdam Protocol, the Commission indicates that the test would be satisfied where prescribed output does not meet the 'democratic, social and cultural needs of each society'.[149]

[143] Armstrong, M and Weeds, H, 'Public Service Broadcasting in the Digital World' in Seabright and von Hagen (eds), *The Economic Regulation of Broadcasting Markets: Evolving Technology and Challenges for Policy* (Cambridge University Press, 2007) 15.

[144] See, for example, the equation of them in Mastroianni, R, 'Public Services Media and Market Integration' in Cremona, M (ed), *Market Integration and Public Services in the European Union* (Oxford University Press, 2011) 163.

[145] Armstrong and Weeds (n 143) 25. Conceivably, the same might be said of many other media, and perhaps even more so in relation to online sources of information on news and current affairs today.

[146] [1997] OJ C340, p 109.

[147] Communication from the Commission, on the application of State aid rules to Public Service Broadcasting, 15.11.2001 [2000] OJ C320/05, p 5.

[148] [2000] OJ C257, p 1, §7.

[149] ibid, §48.

3. Digitalisation and the Emergence of the Consumer Sovereignty Paradigm

(a) The Transformation of Broadcasting Through Digitalisation

As with telecommunications, the digital revolution has had enormous effects on every aspect of the technology of broadcasting.[150] With respect to transmission, digitalisation has increased the variety of products on offer, as well as the number of networks capable of providing those services. As a result, the problem of natural monopoly as justification for entry restrictions has been overcome. Separately, digitalisation enormously boosted the channel dividend from equivalent amounts of spectrum. Perhaps more importantly, it has transformed the capacity of satellite cable and other wired networks both in terms of the number of channels on offer and their ability to support interactive services. Competition by way of a much larger number of channels has enhanced content diversity very considerably. Separately, with the advent of digitalisation, the problem of excludability is much more easily solved, not least through the use of encryption.[151] Finally, improvements in device capability and of memory capacity have given consumers much more control over personal choice, a process that has now culminated in ubiquitous on-demand television services.

(b) The Erosion of the Market Failure Case for Intervention

The effect of technological change, and in particular the impact of digitalisation on the market failure case for intervention in broadcast markets, was first comprehensively articulated in the Report of the Peacock Review of the BBC delivered to the UK government in 1986.[152] Although the remit of the committee, headed by the economist Alan Peacock, was to report on the funding of the BBC, its overall emphasis was on the movement of the entire system of broadcasting towards the consumer sovereignty paradigm.[153] As a result, the role of the BBC and other UK broadcasters was to be subordinated to that purpose. While aspects of the Peacock Review were highly controversial, including the proposal for a three-stage transition to a broadcasting market, its real significance lies in the prescience with which it deconstructs the validity of the market failure justifications for intervention in broadcasting in the light of the then technological changes. In particular, it emphasised the importance of freedom of entry for programme makers, the potential for their output to be carried on a proliferation of channels, and in turn the ability of providers to operate pay-per-view systems through

150 For an overall summary of the changes, see Armstrong and Weeds (n 143).
151 The alternative has been to extract charges through the taxation systems.
152 Report of the Committee on the Financing of the BBC (Peacock Report) (Cm 9824, 1986).
153 ibid, §592.

digital encryption.[154] At all stages, the provision of PSB content was assured, but with the ultimate objective of making public funding available to commission content on a variety of channels and not just the BBC.[155] Ultimately, only some of the recommendations of the Peacock Report were taken forward but it remains an exemplar of a market and government critique of public service organisation and provision.

Consistent with the recognition by his committee of the enduring role of PSB, in subsequent writings Peacock acknowledged that a society could take a collective decision that certain types of programming were especially worthwhile, and in turn deserving of public support.[156] While recognising the merit goods justification for PSB, through his overarching support for 'workable' competition Peacock was concerned to ensure that the impact of government intervention was much more effectively targeted. In particular, Peacock exposed what he regarded as the non sequitur that most or all of public funding for public service broadcasting should go to a single monolithic provider.[157] As to the nature of those outputs, Peacock ultimately regarded this as a question for democratic determination but with a pronounced scepticism concerning the incentives of specialist regulatory agencies delegated that task to get it right.[158] He saw the potential for more individualised consumption decisions to drive diversity and quality: in effect, constituting the consumer sovereignty paradigm. The inevitable result would be a reduction and reorientation in the nature of PSB as the market produced greater variety while competition reduced the cost of access.

It is noteworthy that several of Peacock's more prominent opponents in the UK debate over public service broadcasting subsequently adopted the market failure rationalisation for PSB. In doing so, Graham and Davies argued that technological advances would create new forms of market power affecting the broadcasting sector and that far from weakening the case for broadcasters with a distinct public service ethos, it would strengthen it.[159] In addition, it has been argued that plurality concerns are not adequately safeguarded through competitive processes and competition law.[160] In the light of what digitalisation has now delivered, that is far from clear. More generally, and at least in the UK, the emphasis has switched

[154] ibid, §598.

[155] For a defence of the Peacock Report's actual support for PSB as a merit good, despite an overwhelmingly reformist agenda, see Potschka, C, 'Broadcasting and Market-Driven Politics in the UK and Germany: The Peacock Committee in Comparative Perspective' (2013) 19(5) *International Journal of Cultural Policy* 595–609.

[156] See Peacock, A, 'Public Service Broadcasting Without the BBC?' (2004) 133 *Occasional Papers—The Institute of Economic Affairs* 33–53, 41–42.

[157] That was to be achieved by requiring greater amounts of production to be independently produced, in the process undermining any scale and scope advantages of the BBC and ITV in the UK as vertically integrated providers.

[158] A particular concern (and this has special resonance in the context of Art 106(2)) was the public service provider effectively determining its own outputs and with ineffectual supervisory mechanisms.

[159] Graham, A and Davies, G, *Broadcasting, Society and Policy in the Multimedia Age* (University of Luton Press, 1997).

[160] See Ofcom, Review of Media Ownership Rules, 2006, §§2.15–2.19.

to PSB as enabling democratic participation as part of a more general argument that PSB constitutes a cornerstone of national identity and citizenship.[161] To some degree, that was exemplified by the seeming prioritisation of the citizen over the consumer in the UK's Communications Act 2003.[162]

4. PSB and Market Feasibility Under Article 106(2)

(a) Defining PSB and its Treatment as a Conclusive SGEI

In order to assess the approach of the Commission, it is necessary to place the evolution of its approach concerning PSB in context. Historically, the Commission was confronted with almost all of the Member States organising the provision of PSB, but in many instances subject to very significant autonomy on the part of the provider. During the 1990s, the Commission was sceptical about claims that PSB providers should automatically be accorded SGEI treatment in respect of their activities. In a 1991 Decision concerning the European Broadcasting Union the Commission was non-committal about whether the activities of public broadcasters in the various Member States amounted to an SGEI.[163] That reticence was also apparent two years later in *EBU/Eurovision*.[164] In 1997, in *Flanders Television Advertising*, although seemingly acknowledging the underlying PSB obligation as an SGEI, the Commission made a distinction between general broadcasting obligations applicable to all broadcasters and specific requirements as to the nature of programming, with only the latter to be regarded as an SGEI.[165] It seemed to portend careful vetting of SGEI claims through a focus on actual deliverables. That never transpired, however, not least following the introduction of the Amsterdam Protocol on Public Service Broadcasting.[166]

Prior to considering the effects of the Protocol, the General Court's indication in *SIC* that a typical PSB remit in an SGEI is significant, not least because of its

[161] 'The choice for Government is likely to be a stark one: if the market failure arguments do not work, they may simply have to build a case for public communications provision based on the traditional values of education, pluralism, culture and citizenship'. Tambini, D and Cowling, J 'Living in Cloud Peacock Land', *Financial Times*, Creative Business, 11 March 2003. This approach suggests a somewhat opportunistic attitude to the entire issue. Even if it does not, the lack of market failures specific to broadcasting at least raises the issue of whether there might be better candidates for the receipt of public subsidies in connection with underpinning those values.

[162] See Livingstone, S, Lunt, P and Miller, L, 'Citizens and Consumers, Discursive Debates During and After the Communications Act 2003' (2007) 29(4) *Media Culture and Society* 613–38.

[163] Commission Decision 91/130/EEC, *Screensport*, §69.

[164] Commission Decision 93/403/EEC, *EBU/Eurovision System*, §78. Note, however, that the Commission granted an Art 101(3) exemption for the arrangement.

[165] Commission Decision 97/606/EC, *Flanders Television Advertising*, §14.

[166] Niejahr attributes the adoption of the Amsterdam Protocol to the Commission's publication in 1995 of a first draft of guidelines in relation to PSB, which triggered a political response by the Member States. See Niejahr, M, in Säcker and Montag (eds), *European State Aid Law—A Commentary* (CH Beck, Hart, and Nomos, 2016) 1219.

elaboration of the reasons. In particular, the General Court emphasised that it was not so much any commercial dimension to broadcasting as the impact of PSB on the 'otherwise competitive and commercial broadcasting sector' that determined the position.[167] It then goes on to what it says is the Amsterdam Treaty's acknowledgment of PSB as meeting political, social and cultural needs. Although directed at the issue of whether or not an SGEI concession need be awarded on a competitive basis, the suggestion appears to be that the activity (or PSB provision) is not per se economic because of its intrinsic purpose.[168] Echoing *Sacchi*, that understanding would appear even to disregard the nature of any obligations imposed. Recourse to the intrinsic purpose of any activity should hardly be dispositive for these purposes. After all, the development and manufacture of life-saving drugs has many purposes (including an underlying intention to help save lives, for profit) but that hardly renders the activity non-economic on the basis that other drugs may have many fewer existential benefits.

The effects of the Amsterdam Protocol are especially apparent in relation to the issues of definition, supervision and enforcement of PSB obligations. On the issue of definition, and even making allowances for Member States' primacy, it has always been a requirement that there be adequate specificity in the delineation of public service tasks. The 2009 Broadcasting Guidelines appear to limit the application of Article 106(2) by only requiring a clear definition of a public service remit underpinned by an explicit act of entrustment.[169] This, it has been argued reflects the terms of the Amsterdam Protocol and means that only the fulfilment and not the definition of the public service remit need be supervised.[170] When, however, it is considered that with respect to fulfilment the Commission is self-restricted to seeing that the remit is determined independently and subsequently supervised at national level, it will be clear that the Amsterdam Protocol has the ability largely to deprive Article 106(2) of any useful effect in this field.

In its 2004 Decision in *TV2/Denmark* the Commission acknowledged that the obligations imposed on TV2 were qualitative in nature and, despite the absence of effective monitoring, still found that nearly all of its output (apart from Internet-related commercial services) constituted an SGEI.[171] A similar approach is taken in a 2006 Decision concerning ad hoc financing for Dutch public service broadcasters, which were referred to by the Commission as 'rather broadly defined', but which nevertheless were accepted as constituting an SGEI, even in the absence of any significant domestic supervision.[172] As a result, the 'particular tasks'

[167] T-442/03 *SIC* [2008] ECR II-1161, §53.

[168] This claim is repeated by the General Court subsequently in Joined Cases T-568/08 *M6 v Commission* and T-573/08 *TFI v Commission* [2010] ECR II-3997, §123.

[169] That is despite flagging the dangers of accepting general statements as to the PSB remit. See Commission Communication from the Council on the Application of State Aid Rules to Public Service Broadcasting, 27.10.09 ('the 2009 Broadcasting Guidelines'). That is despite flagging the dangers of accepting general statements as to the PSB remit. See 2001 Broadcasting Guidelines, §37; 2009 Broadcasting Guidelines, §45.

[170] See Gerlach, C and Pikio, D, 'Aid to Broadcasting, Culture and Sport' in Werner and Verouden (eds), *EU State Aid Control* (Wolters Kluwer, 2017) 722–23.

[171] Commission Decision 2005/217/EC, *TV2 Danmark*, §85.

[172] Commission Decision 2006/136/EC, *Lead and Cadmium*, §122.

requirement under Article 106(2) is effectively blunted by the operation of the Amsterdam Protocol. In this regard, an elementary confusion arises with respect to the process by which or the forum in which specific tasks are defined (which should be nationally determined) and the requirement that they be defined with some specificity. The Protocol should not be an excuse for failing to do the latter.

In parallel, the Commission (and the General Court) have also deployed a slightly more grandiose defence of this 'hands-off' approach, grounded in the requirements of the European Convention on Human Rights and, in particular, the freedom of expression guarantee. In 2008 that was endorsed by the General Court judgment in *TV2/Danmark*.[173] Although it annulled the underlying Decision, the General Court upheld the Commission's verification of the PSB remit as an SGEI. Before citing Article 10 of the Convention, the General Court held that 'In this respect, the EBU, intervener in support of the Commission, was right to stress the importance, for protecting freedom of expression, of the public service broadcaster's editorial independence from public authority …'.[174] This is an assertion that the implied freedom of expression right of the PSB provider is inconsistent with the detailed specification of its public service remit.[175]

The General Court's approach in *TV2/Danmark* amounts to privileging the PSB providers' position and effectively assumes that public accountability will lead to corrosive political control. A human rights overlay is being used to justify the failure to pay closer attention to the specification of the general interest. While the concern for editorial independence is most acute in relation to news programming, that can be adequately safeguarded through more generalised regulatory measures, such as those directed at fairness and balance. That is well illustrated by the Commission's consideration of that issue in insisting on better specification of the PSB through entrustment in Germany.[176] In recording its acceptance of proposed reforms in 2007 to close a State aid investigation, the Commission rightly distinguished supervision through adequate specification of particular tasks from respect for editorial independence.[177] That prudence would now appear to be at an end in the light of the *TV2/Danmark* judgment, in the process overlooking the instrumental raison d'être of PSB providers.[178]

[173] T-309/04 *TV2/Danmark* [2008] ECT II-2935.

[174] ibid, §118.

[175] There is undoubtedly some element of spillover from German constitutional law as it applies to broadcasting and this freedom of expression paradigm. Art 5 of Germany's Basic Law has been interpreted as preventing any external attempts to influence content. Separately, the *Länder* control broadcasting policy, with broadcasting freedom regarded as an institutional right of the PSB providers in Germany. See Steemers, J, 'In Search of a Third Way: Balancing Public Purpose and Commerce in German and British Public Service Broadcasting' (2001) 26(1) *Canadian Journal of Communication.*

[176] State Aid E 3/2005, C(2007)1761 final.

[177] ibid, §251.

[178] This is not to doubt that the Commission has faced some difficult situations where constitutionally framed interest of Member States are at issue, as in Germany, where the question of supervision of PSB providers and its discharge independently of them was at issue. See State Aid E 3/2005, C(2007) 1761 final, §§373–74.

(b) Renouncing Market Feasibility

Unsurprisingly, in the light of the Amsterdam Protocol and more generally the superficiality with which Article 106(2) is applied in relation to PSB, any semblance of requiring the Member States to first assess market provision before specifying the PSB is defunct. Either a market failure or a merit goods approach to the definition of PSB necessarily requires a comparison with market-generated outputs. The absence of recourse to such a market comparison means that economic analysis is effectively precluded in the supervision of the SGEI qualification for PSB. The rejection of a market counterfactual approach can be traced back to two significant Decisions of the Commission in relation to the BBC. The first from 2000 concerned the introduction of a 24 hours news service to rival that of CNN and Sky and for which the BBC was being permitted by the UK authorities to use licence fee funding.[179] The Commission emphasised that for the purposes of qualifying as an SGEI under Article 106(2), it was important to consider that this service would enhance the choices available to consumers. That was framed more as a way of safeguarding plurality in news supply than responding to any specific concerns about market power on the part of the then existing players. The Commission claimed that 'the specific features of the service cannot be found in services provided by private operators' before proceeding to rely on both the absence of advertising and of charges for the service as the distinguishing features.[180] That is not entirely convincing given that both of these features become inevitable once a decision is made to include such a service within the BBC's PSB remit. News 24 had no advertising and was free of charge so it was treated as an SGEI and because it was an SGEI it was advertising free and free from direct charges. This is an illustration of a stylised delivery characteristics approach to SGEI qualification obscuring the investigation of market feasibility, leading to a circular justification of the treatment of the activity as an SGEI.[181]

The Commission took a similar approach in *BBC Digital Curriculum* in 2003.[182] Again, the proposal was to extend the remit of the BBC, this time in relation to online educational services. The service included the provision of a virtual learning environment complementing regular school curricula. The Commission noted that at that time, there were at least four existing providers of managed online education services, as well as considerable competition from a number of other less advanced providers. Again, as was the case for *BBC News 24*, the proposal was that the service

[179] NN 88/98 *BBC News 24*. It is noteworthy that no additional licence fee funds were to be made available to the BBC in respect of the service, but instead, an entirely new service, which according to the Commission would have significantly greater overheads than its commercial rivals (at least in terms of headcount) was to be financed from envisaged savings and efficiencies. This perhaps reveals a very generous approach to PSB funding. In effect, output was to be expanded to meet the already sanctioned level of public support.

[180] ibid, §53.

[181] Instead, it may have been better to have only relied upon the plurality concern in the light of the BBC's distinctive impartiality obligations.

[182] N 37/2003 C(2003) 3371 final, *BBC Digital Curriculum*

would be provided on a fully open basis with no charges. The Commission's Article 106(2) analysis was perfunctory.[183] The Commission recorded the UK's acknowledgment that there would be significant effects on the existing market, but noted that a number of conditions were to be imposed on the BBC, as a result of which the Commission accepted that Article 106(2) could be relied upon in full.[184] In particular, the Commission emphasised that those conditions would ensure that the services would be 'distinctive' and 'complementary' to those provided by competitors.[185] While the language has connotations of market comparison, the BBC's proposals appear to have been highly duplicative.[186] Moreover, the subsequent history of this initiative, which became known as BBC Jam, appears to indicate that the spillover effects were much greater than initially represented, with the BBC Trust eventually intervening to end this service in 2007.[187]

The ultimate demise of any market comparison for PSBs occurred in the judgment of the General Court in *TV2/Denmark*, where a number of objections were made to how the Commission had deferred to Denmark concerning the definition of PSB, and in turn its acceptance as an SGEI.[188] The applicant argued that all broadcasters were the subject of PSB obligations and that as a result there was no reason to privilege just one with public support. In rejecting this, the Court upheld the Commission's comparison of obligations by reference to the qualitatively different burdens imposed on TV2 alone. In that regard, it dealt with the separate claim that since TV2's output was largely indistinguishable from those of its commercial rivals, it should not have been accepted as a PSB, and in turn as an SGEI. Having mentioned the Amsterdam Protocol, the General Court responded to as follows:

> To accept that argument and thereby to make the definition of the broadcasting SGEI dependent—through a comparative analysis of programming—on the range of programming offered by the commercial broadcasters would have the effect of depriving the Member States of their power to define the public service. In fact, the definition of the SGEI would depend, in the final analysis, on commercial operators and their decisions as to whether or not to broadcast certain programmes. As TV2 A/S rightly submits,

[183] ibid, §40.

[184] Niejahr (n 166) 1229, cites this as an example, together with the Commission decision in *Chaine française d'information internationale* as an example of the Commission not treating the service as meeting the democratic, social or cultural needs of society, within the terms of the Broadcasting Communication 2001, but instead treating it as an SGEI under Art 106(2). This exemplifies the extent to which the Amsterdam Protocol has pushed the definition of PSB outside of Art 106(2). See N54 of 2005 of 7/6/2005.

[185] ibid, §41.

[186] See *contra*, Wiedemann, V, 'Public Service Broadcasting, State Aid, and the Internet: Emerging EU Law' (2004) 4 *European State Aid Law Quarterly* 597, who refers to this as a 'market failure'-type approach that is at odds with the European model of society.

[187] 'BBC Trust suspends BBC Jam', Press Release of the BBC Trust, 14 March 2007. Among the reasons identified by the Trust included pending complaints to the European Commission that its decision and the conditions that it had imposed had not been respected. www.bbc.co.uk/bbctrust/news/press_releases/2007/bbc_jam.html.

[188] Case T-309/04 *TV2/Danmark* [2008] ECT II-2935.

> when the Member States define the remit of public service broadcasting, they cannot be constrained by the activities of the commercial television channels.[189]

This is a remarkable assertion by the General Court, not least because it effectively concedes that the Member States are free to intervene to procure the delivery of content, even when that is generally available in the market on satisfactory terms.[190] It does not even appear to matter what the underlying justification for the PSB is (market failure, merit good or participatory citizenship) because the realisation of any such objective has no constraining comparator. In other sectors the fact that other players are providing services on satisfactory terms obviates the case for public intervention.[191] The General Court's objection is asserted as a matter of principle and it is categorical in that it admits of absolutely no constraint on the scope or content of PSB, irrespective of the market provision, even where that duplication is in the form of free-to-air transmission.[192] That is not to say that such provision should operate as an absolute constraint in all cases, but to reject its relevance out of hand is to risk wasteful subsidy of duplicative content under the pretext of SGEI provision.[193] As a result, it is difficult to quibble with Grespan's characterisation of PSB as the most 'special' SGEI of all.[194]

5. Digital Switchover and Market Failure

Despite the availability of digital broadcasting since the early 1990s, terrestrial broadcasting networks in particular have been slow to convert to digital. This is due largely to the need to change frequencies, which in many Member States has raised complex cross-border co-ordination challenges. Despite that, broadcasters have gradually migrated, in particular through the deployment of the DVB-T standard that has become harmonised across Europe.[195] As a result, the Commission has walked a fine line between support for this standard and policing the State aid rules. Under the 'eEurope' 2005 strategy adopted in 2002, the Member States were pressed to announced target dates for cutover to DVB-T by December 2003.[196] In its 2003 Switchover Communication, the Commission indicated in general

[189] ibid, §123.

[190] The General Court also referred to a Council Resolution of 25 January 1999 on PSB, which, inter alia, refers to diversification of the activities of PSBs in the digital age. Official Journal C 030, 05/02/1999 P. 0001— 0001.

[191] See, for example, Commission Decision 2001/851/EC *Tirrenia di Navigazione*, §30 and Commission Decision 2011/98/EC *Scottish Ferries*, §§272–77.

[192] In other words, there is no accessibility concern as would arise with respect to comparable offerings provided on a pay television basis.

[193] With respect to entrustment, the Commission has quite correctly pointed out that 'self-commitment' does not suffice for the purposes of entrustment. See State Aid E 3/2005, C(2007) 1761 final, §§245–52. Even if Member States have primacy in terms of defining the remit it makes no sense that commercial offering appear now to be entirely irrelevant for that purpose.

[194] Grespan, D, 'A Busy Year for State Aid Control in the Field of Public Service Broadcasting' (2010) 1 *European State Aid Law Quarterly* 79–85.

[195] This is a European-developed broadcasting standard for digital terrestrial television.

[196] COM (2002) 263 final.

terms the potential relevance of market failures in relation to the problem but was not clear as to whether that was specific to Article 106(2) or Article 107.[197] Subsequent State aid cases confirmed the relevance of market failure concepts and the seeming inability of Article 106(2) to overturn the market failure-driven Article 107(3)(c) analysis.[198] This is reflected in two decisions concerning the introduction of the DVB-T standard in Germany: *Berlin Brandenburg DVB-T* and *North Rhine-Westphalia DVB-T*.[199] Given the factual, legal and economic similarity of the two cases, only the former is considered in detail.

In *Berlin Brandenburg DVB-T* the local regulatory agency, MABB, awarded spectrum for free to Germany's two principal commercial broadcasters, ProSieben and RTL, and provided them with direct funding to offset the cost of switching to DVB-T for a period. In considering the availability of Article 107(3)(c), the Commission faced a number of arguments justifying the intervention. Those included the co-ordination challenge posed by the need to change spectrum, the positive externalities associated with the move (such as the freeing up of spectrum for other uses), the strengthening of competition between platforms, overcoming the risk to the network operator, and the promotion of innovation. Although accepting that the first two concerns were genuine market failures (ie efficiency derived) that could in principle justify intervention, the Commission found that neither justified the financial assistance provided considering the materiality of the aid, which for a period covered nearly half of the transmission costs of the broadcasters.[200] The strengthening of competition, which was really a market power argument, was rejected on the basis that there was vibrant competition from other platforms and that the emergence of new ones could be jeopardised.[201] The risk of roll-out of DVB-T was not regarded by the Commission as exceptional and had subsequently been initiated elsewhere without public support. Finally, the argument for innovation was rejected on the basis that DVB-T was being supported for television only, with significant doubts about ancillary uses, such as on mobile devices.

A notable feature of the *Berlin/Brandenburg DVB-T* Decision is how the Commission dealt with Germany's SGEI argument. The claim was that the mere act of transmission of channels (albeit not PSB channels) on digital was an SGEI

[197] COM (2003) 541 final. At p 11, the Commission is non-committal in stating that '[n]on-intervention can result in market failure and jeopardise general interest goals in the sense explained above'.

[198] Despite that, in respect of the Spanish conversion to DVB-T, although the existence of a market failure in parts of Spain was not in dispute, the existence of a PSO (again equated with an SGEI) was denied by the Commission largely on the basis that the operation of DTT networks had not been specifically declared to be a public service and that the principle of technological neutrality had not been respected in the funding process. See Commission Decision 2014/489/EU, *Spanish DTT Conversion*, §§119–24.

[199] Commission Decision 2006/513/EC *Berlin-Brandenburg DVB-T*, and Commission Decision 2008/708/EC, *DVB-T North Rhine-Westphalia*, respectively. Several of the SGEI arguments featuring in *Berlin Brandenburg DVB-T* under Art 106(2) analysis are rolled up into the Art 107(3)(c) assessment in *North Rhine-Westphalia DVB-T*.

[200] *Berlin-Brandenburg DVB-T*. At §100 the Commission makes express reference to the need for the market failures to be efficiency derived and real, in the sense of being factually verified.

[201] ibid, §110.

on the basis that it promoted technological innovation through mobility and portability, safeguarded competition between platforms and promoted plurality across them.[202] The Commission easily dealt with the innovation argument, largely relying on the preceding Article 107(3)(c) analysis to the effect that moving to DVB-T was not a technological step change. In addition, the Commission pointed out that digitalisation was not unique to terrestrial television and was a challenge for all transmission platforms, including cable. The Commission's approach to the seemingly distinct competition and plurality points was to roll them into one. It dismissed Germany's concerns on the basis that there were no structural or other problems in the market, and no reason why abusive conduct on existing platforms could 'hamper the distribution of content and endanger plurality'.[203] Even though Germany invoked a plurality justification on the basis of encouraging the emergence of another platform, the Commission held that the market was already performing adequately from a competitive perspective and that plurality was accordingly assured.

E. Conclusions

Key to the prevention and mitigation of government failure in SGEI definition is recourse to market feasibility testing and in particular the investigation of market failures. Commission decisions from the telecommunications and environmental arenas in particular demonstrate the operation of market failure as a negative screening device, often leading to the rejection of certain general interest claims. A prominent feature of the Commission's approach is considerable strictness with respect to their verification. Member States are not accorded any special deference with respect to what they propose as market failures or qualifying circumstances. While the Commission might be criticised on the basis that in those situations, review is not marginal, its approach can be defended given the greater susceptibility of these issues to objective analysis, not least because distributional goals are not engaged.

The relative strictness of manifest error control for efficiency-related claims is best exemplified by the environmental sector, in particular by decisions such as *WRAP Newsprint* and *Tierkörperbeseitigung*. In both instances, the Commission treated the assessment of market failures as technical issues, as to which it is fully prepared to second-guess the Member States. By contrast, and as exhibited by the *Pyrénées-Atlantiques* and *MANS* Decisions, when it comes to cohesion concerns, there is clearly greater deference, although now constrained for broadband funding by increasingly prescriptive guidelines. Somewhat confusingly, those guidelines

[202] ibid, §123.
[203] ibid, §128.

are presented as a market failure-based approach when it is clear that they go well beyond the resolution of efficiency-related market failures. Unsurprisingly, in *Colt* the General Court took the Commission's terminological looseness at face value and has asserted that the existence of a market failure is a prerequisite of SGEI qualification.[204] Instead, that judgment is better understood in government failure terms as recognition that the viability of general interest goals must be tested using a market feasibility framework.

As with the general position for Article 106(2) in the Treaty scheme, the role of market failure under Article 106(2) displays significant contingency. That is apparent from a comparison of the three sectors reviewed. In the field of telecommunications, market failure analysis for broadband support occurs predominantly under Article 107(3), in large part because the Commission has so greatly constrained the nature of permissible SGEIs in the field. As a result, the first *Altmark* criterion is frequently not satisfied. By contrast, in the environmental arena, where distributional and cohesional goals are not quite as prominent, there is greater recourse to market failure analysis under Article 106(2), but that too depends on the absence of specific Article 107(3)(c) guidelines. Completing the picture, the market failure case for PSB has been largely eroded. Constitutional change has been interpreted as precluding recourse to even elementary market comparisons so as to calibrate the nature and extent of public provision with respect to other, largely non-economic, bases for intervention. As a result, economic analysis in framing the nature or context of PSB as an SGEI is effectively defunct. The contrast with the assessment of public support for broadband could not be any clearer, even taking account of the pseudo-market failure approach of the Commission for that purpose.

In considering the role of market failure under Article 106(2), it should be emphasised that sometimes the resolution of a market failure does not take the form of a classic SGEI with stylised delivery obligations that are frequently the hallmark of distributional or cohesion goals. Those obligations may lead to an irresistible conclusion that there is a valid underlying general interest objective, not necessarily as apparent in respect of the resolution of a market failure. As a result, the Commission Decisions in *German Ecological Reserves* and *Netherlands Ecological Reserves I* are significant, not just as examples of environmental public goods, but also because they demonstrate that particular tasks under Article 106(2) need not take the form of stylised delivery obligations for conventional services in order to make a direct contribution to the fulfilment of the general interest. Contingency aside, this innovation could be essential to the suitability of market failure analysis to play a more prominent role in Article 106(2), in the process helping to further mitigate the degree of government failure.

The contrasting situations in the environmental and broadcasting fields are very revealing from a constitutional perspective. Constitutional change, such as

[204] T-79/10 *Colt* ECLI:EU:T:2013:463, §154.

the introduction of the 'polluter pays' principle, has given impetus to the use of market failure analysis. By contrast, in relation to broadcasting and albeit limited to PSB, a protocol dating back to the introduction of the Amsterdam Treaty has been misused to oust recourse to market feasibility in their construction. It is therefore difficult to better Niejahr's characterisation of the situation as one where 'the competition rules will therefore continue not to be a catalyst for structural change in the broadcasting area'.[205] While Article 106(2) remains to the fore, market feasibility testing has been completely eviscerated. The price in terms of government failure is considerable, not least because so many Member States continue to use taxpayer money to subsidise ill-defined and inadequately policed PSB remits. That is at a time when vertically integrated broadcasting is likely incapable of delivering general interest objectives in a digital economy where the sourcing and authenticity of content has become the paramount consideration. The fact that PSB providers are likely viewed by the political classes as especially deserving of protection, and in turn the symbiotic nature of the relationship between politicians and PSB providers, poses an especially acute challenge from a government failure perspective.

We now live in a world where the transmission costs of information have gone to virtually zero, thereby massively increasing its supply, but possibly at the price of accuracy, and with no corresponding mass improvement in the ability to filter by reference to quality. At the same time, actual sources of journalistically constructed, on-the-ground news gathering continue to decline. Yet, government policy in so many EU countries remains almost exclusively focused on support for vertically integrated PSB providers, with a heavy weighting on the production and airing of content that is generally accessible elsewhere. There may well be an important and much more optimal role for government in this area, not as editor-in-chief or funding underwriter of a national champion, but instead as guarantor and supporter of conditions under which the origination of democracy-sustaining outputs is supported into more widely competitive markets.[206] An informed citizenry would demand no less.

[205] Niejahr (n 166) 1236.

[206] As an example of a more targeted innovative approach to State aid in support of pluralism, see State aid SA.36366 (2013/N)—Denmark—C(2013) 7870 final.

6

Government Failure in Disapplication Review

A. Introduction

This chapter is an assessment of government failure in disapplication review under Article 106(2) TFEU. Disapplication review, it will be recalled, is the process through which a decision is reached that other Treaty rules should not be applied because otherwise it would obstruct the performance in fact or line law of the SGEI. Given the manner of their organisation and typical content, SGEIs are susceptible to the particular forms of government failure that I outlined in Chapter 2. Critical to the establishment and mitigation of government failures are transparency challenges, whether in the form of non-existent information, or, as is more frequently the case, acute information asymmetries. The latter may give the SGEI provider an insuperable advantage over governments by obscuring both necessity and proportionality review under Article 106(2). Similarly, the lack of pertinent information, and in particular of meaningful comparators, can make distinct efficiency scrutiny effectively impossible. While efficiency can be treated as an aspect of proportionality review, such is its growing prominence and cross-cutting significance that I treat it on a stand-alone basis in this chapter. As will be apparent, the position with respect to transparency and proof affects the assessment with respect to necessity and proportionality, and in turn, efficiency, to a considerable extent.

As I set out in this chapter, critical in the prevention and mitigation of government failure in the application of Article 106(2) are information asymmetry and related organisational issues. It is, moreover, the case that the application of the competition rules (which Article 106(2) is frequently used to disapply) frequently takes place in sectors that are subject to economic regulation of varying types and degrees of sophistication. The EU has a practice of intervention in traditional utility sectors, not least in telecommunications, which remains the sector subjected to the most comprehensive system of economic regulation. Critical to the prevention of government failure is the transfer of know-how and fundamental economic insights between sectors. Given the organisation of the EU, we might expect significant cross-deployment of that know-how and, at least to some degree, its incorporation into the Article 16(2) *acquis*. In that regard, the *Altmark* judgment looms large. It represents an embryonic form of economic regulation, albeit developed solely for the identification of advantage for the purpose of the State aid rules. While it has contributed to the contingency of Article 106(2) as described in Chapter 4, it has also heralded a collateral, albeit partial, revival in the potential for the mitigation of government failure through disapplication review under Article 106(2). The convoluted process by which that outcome was arrived at is at the core of this chapter.

The following are the elements of this chapter. The next section describes the initial period leading up to the judgment in *Corbeau*, which is referred to as the 'strict exception' phase in line with rhetorical claims by the European Court and the European Commission during that phase. In the following section, I track a second phase, beginning with *Corbeau* and leading up to *Altmark*, during which Article 106(2) went from being a strict exception to becoming much more of a permissive derogation. The subsequent section is a consideration of *Altmark* and its later implementation in terms of the implications for disapplication review under Article 106(2) from a government failure perspective.

B. The First Phase—The Strict Exception

1. Introduction

In this section, the issues of transparency and proof, necessity and proportionality, and, finally, efficiency are considered with respect to Article 106(2) for the period running from the establishment of the EEC up to just before the handing down of the Court of Justice's judgment in *Corbeau*. In this period SGEIs were largely untouched by EU law. Nevertheless, judicial and administrative determination to operate Article 106(2) as a strict exception is apparent. That said, the first phase is characterised by the Commission not taking on genuinely difficult cases where distributional objectives were implicated, and equally, in the same period the Court of Justice was not confronted with any preliminary references that really tested the accuracy of the strict exception label. Nevertheless, the foundation blocks for making that claim a reality were laid, not least with respect to transparency and proof, where the judgment of the Court in *Ahmed Saeed* stood as a model exposition of how the judicial function can be used to mitigate government failure under Article 106(2).

2. Transparency and Proof

As considered in Chapter 2, information deficits and asymmetry problems are rife in Article 106(2) cases. At best these are only partially soluble through judicial intervention, perhaps in part through the deployment of presumptions.

In relation to Article 106(2), the resolution of information asymmetries becomes a challenge, mainly for the Commission in respect of which it enjoys a specific competence under Article 106(3). The Commission's first use of that power occurred in 1980 when it adopted Directive 80/723/EEC ('the Transparency Directive').[1] The Transparency Directive was primarily envisaged as a necessary intervention for the purposes of State aid control.[2] It included reference to the desirability of transparency with respect to compensation for burdens associated with the pursuit of ends 'other than commercial ones' but made no explicit references to SGEIs.[3]

The Transparency Directive required the Member States to collect basic accounting information concerning their financial relations with public undertakings (broadly defined) as well as on the financial performance of those entities, including details of compensation for non-commercial burdens.[4] Despite its scope, the Transparency Directive included a prominent exclusion for public undertakings that operated in the water, energy, postal, telecommunications and transport sectors.[5] As a result, many of the fields generating archetypal SGEI claims fell outside the terms of the Transparency Directive, albeit temporarily. That deficiency was subsequently rectified by the first revision to it in 1985, which ended those sectoral exclusions. The Commission justified this extension on the basis of 'developments in the competitive situation in the sectors concerned and the progress made towards closer economic integration'.[6]

Despite the limitations of the Transparency Directive from an SGEI perspective, in 1989 the Court of Justice took the strict exception characterisation of Article 106(2) to its logical conclusion concerning the nature of proof that was required in order to establish that the competition rules should be disapplied by reason of Article 106(2). This occurred in *Ahmed Saeed*, which concerned the tariff-setting arrangements between airlines and efforts to circumvent them through the sale of tickets to German residents for flights not originating in Germany but which stopped there.[7] The Court of Justice was faced with difficult questions as to the direct effect of Articles 101 and 102, as well as the duty of national authorities under Article 106(1) when it came to tariff approval. With respect to those duties, the Court acknowledged the potential relevance of Article 106(2) considering the obligations of certain airlines to operate non-commercial routes in the general interest.[8] The Court held that a direct link needed to be established between specific PSOs and the overall tariff system in order to qualify under

[1] Directive 80/723/EEC on the Transparency of Financial Relations between Member States and Public Undertakings of 20 June 1980.

[2] ibid, see recitals 4, 5, 6.

[3] ibid, recital 12.

[4] ibid, Art 3.

[5] ibid, Art 4.

[6] Recital 3, Commission Directive 85/413/EEC of 24 July 1985 amending Directive 80/723/EEC on the Transparency of Financial Relations between Member States and Public Undertakings.

[7] C-66/86 *Ahmed Saeed* [1989] ECR 803.

[8] ibid, §55.

Article 106(2). More specifically, the Court held that 'without effective transparency of the tariff structure it would be difficult, if not impossible, to assess the influence of the task of general interest on the application of the competition rules in the field of tariffs'.[9] Although it went on to acknowledge that ultimately the assessment was for the national court, the obvious inference was that absent the necessary proof, arguments for the disapplication of the competition rules should be rejected.[10]

From a government failure perspective, the judgment of the Court of Justice in *Ahmed Saeed* was very significant. First, the Court was live to a critical information problem, although not one that was very prominent in the argument of the case.[11] Second, the Court's stipulation that the impact of any SGEI needed to be demonstrated with reference to the tariff structure was directed at the role of the national authorities. It correctly focused attention on the only meaningful way of determining the case for an exemption from the competition rules. Third, the Court's stipulation also indicated the likely limits of feasible judicial intervention on this issue. EU experience from many sectors has since demonstrated that the quantification of the burdens and benefits associated with SGEI delivery is often complex, necessitating a range of accounting and economic techniques.[12] It would be too much to expect the Court to be any more prescriptive than it was. Finally, and perhaps crucially, by raising the inference concerning a failure to substantiate the impact of the SGEI on the tariff structure the Court was giving the Member States a compelling incentive to adhere to elementary accounting transparency.

3. Necessity and Proportionality

(a) The General Position

In general terms, Article 106(2) sets the substantive standard for determining the extent to which the disapplication of other Treaty rules is to be judged. Their application must give rise to obstruction of the performance of the SGEI mission, either in law or in fact. For its part, in some of the earlier Article 106(2) cases, the Court of Justice tended to take an uncompromising stance, although arguably necessity was not seriously in issue in those cases. Faithful to the literal wording of Article 106(2), in cases such as *CBEM/CLT Höfner* and *Porto di Genova*, the Court emphasised that there needed to be a demonstration of how the application of other Treaty rules would 'obstruct' in the sense of being 'incompatible'

[9] ibid, §57.

[10] ibid.

[11] It does not feature at all in the opinions of AG Lenz on 28 April 1988 and 17 January 1989.

[12] In the field of telecommunications, Art 5 and Annex III of Directive 97/33/EC on Interconnection and Open Network Provision established, for the first time, specific rules for the calculation of the costs of universal service provision. This was based on the net cost methodology, namely the difference between operating with and without the SGEI.

with the performance of the particular tasks arising from the SGEI.[13] According to the Court, there needed to be proof of how the application of other Treaty rules was incompatible with the discharge of the particular tasks associated with the SGEI. Framed in this way, necessity review appeared to mitigate the potential for government failure, although in the absence of testing cases, the Court was not challenged in a serious way.

Taking its cue from the Court of Justice's characterisation of Article 106(2) as a strict exception, during the strict first phase, the Commission usually took a hard-line approach to necessity under Article 106(2). In *NAVEWA-ANSEAU*, for example, the Commission indicated that it would only countenance a limitation on the rules on competition when 'the undertaking concerned has no other technically and economically feasible means of performing the particular tasks'.[14] In *BT-Telespeed* the Commission asserted that it was not sufficient that compliance with other Treaty rules made the performance of the SGEI difficult.[15] Similarly, in *Ijsselcentrale* the Commission dismissed the argument that ending restrictions on imports of electricity could make distribution planning more complicated. That was on the basis that to permit imports required no more than an intensification of planning that the network operator already needed to undertake in order to take account of authorised self-suppliers.[16] In the same spirit, in *EBU/Eurovision System*, the Commission held that although the airing of international sports content would be made more difficult for public broadcasters by applying the competition rules, it would not be rendered 'impossible'.[17]

During the first phase, when the Commission faced distributional objectives (and this may have affected its choice of cases), it was fortunate that those goals were formulated in ways that facilitated strict necessity review. In *Ijsselcentrale*, the Commission was able to rely on the fact that a customer proposing to rely on imports for part or all of its requirements could no longer automatically fall back on the default 'absolute obligation to supply'.[18] Similarly, in *Netherland Express Delivery Services*, in censuring the extension of PTT Post BV's dominant position, the Commission pointed out that the incumbent was not actually subject to an obligation to provide services at uniform rates throughout the Netherlands.[19] While the Commission could control the cases that it took forward, availing itself

[13] C-311/84 *CBEM* [1985] ECR 3261, §17; C-41/90 *Höfner* [1991] ECR 1979 §25; C-179/90 *Porto di Genova*, §26.

[14] Commission Decision 82/371/EEC, *NAVEWA-ANSEAU*, §66. The SGEI in question (operation of a public water system) was quite remote from the practices in question, which concerned the labelling of washing machines.

[15] Commission Decision 82/861/EEC, *BT-Telespeed*, §42.

[16] Commission Decision 91/50/EEC, *Ijsselcentrale*, §44.

[17] Commission Decision 93/403/EEC, *EBU/Eurovision System*, §79, but note the Commission cleared the arrangements under Art 101(3).

[18] *Ijsselcentrale*, §44(a) and (b). The supplier of last resort was at the core of the assumed SGEI.

[19] Commission Decision 90/16/EEC, *Dutch Express Delivery Services*, §17. This decision was subsequently annulled on procedural grounds. Joined Cases C-48/90 and C-66/90 *Netherlands et al v Commission* [1982] ECR I-565.

of Article 106(3), which likely entailed a consideration of Article 106(2), it had no control over questions concerning necessity and proportionality that might reach the Court of Justice through the preliminary reference procedure.

Finally, the position on the choice of means is unknowable with respect to the first phase given the absence of decisions or cases directly on point. While the strict exception characterisation of Article 106(2) might be regarded as leading inevitably to a proportionality standard based on the deployment of the least restrictive means, this is conjecture only. EC legislative intervention in sectors featuring SGEIs only began to proliferate in the wake of the adoption of the 1986 Single European Act.[20] It was from then on that liberalisation began to impact on sectors where SGEI claims were likely. As a result, it is unsurprising that in the first phase neither the Commission nor the Court was faced with resolving the most contentious element of disapplication review, namely whether the proportionality standard required recourse to the least restrictive means.

(b) Pragmatism Portended

The advent of liberalisation of various network industries was to have very considerable implications for the analysis of necessity under Article 106(2). Beginning with the telecommunications sector from the mid-1980s, liberalisation was introduced in the utilities and network industries. By the early 1990s these developments drew much more forensic attention to the feasibility of continuing to implement important distributional objectives while pursuing liberalisation, and in turn, giving full effect to the competition and free movement rules. In particular, the questions of necessity and proportionality under Article 106(2) came to the fore. The displacement of the competition rules was assumed to facilitate SGEI provision in many sectors. Whether in practice that was essential for the maintenance of the SGEI was far less obvious. In the Terminal Equipment Directive, the Commission had asserted boldly that even if the provision of the underlying telecommunications network was an SGEI, the abolition of special or exclusive rights with respect to importing and marketing terminal equipment would have no impact on universal network provision.[21] That kind of declaratory approach would not be defensible with respect to the liberalisation of telecommunications services.

There were indications during the first phase that an absolutist approach to necessity and proportionality might not be sustained. One such sign came in the form of the Commission's assessment of the scope of the exclusive privilege that might be necessary in order to allow the liberalisation of telecommunications services to begin. With its adoption of the Telecommunications Green Paper in 1987,

[20] It set a deadline of 31 December 1992 for the completion of the internal market.

[21] See Commission Directive 88/301/EEC on Terminal Equipment, recital 11. Obviously there may have been monopoly profits on equipment that cross-subsidised underlying network provision, but presumably not of a magnitude as would threaten the viability of underlying network provision.

the Commission signalled how it would use its margin of appreciation under Article 106(3) in order to liberalise the sector.[22] The Commission approached the issue of the necessity of exclusive rights on the basis of two considerations. The first was in the context of maintaining then prevailing USOs and associated tariff structures.[23] The second, and arguably more prominent, consideration was that monopoly profits from exclusive rights were considered crucial for investment in digitalisation.[24] As a result, an overarching concern to ensure the survival of the incumbent firms as principal providers of ubiquitous services is a dominant sub-text, with the need for investment and the introduction of competition framed at least in part in oppositional terms.[25] No consideration is given to whether earlier competition would have provided even greater incentives to invest.

In the light of those considerations, the Commission adopted a pragmatic if over-generous approach.[26] It concluded that since most countries gave incumbents a monopoly over basic network provision and voice services, this could serve to delineate the extent of necessary exclusive rights considering the network investment challenges common to them all.[27] The immediate concern was not a significant contraction of existing rights but the curtailment of their extension. On that basis, the Commission proposed to use Article 106(3) to liberalise all fixed services, apart from what came to be termed 'voice telephony' services.[28] Other services regarded as 'value added' in nature were to be open to provision by competing undertakings, with a general date for full liberalisation of all voice services set for 1 January 1998.[29] If nothing else, the experience in telecommunications served to demonstrate the difficulties presented by necessity and proportionality review in mitigation of government failure in a complex and dynamic sector, even for a technically sophisticated bureaucracy like the Commission.[30] It also portended a possible revision in the Court's generally absolutist stance on necessity and proportionality review during the first phase once distributional goals were implicated in a way that engaged those tests in a critical way in an Article 106(2) case.

[22] COM (87) 290 final.

[23] ibid, 74.

[24] At least at EU level this did not subsequently result in any significant enhancement in the nature of the USO obligation in line with the progressive digitalisation of networks.

[25] The Telecommunications Green Paper refers to these as 'partially contradictory' considerations, p 49.

[26] See in that regard, Buendía Sierra, JL, *Exclusive Rights and State Monopolies under EC Law* (Oxford University Press, 2000) 309–14.

[27] The fact that in many cases those exclusive rights long pre-dated even the prospect of ubiquitous digitalisation did not appear to matter.

[28] This was subsequently defined quite narrowly in Art 1 of Commission Directive 90/388/EEC as 'the commercial provision to the public of the direct transport and switching of speech in real time between public switched network termination points …'.

[29] See Commission Directive 96/19/EC of 13 March 1996, amending Directive 90/388/EEC with regard to the implementation of full competition in telecommunications markets. Prior to that, the Commission had liberalised satellite, cable and mobile services.

[30] The preponderance of state ownership of incumbents may also have been significant in the negotiating dynamic.

4. Efficiency—The Manifest Incapacity Doctrine and Article 106(2)

Although perhaps not readily apparent from the wording of Article 106(2), questions of efficiency are very heavily implicated in its operation. The specification of the SGEI may involve the realisation of goals that unavoidably have efficiency implications, depending on the incentives of providers. Especially serious efficiency failures may arise where an SGEI is supported through the grant of exclusive rights. Absent economic regulation, an exclusive rights holder will be free to limit output by setting excessive prices, leading to allocative inefficiency.[31] In addition, not having the spur of competitive rivalry to keep costs down, frequently monopolists are productively inefficient.[32] Furthermore, a monopolist may be impervious to changes in the nature of demand and in turn fail to innovate, leading to losses in dynamic efficiency.

The question then arises whether Article 106(2) has a bearing on either the censure or toleration of such inefficiencies. During the strict exception phase of Article 106(2), it appeared that even if an intervention qualified as an SGEI, Article 106(2) would not be available to excuse certain types of failure and non-performance that in very general terms might be regarded as forms of inefficiency. Those would include output restrictions and failures to innovate. The basis for the doctrine, referred to as manifest incapacity to satisfy demand ('the manifest incapacity doctrine'), was a prior finding of an Article 106(1) violation in conjunction with Article 102, but with the Court of Justice effectively refusing to extend the benefit of Article 106(2)—where it was applicable—to excuse the inefficiency.[33]

The manifest incapacity doctrine is exemplified by the *Höfner* judgment of the Court.[34] There the federal agency that had been given a monopoly over employment placement services tolerated the activities of competing business executive placement agencies. Liability in *Höfner* turned on the Court being able to specify actual abuses that had already occurred, while implicitly finding that they were

[31] The position is separately more complicated for network industries (where SGEIs are common) since marginal costs are frequently less than average costs and as a result pricing on that basis would not ensure solvency in the presence of significant fixed costs. While two-part tariffs based on price discrimination using inverse elasticities of demand are a potential solution, they too have significant drawbacks, not least the difficulty of calculating them. Furthermore, frequently SGEIs entail mandates to implement uniform or non-discriminatory pricing, which is at odds with systems based on inverse elasticities. See generally, Pierce, R and Gellhorn, E, *Regulated Industries*, 4th edn (West Group, 1999) ch 7.

[32] The potential for productive inefficiency in the operation of networks goes beyond possible overstaffing and lack of productivity that may arise under monopoly. In addition, and depending on how prices are set through regulation, there may be extra incentives to inflate the reckonable asset base, in particular if the regulator permits a rate of return in excess of the cost of capital. This is referred to as the Averch Johnson effect. Averch, J and Johnson, L, 'Behaviour of the Firm Under Regulatory Constraint' (1962) 52(5) *American Economic Review* 1052–69.

[33] This is referred to as such in Van Bael and Bellis, *Competition Law of the European Union*, 5th edn (Kluwer, 2010) 913.

[34] C-41/90 *Höfner* [1991] ECR-1979.

directly attributable to the grant of exclusive rights by the Member State. In *Höfner* the Court stipulated that there would be a violation of Article 106(1) in conjunction with Article 102 where a dominant firm was 'manifestly not in a position to satisfy demand'.[35] *Höfner* is a case of 'seeing is believing', with the Court being presented with clear evidence of monopoly non-provision.[36] By focusing on manifest failure to meet demand, the Court of Justice appeared to be capable of having it both ways: the conferral of special and exclusive rights was not automatically condemned under Article 106(1) in conjunction with Article 102, but could be, depending on market outcomes.[37] In *Höfner* the Court was quick to confirm the existence of an SGEI, but having identified the possibility of a manifest failure to meet demand, the Court was equally clear that Article 106(2) could not justify any derogation from the principle of effectiveness as applied to the competition rules.[38] As a result, it appeared that Article 106(2) could not be used to excuse certain kinds of government failure, especially if they were egregious.

The potential shortcomings of relying on outward manifestations of abuse become apparent when comparing the argument in *Höfner* with those recorded in the later judgment in *Italian Job Centres*.[39] *Höfner* proceeded on the basis that the mere existence of executive placement services (which were tolerated by the German authorities) highlighted the manifest failure to meet demand. In *Italian Job Centres*, relying on statistics, the Italian authorities made a valiant effort to argue that the public jobs placement service was at least performing adequately. In its intervention, the Commission claimed that the nature of the market was such, both in terms of size, differentiation and evolution of the labour being procured, that it was impossible to imagine that a single provider could meet all demand.[40] Rather than abandoning the inevitable abuse doctrine, Advocate General Elmer instead broadened and deepened the inquiry by carrying out a globalised review of the nature of the jobs placement market and the degree of specialisation witnessed in liberalised markets.[41] For its part, the Court adopted the Commission's assessment of the varied and dynamic nature of placement services, emphasising the challenges for a public undertaking in responding to a market undergoing significant changes.[42]

[35] ibid, §24.

[36] In *Höfner* executive recruitment appears to have been left to the private sector.

[37] Historically, this has been a vexed and fluid issue in EU law, see Buendía Sierra, JL, 'Article 106—Exclusive or Special Rights and Other Anti-Competitive State Measures' in Faull and Nikpay (eds), *The EU Law of Competition*, 3rd edn (Oxford University Press, 2014) 824–34.

[38] C-41/90 *Höfner* [1991] ECR-1979, §§24, 25, respectively.

[39] C-55/96 *Italian Job Centres* [1997] ECR I-7119.

[40] This is only one step away from a first-principle argument that absent special circumstances a monopolist is always likely to restrict output, fail to innovate, and more generally not satisfy demand except at supra-competitive prices.

[41] In the same vein, see AG Gulmann in *Crespelle*, where he addressed arguments to the effect that various co-operatives given exclusive rights over bovine artificial insemination were not offering a comprehensive service and were overcharging customers. In addressing claims of overcharging he suggested that 'such examples are of interest only if they may be regarded as evidence that the system itself—as a whole or as regards sufficiently important aspect of it—is contrary to community law'. See C-323/93 *Crespelle* [1994] ECR I-5077, Opinion of 4 May 1994, §29.

[42] C-41/90 *Höfner* [1991] ECR-1979, §§33–35.

As will be considered in the next section, ultimately Article 106(2) was made available to excuse inefficiencies in SGEI delivery. As a result, an alternative market failure interpretation of the underlying facts of *Höfner* allows for the extraction of a more coherent government failure-driven explanation of the result. Employment markets are prone to market failures on the basis of possible information asymmetries and co-ordination difficulties. This is particularly the case where a Member State wishes to offer economy-wide placement services. At most, that general interest objective serves to justify a monopoly over the gathering of information on the availability and requirements of job seekers and prospective employees. Although Germany wished to offer a federally run universal and free service (at the point of access), that did not necessitate the grant of across-the-board monopoly rights covering information gathering, matching services and ultimately placement. As a result, if the Court had reasoned out from what was required to sustain the SGEI in the light of those market failures, it could have determined in a more convincing manner the extent of the necessary exclusivity.[43]

C. The Second Phase—Permissive Derogation

1. Introduction

The second phase in the analysis of disapplication review from a government failure perspective runs from the handing down of the judgment in *Corbeau* in 1993 up until just before the judgment in *Altmark* in 2003. Although this period only covers 10 years, it includes a wide range of developments, which, with a small number of exceptions, disclose not just a marked change in sentiment, especially in the language of the Court, but also subtle and sometimes profound adjustments in the direction of Article 106(2). Despite some compensating legislative interventions by the Commission, particularly directed at transparency, by the end of this phase Article 106(2) was not as significant a backstop against government failure as it once was. It had become a much more permissive derogation. The strict exception mantra was shown to be an empty claim.

2. Transparency and Proof

As previously considered, the first and second iterations of the Transparency Directive did little to overcome the informational challenges inherent in disapplication

[43] An objection to reasoning out from Art 106(2) is that it may lead to a failure to fully particularise breaches of Art 106(1) in conjunction with another Treaty provision. For a criticism of this 'burden shifting', see Van Bael and Bellis (n 33) 916–17.

review under Article 106(2).[44] It was not until 2000 that the position was changed in several important respects, through the adoption of Directive 2000/52/EC. As reflected in its amendment of the title to the Transparency Directive, this legislation extended the underlying requirements to all undertakings engaged in SGEI provision, while also introducing a requirement that separate accounts be maintained.[45] Significantly, in terms of what was to come to pass later, Directive 2000/52/EC contained an exclusion from its requirements for SGEI support 'fixed for an appropriate period following an open, transparent and non-discriminatory procedure'.[46] In line with an approach that in overall terms was indulgent, it was not framed so as to require that a tender be run on the basis of lowest cost.[47]

Despite SGEIs being the paramount concern of the amendments to the Transparency Directive made in 2000, the separate accounts requirement was undercut by a lack of specificity as to the precise method of cost and revenue allocation. While it may be unfair to impugn that approach by reference to current standards, by 2000 the regulation of telecommunications in particular (and post, electricity and gas to a lesser extent) had generated a significant amount of know-how and legislative prescription in relation to these issues.[48] The Commission did not bring that know-how or specificity to bear in its amendments to the Transparency Directive, although by then, there were latent political strictures on recourse to Article 106(3). More generally, those sectors had demonstrated the indispensability of targeted interventions directed at the informational problem in the context of quantifying necessary support for SGEIs in classic USO form. Furthermore, the revisions to the Transparency Directive in 2000 did not include any provision to the effect that non-compliance with its terms would mean that the benefit of Article 106(2) would be denied.[49]

In the absence of a sufficiently comprehensive Transparency Directive, much would turn on whether the approach in *Ahmed Saeed* would continue to be maintained. With its 2000 judgment in *Deutsche Post*, the Court began a significant retreat.[50] *Deutsche Post* concerned the non-physical re-mailing of credit card-related data, which Citibank undertook by delivering letters to the Dutch Post Office for final delivery by Deutsche Post to customers in Germany. Although Deutsche Post was paid a terminal due for final delivery, it appears to have been

[44] A third revision to the Transparency Directive in the form of Directive 93/84/EEC did not alter the position in that regard. It was principally concerned with the manufacturing sector.

[45] Commission Directive 80/723/EEC of 25 June 1980 on the Transparency of Financial Relations between Member States and Public Undertakings as well as on Financial Transparency within Certain Undertakings.

[46] Inserted as the new Art 4(2)(c) of the Transparency Directive. See also Recital 11.

[47] The process is not expressly referred to as tendering.

[48] Under Art 7(2) of Directive 97/33/EC, the Commission was permitted to draw up guidelines on cost accounting systems and accounting separation in relation to interconnection. Similarly, Art 18(3) of Directive 98/10/EC of the European Parliament and Council on the Application of Open Network Provision to Voice Telephony and on Universal Service contains relatively precise rules for cost allocation in relation to voice telephony.

[49] That would have put the result in *Ahmed Saeed* on a legislative footing.

[50] C-147/97 and C-148/97 *Deutsche Post* [2000] ECR I-825.

accepted before the referring German court that, nevertheless, Deutsche Post incurred a loss in respect of this kind of mail. As a result, it attempted to impose a surcharge, in purported operation of an international convention on postal charges, which was set at the price of the standard charge of mailing for a regular letter in Germany.[51] This resulted in the referral of several questions to the Court, including as to a possible violation of Article 106(1) in conjunction with Article 102.

In his opinion in *Deutsche Post*, Advocate General La Pergola pointed out that based on the evidence before the Court, it was not apparent that Deutsche Post operated an appropriate cost allocation system, which would have been essential to assess the proportionality of levying a surcharge on all foreign-originated mail based on standard postal charges.[52] He expressly adopted the Court's previous ruling in *Ahmed Saeed* to the effect that absent this kind of transparency, it could not be inferred that the conditions of Article 106(2) were satisfied.[53] In other words, the proportionality of the charge would not be assumed simply because there was a plausible argument that some level of recovery was appropriate to support Deutsche Post's USO.

The Court of Justice declined to follow the opinion of its Advocate General. It pointed to the fact that while such a system of cost transparency would be required, the relevant Directive was not then in force. Without it, and given the absence of an international agreement on the appropriate system of charges between operators, the Court refused to rule that the principle of a surcharge was not justified under Article 106(2).[54] In effect, the information asymmetry worked to the advantage of the SGEI provider. While it is true that the Advocate General's approach is 'all or nothing', it is justified considering the underlying information asymmetries. By contrast, the Court of Justice's stance appears indulgent considering that at the relevant time, Deutsche Post had not been complying with its recruirements under the Postal Services Directive, which required it to separate out the costs of each element of universal service provision.[55] Compliance with those requirements would have likely disclosed that any losses on the service at issue in the proceedings could have been offset by profits from elsewhere, thereby not jeopardising the SGEI.[56]

From the perspective of proof, just over a year after *Deutsche Post* Article 106(2) was further undermined by *TNT Traco*.[57] It concerned a challenge to a practice of

[51] Subsequently, Deutsche Post moderated its claim to a surcharge based on the standard charge less the actual amount received from the originating postal service in respect of each letter.

[52] Opinion of 1 June 1999 in C-147/97 and C-148/97 *Deutsche Post* [2000] ECR I-825, fn. 59.

[53] ibid.

[54] Conceivably, the Court could have taken the terms of the Directive as prima facie evidence of what a proportionate response might be. See an example of that approach with respect to security of supply for electricity in *Jahrhundertvertrag*, where a proposed provision of a draft Directive permitting a 20% reservation for domestic energy sources was used by the Commission to clear a measure under Art 106(2). Commission Decision 93/126/EEC, *Jahrhundertvertrag*, §30.

[55] Art 14(2) of Directive 96/67/EC.

[56] For a detailed criticism of the approach of the Court of Justice, see Bartosch, A, 'Joined Cases C-147/97 and C-148/97' (2001) 38 *Common Market Law Review* 195–210.

[57] C-340/99 *TNT Traco* [2001] ECR I-4109.

the incumbent Poste Italiane in levying a surcharge on rivals equal to its standard postal charge, even when its infrastructure and services were not being used. In addition to questioning the abusiveness of the charge, the referring court drew attention to the fact that although there were domestic legal requirements concerning the separate presentation of the revenues and costs of monopoly and competitive services, there was no regulatory mechanism to prevent the allocation of subsidies from the funding of the SGEI (including the levies) to competitive services. TNT Traco argued that the latter should have prevented recourse to Article 106(2). In rejecting this, the Court of Justice held that absent EC rules, reliance on Article 106(2) was, as was the case for Article 102, to be determined in accordance with national law.[58] As a result, the lack of domestic measures prohibiting cross-subsidies did not mean that the conditions of Article 106(2) were not met.[59] That was despite the Court of Justice stipulating that the contested surcharge also needed to be levied on Poste Italiane's own competing services, something not provided for in domestic law.[60]

The effect of the Court's approach was that Article 106(2) could be satisfied through a demonstration with reference to the separate accounts requirement only. In *TNT Traco* Advocate General Alber had advised that in the absence of European rules, this issue was to be determined in accordance with national procedural rules, subject to the usual equivalence protections.[61] The difficulty with this is its characterisation of this issue as procedural, considering that it went to the essence of what needed to be demonstrated in order for Article 106(2) to apply.[62] By asserting that the position under Article 106(2) was the same as for Article 102, the Advocate General and the Court both overlooked the acute information asymmetry problems arising in SGEI litigation. As a result, the claim in *TNT Traco* that the burden of proof rests on the party seeking to rely on Article 106(2) is exposed as empty rhetoric.[63]

3. Necessity and Proportionality

(a) *The Necessity of the Intervention*

In the second phase, the issue of necessity underwent very significant change. While the strict exception conception of Article 106(2) may have been overstated, it was based on a general objectification of the SGEI mission, a default presumption in

[58] ibid, §§61–62.

[59] ibid, §62.

[60] ibid, §58.

[61] ibid, Opinion of AG Alber, 1 February 2001, §116.

[62] AG Alber also relies on C-242/95 *GT-Link* [1997] ECR I-4449 as authority for the fact that procedural issues under Art 106(2) are to be determined by national law in the absence of EU harmonisation. Arguably, *GT-Link* only does so in respect of Art 102.

[63] C-340/99 *TNT Traco* [2001] ECR I-4109, §59.

favour of competition provision and the operation of markets, and finally, a pronounced willingness to hold Member States to account. The crumbling of these keystones of necessity review during the second phase will now be considered.

From SGEI Provision to the Stability of the SGEI Provider

The judgment in *Corbeau* marks the start of a distinct second phase in disapplication review under Article 106(2) from a government failure perspective. *Corbeau* concerned the operation of a rapid delivery service in Liège in competition with that of the publicly controlled provider, Régie de Postes (RdP). RdP claimed damages on the basis that the services provided by Corbeau infringed upon its monopoly over a basic postal service. That led to questions about the validity of the underlying monopoly under Articles 102 and 106 by a local court.

The Court of Justice found that there was an SGEI to collect, carry and distribute mail on behalf of users throughout Belgium. As has already been pointed out, in *Corbeau* the Court did not particularise, but appeared to assume an automatic violation of Article 106(1) in conjunction with Article 102.[64] Furthermore, the Court of Justice might be said to have 'reasoned out' from requirements that it saw as flowing from the underlying SGEI, namely the operation of a national postal system. It referred to the activities of competitors such as *Corbeau*, which, it noted, were free from the obligation to operate a system of internal subsidies.[65] By contrast, the 'economic equilibrium' of the provider was based on the ability to offset losses on unprofitable activities through monopoly profits from reserved services.[66] It left the referring Court to determine whether Corbeau's activities were directly competing services or instead value-added services.

It is important to understand the nature of the concession made by the Court in *Corbeau* to SGEI providers. In essence, the focus moved from what was required to ensure the provision of universal service to guaranteeing conditions for the survival of the SGEI provider.[67] Although not necessarily intended to collapse the necessity test into a consideration of what was needed to protect the incumbent, the emphasis on 'equilibrium' and its subsequent deployment had that effect.[68] Furthermore, it is not apparent that the Court needed to do any of this to resolve

[64] Buendía Sierra (n 37) 831. See also, and by way of criticism, Van Bael and Bellis (n 33) 906–07.

[65] C-320/91 *Corbeau* [1993] ECR I-2533, §18.

[66] ibid, §19.

[67] An alternative approach by the Court could have been to indicate that if exclusivity was strictly necessary for the underlying SGEI, then the incumbent would have had sufficient incentives to respond comprehensively to the demand for rapid delivery services, which it did not.

[68] This, for example, is how AG Darmon interprets *Corbeau* in his opinion in C-393/92 *Almelo*, §146. He suggests that the competition rules did not apply either where they would jeopardise the provision of the SGEI or, with reference to the provider, 'where they jeopardise its financial stability'. This concern for financial stability would always persist unless the actual burden of SGEI provision was quantified. Furthermore, although in the *Gas and Electricity Cases*, the Court had been induced by the Commission's line of argument to indicate that it would not be necessary to show that without exclusive rights (in that case) the provider would not survive, in effect the *Corbeau* equilibrium formula was little more than a superficially alluring label for taking no chances with the survival of the SGEI provider.

the issues before it. Advocate General Tesauro correctly characterised the dispute as a factual one, essentially concerned with whether Corbeau was providing rapid delivery services. On that basis the reference questions were soluble without relying on the 'equilibrium' formula.[69] Despite that, the Court introduced a double protection for RdP by stipulating that even if Corbeau's offering was a rapid delivery service, it needed to be shown that its provision would not affect RdP's economic equilibrium.[70] That even went beyond Belgium's own assessment of what was necessary prospectively, given that it had made a decision to liberalise all rapid delivery services.[71]

The contrast in substance and sentiment with *Ahmed Saaed* is apparent, where the Court objectivised the requirements of SGEI delivery in a manner that avoided its conflation with the survival of the SGEI provider in accordance with *Corbeau*. In this regard, a later judgment of the General Court in *Air Inter* is revealing, not least because it resisted the equilibrium formula by insisting that Article 106(2) was not available simply because competition would hinder or make the task of the SGEI provider more difficult.[72] In that case, the General Court was even more dismissive of generalised assertions as to the need for a system of internal subsidies (in effect the equilibrium argument in more elaborate form), finding that a loss of revenues from competition had not been particularised.[73] Moreover, there had been no demonstration that any such losses would lead to the discontinuance of the route.[74] Despite this, *Air Inter* is really an outlier judgment in this period (like *Ahmed Saaed*, it concerned aviation, where there had been legislative intervention), with the generic equilibrium standard usually holding sway. With the benefit of hindsight, subsequently the Commission only made things worse in pursuing the *Electricity and Gas Case*, by arguing against France that it needed to demonstrate that there would be no financial imperilment of the incumbent if the contested bans were removed.[75] The Court had probably no option but to reject that contention.[76] As a result, for the duration of the second phase, the Commission was generally tied to the equilibrium standard, and was usually only able to overcome it where those claims were loosely asserted or where they stretched credulity.[77] *Corbeau* casts a dominant shadow over the second phase and provided essential context for the rulings in *Deutsche Post* and *TNT Traco* with respect to transparency and proof respectively.

[69] Opinion of AG Tesauro of 9 February 1993, §§21ff.

[70] §19. Furthermore, it appeared that this assessment would need to be undertaken on a market-wide basis.

[71] A Law of 21 March 1991, which would be effective after the period relevant in the case, provided for the liberalisation of rapid delivery services. Presumably, Belgium considered that this could occur without jeopardising the SGEI. For background, see the opinion of AG Tesauro of 9 February 1993, §1.

[72] T-260/94 *Air Inter* [1997] ECR II-977.

[73] ibid, §139.

[74] ibid.

[75] C-159/94 *Commission v France*, §90.

[76] ibid, §95.

[77] See, for example, Commission Decision 1999/695/EC, *REIMS II*, §92.

Ignoring the Contradiction of Necessity

A concerning feature of the second phase is the extent to which the necessity of disapplying other Treaty rules is negated by available facts but they are ignored in the application of Article 106(2). To some degree that phenomenon begins very subtly with *Corbeau*. There, General Tesauro had pointed out that in the Commission's 1991 Green Paper on postal liberalisation, it had found that rapid delivery services had been liberalised in all but three of nine Member States studied by the Commission.[78] The Court attached no special significance to Belgian's prospective assessment (proposing the abolition of exclusive rights over rapid delivery services) and required a demonstration that even if the impugned services were of the rapid delivery kind, RdP's equilibrium would not be imperilled.[79] While Belgium's proposal was prospective, thereby requiring such a demonstration for the prior period of Corbeau's infringement, given the close proximity in time, the Court's concern appears to have been misplaced. The experience of other Member States that had liberalised these services suggested that their liberalisation was not incompatible with the underlying SGEI being sustained.

Disregard for evidence that the disapplication of other Treaty rules is not necessary emerges even more clearly from the facts in *Ambulanz Glöckner*, and with it inevitable government failure.[80] The case concerned the refusal to continue the authorisation of Ambulanz Glöckner to provide non-emergency medical transport services in competition with the four medical aid organisations operating in the region. The Court of Justice's approach followed the *Corbeau* equilibrium formula on the basis of it being satisfied, albeit in somewhat muted terms, that revenues from non-emergency transfers were necessary to help underwrite the costs of emergency transfers carried out under uniform conditions.[81] On that basis, Article 106(2) appeared to justify the refusal of authorisation to Ambulanz Glöckner, but that was subject to there being no manifest inability to meet demand.[82] As against that, according to the national court, Ambulanz Glöckner's participation in the sector had proceeded without any adverse effects for seven years prior to the introduction of new legislation.[83] The amending legislation made provision for refusing authorisation for non-emergency services in the event that this posed a risk

[78] See §19 of his Opinion of 9 February 1993 in C-320/91 *Corbeau* [1993] ECR I-2533. Although much of his analysis is concerned with showing that rapid delivery services were not subject to the same regulatory constraints as basic postal services, his reliance on liberalisation in other Member States served to implicitly demonstrate that a flow of subsidies from monopoly profits to those services was not necessary to sustain basic postal services.

[79] Taken literally, the Court appears to suggest that *Corbeau* needed to make this demonstration, something that would clearly be beyond Mr Corbeau given the information asymmetries. Even if it that was not the case, the subsequent reversal of *Ahmed Saaed* meant that exclusive rights holders enjoyed great latitude.

[80] C-475/99 *Ambulanz Glöckner* [2001] ECR I-8089.

[81] ibid, §58.

[82] ibid, §65.

[83] ibid, §14.

(the degree not being specified) to the ability of the medical aid organisations to go on providing a public medical transport service.[84] It also provided that existing special rights holders would be consulted on any applications for authorisation.[85] From a government failure perspective, such a mechanism is fraught with risks of special pleading and exemplifies the triumph of provider interests over the general interest. Seen in overall terms, the Court may have been swayed by the argument that to invalidate the exclusive rights might have increased the overall cost to the public authorities of the service.[86]

More striking examples of government failure, particularly in the process for establishing necessity (or to be more accurate, for admitting exceptions on the basis that adherence to a scheme of restrictions is not necessary in a given case) are provided by the outcomes in the *Albany*, *Brentjens* and *Drijvende Bokken* cases. The context was the grant of de facto exclusive rights to supplementary retirement funds through the imposition on employers in certain sectors of an obligation to insure their employees with a specific fund. In each case, the Court emphasised the risk of certain providers targeting businesses with younger healthier workers. That appears to ignore the likelihood that in distinct economic sectors individual workforces might have had roughly homogeneous risk profiles.[87] In *Albany*, Advocate General Jacobs drew the attention of the Court to evidence that similarly obligated pension funds had been operating successfully in other sectors without recourse to special or exclusive rights through compulsory membership.[88] As a result, there appeared to be strong prima facie evidence that in the real word, competition was viable while at the same time respecting the special terms of cover for supplementary schemes. In short, there was no necessity to disapply the competition rules. That did not persuade the Court, however, which appears to have been more swayed by Member State conjecture as to the incompatibility of competitive provision with the realisation of the general interest than it was by empirical evidence of market feasibility.

While it would be going too far to suggest that in each of these instances the Court of Justice should have taken the available evidence dispositive, that may have been defensible, at least in *Albany*, *Brentjens* and *Drijvende Bokken*. An alternative

[84] Although the incumbent providers were 'not for profits', it would seem naïve to exclude self-interested exclusionary intent.

[85] At most, the public authorities needed to be able to procure necessary information while being aware of the incentives of the incumbent providers.

[86] C-475/99 *Ambulanz Glöckner* [2001] ECR I-8089, §53. See Opinion of AG Jacobs of 17 May 2001, §182.

[87] This approach to risk is fairly typical of the Court in insurance-related cases where it appears unwilling to stipulate that Member States engage in some form of probability assessment. Instead, usually it is prepared to accept a possible risk, no matter how fanciful or unsubstantiated, as justification for exclusive rights or other interventions.

[88] See Opinion of AG Jacobs in C-67/96 *Albany* [1999] ECR I-5751, §432. Furthermore, attempts by the Dutch government to explain away that example do not appear to have been successful, at least in the eyes of AG Jacobs, who recommended that the entire issue of 'obstruction' needed to go back to the national court. See §§433–35.

approach would have been to rely on that evidence to establish a strong presumption for the referring tribunal that the disapplication of the competition rules was not necessary. That is distinct from saying that the burden of proof always lies on the party seeking to rely on Article 106(2). More specifically, the Court of Justice could have insisted on the referring court being satisfied to a high degree of certainty through sufficiently cogent evidence that competition was not reconcilable with adherence to specification of cover. That would have avoided the *Ambulanz Glöckner* scenario, where the Court itself appeared only to confirm the plausibility of the underlying financial case. In the presence of significant risks of government failure, the position can only be made worse by effectively resolving difficult evidential issues summarily in a preliminary reference (*Ambulanz Glöckner*), or conversely, delegating their determination with vague guidance only to national courts (*Corbeau*).

As will be apparent from several of the cases considered, necessity review under Article 106(2) is frequently a question of risk appraisal. Seen that way, and considering the nature of judicial review at the EU level, there are significant limits on the ability of the EU Courts to scrutinise such assessments for government failure. As an alternative, they might be expected to ensure adequate protection by way of robust national scrutiny. The opportunity for that was passed over during the second phase in *Albany*, where in respect of exclusive rights for supplementary pensions, an employer wishing to buy cover elsewhere was not allowed to do so. While the possibility of exemption existed, that was only on the basis of an application being made to the holder of the exclusive rights. Unsurprisingly, that was challenged on the basis of a conflict of interest, and more collaterally, by reason of the lack of effective judicial supervision.[89] During the proceedings before the Court of Justice, it became clear that although complaints about the refusal of an exemption could be referred to an independent board, its decisions were not binding, as evidenced by the fund's non-compliance with them in the underlying proceedings.[90] From a government failure perspective, this appears to be an instance of outright regulatory capture. Despite that, the Court considered that the complexity of making an assessment for exemption from compulsory affiliation was such that 'a Member State may consider that the power of exemption should not be attributed to a separate entity'.[91] Instead, the Court specified that after-the-fact judicial review needed to ensure that decision making was not arbitrary, non-discriminatory or otherwise illegal.[92] Tellingly, it stopped short of

[89] The existence of an exemption mechanism might be taken as implicit recognition that the exclusive rights as conferred may not have been strictly necessary.

[90] See C-475/99 *Ambulanz Glöckner* [2001] ECR I-8089 at §110 of the judgment and the Opinion of AG Jacobs at §467. AG Jacobs had no difficulty identifying and condemning the conflict of interest, even considering the 'not for profit' status of these funds. See pp 5853–58.

[91] C-67/96 *Albany* [1999] ECR I-5751, §120. The task was a mixed actuarial and economic one, although hardly beyond the competence of an independent ad hoc expert panel.

[92] ibid, §121.

prescribing a full merits review by the national court. It also left undisturbed the egregious failure to make appeal decisions binding.[93]

(b) Proportionality of Means

In overall terms, the second phase of disapplication review is characterised by significant uncertainty in relation to the proportionality standard and in particular the issue of whether or not proportionality review requires the deployment of the least restrictive means. Obviously, the issue of less restrictive means, and in particular their viability, is closely connected to the issue of the competitive counterfactual which may serve to demonstrate or disprove their suitability. In many of the second-phase cases there is no consideration whatsoever of the possibility of less restrictive means being deployed. In *Corbeau* and *Ambulanz Glöckner*—and leaving aside the fundamental argument about competitive provision—the possible pursuit of alternative regulatory solutions was not part of the debate before the Court of Justice. In neither case was the Court presented with comprehensive argument as to the ability to maintain the SGEI without recourse to exclusive rights. That is not to excuse it from raising these issues of its own motion, which again makes the ruling of the General Court in *Air Inter* so striking.[94] There, as part of rejecting the case for obstruction, the General Court emphasised that there had been no demonstration that there was 'no appropriate alternative system capable of ensuring regional development and in particular that loss-making routes continued to be financed'.[95]

The outcome in *Air Inter* can be usefully contrasted with that in *Albany*, *Brentjens* and *Drijvende Bokken*. There detailed arguments were made about possible recourse to market-based regulatory alternatives to the grant of exclusive rights in the Dutch supplementary pensions cases.[96] It was argued that generally applicable regulation would suffice to secure the desired social outcomes. Conceivably, minimum standards could have been adopted with respect to entitlement and eligibility requirements, as had been the case in respect of the prohibition on prior health screening.[97] The Court did not engage with this contention beyond an assertion that the case concerned social security, as to which Member States

[93] Technically, the Court's holding on this point appears to be that there was no violation of Art 106(1) in conjunction with Art 102 concerning the review mechanism. It is, nevertheless, heavily bound up with the Court's Art 106(2) assessment.

[94] T-260/94 *Air Inter* [1997] ECR II-977. The issue of less restrictive means does not feature in the underlying Commission Decision 94/291/EC, which was an application of sectoral legislation, Council Regulation 2408/92, but equally, does not feature as an issue in the arguments recorded in the judgment. That said, Art 6 of Council Regulation 2408/92 provides for the phasing out of exclusive rights with respect to domestic routes.

[95] ibid, §140.

[96] The final three cases can be treated together since they all concerned supplementary pensions in the Netherlands and were determined by largely identical Court judgments handed down on the same day.

[97] §430 of the Opinion of AG Jacobs in C-67/96 *Albany* [1999] ECR I-5751.

had a significant margin of appreciation.[98] In addition, the Court asserted that in order for the conditions of Article 106(2) to be satisfied in the aggregate, all that needed to be shown was that without the exclusive rights in question, the entrusted undertakings could not perform the particular tasks assigned to them.[99] Taken literally, that reduced disapplication review to simplistic 'but for' causality analysis.

Closer to the approach in *Air Inter* is that taken in *Dusseldorp*.[100] There, the Court of Justice condemned an export restriction for waste recovery as disproportionate. The context was the operation by the Netherlands of a system restricting the export of oil-related waste products to other Member States against a backdrop of significant EU legislation. The Dutch authorities prohibited the export of oil filters for recovery unless it was demonstrated that the destination country operated more technically advanced facilities. They argued that the operation of a dedicated facility to handle this waste was an SGEI. This, they claimed, made it necessary to guarantee it a stable supply of waste fuel, thereby justifying a highly restrictive regime for exports. The Court held that Article 106(2) could only apply if 'without the contested measure, the undertaking in question would be unable to carry out the task assigned to it'.[101] In doing so, the Court expressly adopted the observations made by Advocate General Jacobs to the effect that it needed to be shown 'to the satisfaction of the national court that the objective cannot be achieved equally well by other means'.[102]

4. Efficiency

In *Höfner*, as part of an expansive approach to Article 106(1) in conjunction with Article 102, the Court condemned the operation of an SGEI provider as an exclusive rights holder on efficiency grounds while denying the availability of Article 106(2) to excuse those failings. A critical question in the second phase would be whether the Court continued to refuse recourse to Article 106(2) in that way. More generally, the issue would arise as to whether the Court or the Commission was in a position to require efficiency-enhancing measures as a condition

[98] C-67/96 *Albany* [1999] ECR I-5751, §122. The Court seeks to rely on C-238/82 *Duphar* [1984] ECR 523, which reliance is criticised by Gyselen as the Court's 'most sweeping (and probably most disappointing) observation' considering that *Duphar* concerned basic compulsory cover and the operation of the free movement rules. See Gyselen, L, 'Case Law, Case C-67/96 and Case C-219.97' (2000) 37 *CML Rev* 425–48. Interestingly, although writing in a personal capacity, Gyselen (a former Commission official) indicates that in respect of a complaint to the Commission by Brentjens, prior to the trilogy of judgments, the Commission had anticipated that it would need to be satisfied that no less restrictive means could have been deployed.

[99] C-67/96 *Albany* [1999] ECR I-5751, §107; C-115/97, C-116/97 and C-117/97 *Brentjens'* [1999] ECR I-6025, §107; and C-219/97 *Drijvende Bokken* [1999] ECR I-6121, §97.

[100] C-203/96 *Dusseldorp* [1998] ECR I-4075.

[101] ibid, §67.

[102] Opinion of 23 October 1997, §108.

of the applicability of Article 106(2) so as to mitigate government failures. In the second phase, the limits of the manifest incapacity doctrine became apparent and more formal recognition of Member State control over SGEI definition led to a significant overall weakening of the position on efficiency under Article 106(2).

(a) The Limits of the Manifest Incapacity Doctrine

In *Corbeau*, unsurprisingly, the defendant made a valiant effort to frame the case as a *Höfner*-type failure to meet demand.[103] The essential claim was that RdP had not innovated in terms of catering for rapid delivery services and that a gap in the market was being filled by Corbeau. Those claims were confronted head on in the opinion of Advocate General Tesauro, who acknowledged that although the service provided by the incumbent might be said to be 'indifferent', nevertheless there was an obligation on it to meet all requests for service.[104] He contended that where the exclusive rights were objectively necessary, it was beside the point under Article 106(2) if the monopolist was inefficient.[105] He argued that questions of efficiency were a matter for the national authorities.

In *Corbeau*, while the Court did not go so far as expressly to adopt the Advocate General's position on efficiency, that may be regarded as inherent in the outcome. As a result, contrary to *Höfner*, it appeared that non-performance was excusable and did not rule out reliance on Article 106(2). An important difference in that regard was that in *Corbeau* such inefficiency appeared to benefit from the protection of Article 106(2).[106] This stems from the approach of the Court in 'reasoning out' from Article 106(2) as referred to above. While Advocate General Tesauro's logic appears convincing, nevertheless, the Court could have conditioned its approval on grounds of necessity by reference to RdP's not failing to meet demand in a manifest manner. Buendía Sierra has pointed out that such a stipulation was included in the judgment in *Glöckner*, while acknowledging that it was not subsequently taken forward in the Article 106(2) jurisprudence.[107]

(b) Pre-eminence as to SGEI Definition Precluding Efficiency Scrutiny

While there is undoubtedly a need to respect the ability of Member States to make their own distributional and cohesion-based choices, it is not apparent that this

[103] See Report for the Hearing, *Corbeau*, p 2539.

[104] Section 16 of his opinion of 9 February 1993.

[105] ibid.

[106] Buendía Sierra explains this on the basis that *Corbeau* effectively reversed the burden of proof. Unlike *Sacchi* where exclusive rights were not presumed to be unlawful, the opposite appears to be assumed in *Corbeau* but with Art 106(2) providing the saving justification. See Buendía Sierra, 'Article 106' 832.

[107] Buendía Sierra has argued that *Corbeau* is moderated by *Ambulanz Glöckner* on the basis that the latter qualified Art 106(2) by requiring that it would only apply provided that there was no manifest failure to meet demand in line with *Höfner*. He acknowledges that other judgments do not support this approach. Buendía Sierra (n 37) 860.

should extend to permitting significant levels of productive inefficiency in their fulfilment. Even if the Court's abilities in this regard are heavily constrained, at least in replying to preliminary references, that does not appear to follow for the Commission. At the very least, it has the capacity to grapple with the exact modalities of SGEI provision and in turn possible efficiency implications. Furthermore, such control would appear to be legitimate even considering the hegemonic position of the Member States in respect of the definition of SGEIs. Contrary to this reasoning, in a number of judgments during the second phase, judicial affirmation of discretion with respect to SGEI formulation (in terms of the specification of particular tasks) effectively morphed into the Commission being disabled from taking steps to ensure even productive efficiency in SGEI delivery.

The regression on efficiency in the second phase can be traced back to the setting of the supervision standard for SGEI qualification based on manifest error. Although the manifest error standard was confirmed in *Fred Olsen*, this was predicated on a statement in *FFSA* concerning the amount of discretion vested in the Member State.[108] There, the Court of Justice indicated that 'the authorities of the Member States may in some cases have a sufficient degree of latitude in regulating certain matters, such as, in the present case, the organisation of public services in the postal sector'.[109] At its highest, that was a claim for deference in the specification of particular tasks (eg, delivery targets, number of post offices per head of population, etc). It does not follow that this should have precluded the appraisal of how efficiently the entrusted tasks were performed. The Court went further, however, in *FFSA* and stipulated that

> [i]n the absence of Community rules governing the matter, the Commission is not entitled to rule on the basis of public service tasks assigned to the public operator, such as the level of costs linked to that service, or the expediency of the political choices made in this regard by the national authorities, or La Poste's economic efficiency in the sector reserved to it.[110]

In superficial terms this appears to preclude efficiency as a condition of qualification under Article 106(2). It is worth pointing out, however, that the Court made this pronouncement on efficiency in the context of arguments directed at the specification of the USO in terms of its nature and extent. In particular, it was addressing an argument seeking to question the extent of USO provision (and in turn, the related costs) through requirements as to the number of post offices to be operated by the SGEI provider.[111] In substance, that amounted to impugning the particular tasks assigned to La Poste, as to which deference to the Member

[108] T-106/95 *FFSA* [1997] ECR II-229, §99.

[109] ibid, §99.

[110] The Court relied on the Opinion of AG Tesauro in *Corbeau*.

[111] See §108 of the judgment. Separately, at §86, the General Court records the Commission as having argued that it was not its role to improve the efficiency of the public postal service in France.

States is understandable. The Court could have distinguished deference on the precise tasks delegated to La Poste from an appraisal of its operational efficiency in their execution. Despite the potential for distinguishing those issues in that way, under the *FFSA* approach SGEI providers were entitled to recover compensation based on all of the costs that they actually incurred.[112] This meant that significant productive inefficiencies would continue to be tolerated at EU level to the extent that domestic initiatives or EU regulation did not actively target them. The General Court's excusing of the Commission in this way acted as a significant constraint on the use of efficiency control as a check on government failure.

D. The Third Phase—Partial Revival

1. Introduction

This section explores government failure under Article 106(2) in the wake of the *Altmark* judgment. The relationship between *Altmark* and Article 106(2) is both complex and nuanced. In particular, matters have been complicated by legislative interventions in the wake of *Altmark*. These have come in two rounds: first the 'Monti-Kroes Package' in 2005, and subsequently, the 'Almunia Package' in 2012.[113] As a result, the structure of this section involves a split in the consideration of government failure between the implementation of *Altmark* and the position more generally pertaining under Article 106(2). This section maintains the tracking of the strictness of disapplication review by reference to transparency and proof, necessity and proportionality, and efficiency. The position based on *Altmark* implementation is in turn divided between, on the one hand, measures that fall within the relevant exempting decision, and on the other hand, the corresponding frameworks adopted by the Commission for those that do not. Both the Monti-Kroes and Almunia packages represented progressively more rigorous requirements from an efficiency perspective with respect to the delivery of SGEIs. Whether they herald a wider reorientation of Article 106(2) back towards the prevention and mitigation of government failure remains to be seen.

[112] See, for example, Commission Decision 2002/782/EC, *Poste Italiane*, §133, despite possible indications of efficiency problems. See §131, point (iv).

[113] The Monti-Kroes Package comprised Commission Decision 2005/842/EC of 28 November 2005 on the application of Article 86(2) of the EC Treaty to State aid in the form of public service compensation granted to certain undertakings entrusted with the operation of services of general economic interest, the Community Framework for State Aid in the form of Public Service Compensation (2005/C297/04), and Commission Directive 2005/81/EC of 28 November 2005 amending Directive 80/723/EEC on the transparency of financial relations between Member States and public undertakings as well as on financial transparency within certain undertakings.

2. *Altmark* and the Transformation of Article 106(2)

(a) *Altmark and the Mitigation of Government Failure*

The overall composition and tenor of the *Altmark* ruling evinces a pronounced concern to guard against government failure even though the ruling was rendered as a filter for the identification of advantage as one of the elements of State aid.[114] In line with the nature of SGEIs, however, the PSO requirement of the first test is open ended, although it may ultimately lead to the narrower PSO requirement eventually emasculating the SGEI concept. In addition the requirements of obligation and definition replicate the entrustment requirement in Article 106(2). The second element of *Altmark*—which requires that compensation parameters be arrived at in a transparent manner and that they be determined in advance—can be understood as an attempt to guard against government failure through an emphasis on process. There is clearly a concern about the incentive effects of systems based simply on reimbursement for losses after the fact.[115] The third *Altmark* criterion limits compensation to the costs of PSO provision and makes provision for profit. Both the nature of cost calculation and the precise allowance for profit are left open, which is unsurprising considering the technicality of both.

It is with respect to the fourth test that the Court of Justice displays great subtlety and commendable awareness of the difficulties inherent in PSO funding. This sophistication was likely informed by the fundamentals of utility regulation. Member States are given an incentive to tender based on lowest cost.[116] As an alternative, the Court constructed a quasi-regulatory formula. While stipulating that compensation should be based on the costs of a 'typical' undertaking, this needed to be one that was 'well run'. It at least places some emphasis on productive efficiency, even if that is generous in relative terms. The Court was trying to square a difficult circle. It raised the issue of comparative performance but without setting a hypothetically efficient comparator as the benchmark. Similarly, the reliance on the undertaking being 'adequately' resourced reflects an abiding concern in utility regulation that a provider be properly capitalised.[117] Completing the third

The Almunia Package is more comprehensive and includes Commission Decision 2012/21/EU, on the application of Article 106(2) of the EC Treaty to State aid in the form of public service compensation granted to certain undertakings entrusted with the operation of services of general economic interest, a European Union Framework for State Aid in the form of public service compensation (2012/C8/03), a Communication from the Commission on the Application of the European Union State Aid Rules to Compensation Granted for the Provision of Services of General Economic Interest (2012/C 008/02) and Commission Regulation 360/2012/EU on the Application of Articles 107 and 108 of the Treaty on the Functioning of the European Union to de minimis aid granted to undertakings providing services of general economic interest.

[114] C-280/00 *Altmark* [2003] ECR I-7747, the critical sections of the judgment are §89–93.

[115] ibid, §91.

[116] That is even more prescriptive than Art 4(2)(c) as introduced to the Transparency Directive when amended by Directive 2000/52/EC.

[117] See Pierce and Gellhorn (n 31) 134–44.

test, and possibly drawing (albeit without attribution) on the legislation at issue in *ADBHU*, the Court makes reference to the PSO provider being permitted a reasonable profit.[118]

Despite its very specific purpose, given its subsequent deployment for substantive compatibility assessment, it is interesting to compare the overall effect of the *Altmark* criteria with Article 106(2) during the first two phases. Clearly, it is much closer—not just in substance, but also in sentiment—to Article 106(2) in its strict exception guise. Put otherwise, if the trajectory of the strict exception approach had been maintained, this may have led to the kind of prescription for substantive assessment under Article 106(2) as used to rule out the existence of an advantage under *Altmark*. By contrast, *Altmark* seems far removed from Article 106(2) as a permissive derogation. Given that the case concerned land transport, the Court could not have actually deployed Article 106(2) considering the distinct constitutional and legislative provisions for aid in that sector. Even if it could, however, this kind of approach would have been unthinkable in the second phase. In formulating its judgment in *Altmark*, presumably the Court also understood that in other sectors Article 106(2) would still be available. The immediate question was whether the rigour and specificity of *Altmark* would be mirrored under Article 106(2), or whether the permissive derogation approach would be maintained.

(b) Initial Stasis

Immediately following *Altmark* it appeared as though certain types of aid would inevitably be cleared under Article 106(2), even when one or more of the *Altmark* criteria were not satisfied. Although the Commission proceeded to enforce several of the *Altmark* criteria, and the third criterion in particular, vigorously, it appeared that Article 106(2) would continue to be applied permissively. *BBC Digital Curriculum* provides an example.[119] In that case, the Commission accepted as adequate the UK government's claim largely on the basis that the BBC would not receive all of the money that it had requested for the service (by way of licence fee). This meant that the compensation was not proportionate under Article 106(2).[120] This was despite the lack of any demonstration that the BBC's costs were those of a typical, well-run organisation. The same approach is apparent elsewhere. Accordingly, compensation for credit unions in Scotland that failed the fourth *Altmark* criterion was also cleared under Article 106(2).[121] This was done on the basis that

[118] C-240/83 *ADBHU* [1985] ECR 531. Art 13 of Directive 75/439/EEC specified that the permitted cost indemnities could take into account a 'reasonable profit'. The Court's reliance on 'profit' is distinct from the more usual reliance (in economic regulation) on a rate of return related to the cost of capital.

[119] N 37/2003 *BBC Digital Curriculum.*

[120] That included a requirement to maintain separate accounts and the general prohibition on the BBC using the licence fee for commercial purposes. See §55. Neither of those measures provides any reassurance that the underlying service would be productively efficient.

[121] N 244/03 *Credit Union Access Provision of Access to Basic Financial Services—Scotland.*

compensation would reflect net costs, compliance with which would be systematically verified.

3. Elements of Disapplication Analysis post *Altmark* Implementation

(a) Transparency and Proof

Transparency and Proof under Article 106(2) so as to Avoid State Aid Control

The issue of transparency was not addressed on a stand-alone basis in the 2005 SGEI Decision, but clearly the detailed elaboration of the entrustment requirement is relevant. The 2005 SGEI Decision expanded on the traditional specificity by requiring that the act of entrustment must, in addition to specifying duration, scope and nature, also include parameters for 'calculating, controlling and reviewing compensation'.[122] In addition, and presumably with a view to better specifying the general interest, and possibly minimising the dangers of regulatory capture, Member States were 'encouraged' to consult widely with respect to the SGEI mission. All of these elements are taken forward into the 2012 SGEI Decision, with the addition of a pointed evidential requirement, namely that the act of entrustment must make specific reference to the 2012 SGEI Decision. In addition there is generic reliance on the observation of general cost accounting principles for undertakings providing services of general economic interest. The 2012 SGEI Decision retains those elements and introduces a new provision on transparency for certain undertakings requiring the publication of the amount of aid by year.[123]

Transparency and Proof under Article 106(2) for State Aid Compatibility

As already noted, the 2005 Framework adopted the same approach to entrustment as the 2005 SGEI Framework Decision, subject to the consultation addendum and a stand-alone requirement for separate accounts for undertakings providing several services. That is stated to be without prejudice to the requirements of the Transparency Directive. The 2005 Framework takes a broadly similar approach with respect to the specification of accounting and related requirements, which is maintained in the 2011 Framework. In addition, the 2011 SGEI Framework includes a new section headed 'Transparency'. This introduces a publication obligation with respect to consultation on the specification of the PSO, its details and the amount of funding.[124] The 2011 Framework also creates new reporting

[122] Commission Decision 2005/842/EC, Art 4(d).
[123] Commission Decision 2012/21/EU, Art 7.
[124] [2012] OJ C8/03, §60.

requirements to the Commission, including complaints as to non-compliance with its terms.[125]

Perhaps more importantly for government failure purposes, and considering the wider consideration of transparency in this chapter, the 2011 Framework includes a provision to the effect that non-compliance with the provision of the Transparency Directive means that the aid is regarded as affecting the development of trade contrary to the interests of the Union.[126] This is a very significant change, creating precisely the kind of incentive necessary to secure compliance with its terms. Such an amendment was not included in the Transparency Directive, even when recast as Directive 2006/111/EC. The Transparency Directive had been amended in the immediate wake of the *Altmark* judgment to change the scope of covered undertakings, which had been defined as including SGEI providers that were recipients of State aid. Directive 2005/81/EC simply amended the Transparency Directive to bring within its terms SGEI providers that were in receipt of any form of public service compensation.[127] In turn, Directive 2006/111/EC was largely a codification exercise.[128] By contrast, through the consequences of non-compliance, the 2011 Framework creates an essential and compelling incentive long missing from the transparency regime, at least for some SGEIs.

The Residual Position on Transparency and Proof under Article 106(2)

With respect to the case law on transparency and proof in the period since *Altmark* there have been no fundamental changes. As such, absent the Court of Justice reviving *Ahmed Saeed* or further legislative intervention, there appears to be a significant gap between, on the one hand, compensation that falls within the 2012 SGEI Decision or that is compatible with the 2011 Framework, and on the other hand, measures falling outside. Moreover, as *Deutsche Post* demonstrated in the second phase, not even non-compliance with sectoral legislation has led the Court to conclude that necessity could not be established.

(b) Necessity and Proportionality

Proportionality under Article 106(2) so as to Avoid State Aid Control

In respect of the calculation of PSO compensation, the 2005 SGEI Decision followed the third *Altmark* requirement by stipulating that all revenues derived from the provision of the SGEI must be taken into account. It went further by specifying that all of the variable costs of providing the SGEI could be recovered in addition to a contribution to common costs and an adequate return on capital.[129]

[125] ibid, §62.
[126] ibid, §18.
[127] Art 2.1(d) as inserted by Directive 2005/81/EC.
[128] See recital 1 of Directive 2006/111/EC.
[129] Art 5 of Commission Decision 2005/842/EC.

That could include a 'reasonable' profit, which was linked to that of the average of the 'sector in recent years'.[130] In line with a more economics-oriented approach, the concept of 'profit' was recast as 'a rate of return on capital', for which recourse to benchmarking was permitted.[131] Despite that, the approach to cost recovery remained indulgent. Recital 11 confirmed that the permissible level of cost recovery for SGEIs under Article 106(2) 'should be taken as referring to the actual costs incurred by the undertakings concerned'. As a result, in practice, cost recovery was likely to be based on some form of fully distributed historic costs. This can be contrasted with previously established methods of allowing for the recovery of efficient costs only, such as long run incremental cost (LRIC) models deployed in telecommunications.[132] From the Commission's perspective, initial reserve was likely a pragmatic calculation both in terms of the invasiveness of the intervention and the need to begin reform through the introduction of elementary accounting principles ahead of more efficiency-oriented hybrid economic accounting models such as LRIC.[133]

The 2012 SGEI Decision takes forward these requirements with some additional detail and limitation. It rows back on the limits for compensation that were declared compatible with Article 106(2) and in turn exempted from notification under the 2005 SGEI Decision.[134] Under the 2012 SGEI Decision, allowable costs are limited to avoidable costs for undertakings providing services in addition to the SGEI.[135] There is, however, no suggestion of any limitation of costs to 'efficiently incurred' costs only, even if in principle such an approach can be reconciled with taking the modalities of PSO provision (as expressed through entrustment) as a given. With respect to the cost of capital, the 2012 Decision introduces a safe harbour that in all events, a rate of return not greater than the relevant swap rate plus a specified premium is reasonable.[136]

[130] ibid, Art 5(4). Significantly, the 2005 Decision does not stipulate the return on capital must not exceed its cost.

[131] ibid.

[132] These access-pricing models are designed to simulate marginal cost pricing. It should be acknowledged that in the very early days of access price regulation in telecommunications, approaches such as those based on Fully Distributed Historic Costs were initially permitted as a basis for calculating interconnection prices but by 1998 were being criticised by the Commission as likely producing prices that were not efficient. See Commission Recommendation 98/195/EC on interconnection in a liberalised telecommunications market. (OJ L73/42). More generally, the treatment of common costs is frequently a major issue in the cost of SGEIs. On the nature of possible alternatives (in the context of test for cross-subsidies), see Hancher, L and Buendía Sierra, JL, 'Cross-subsidization and EC Law' (1998) 35(4) *CML Rev* 906–08.

[133] Significantly, the 2005 Decision does not stipulate the return on capital needed to equal the cost of capital.

[134] Art 2 of Commission Decision 2012/21/EU creates a general maximum for annualised compensation at €15 million.

[135] ibid, Art 3(3). In practice this may result in less compensation than on a stand-alone cost basis.

[136] ibid, Art 5(7). Again reference to benchmarking is permitted where an approach based on a rate of return on capital is not feasible.

Proportionality under Article 106(2) for State Aid Compatibility

The 2005 Framework adopted a more or less identical approach to the proportionality of PSO compensation, including the same requirements with respect to cost allocation as contained in the 2005 SGEI Decision. With respect to the calculation of SGEI compensation, it provided that non-SGEI activities must recover at least all of their variable costs, an appropriate contribution to fixed common costs, and an adequate return.[137] The 2011 SGEI Framework specifies an approach to the proportionality of PSO compensation that is in keeping with the 2012 SGEI Decision. With respect to the calculation of compensation, while expressly permitting compensation based on expected costs and revenues, it ties the underlying assumptions to validation by sectoral regulators and other independent agencies.[138] Separately, and by way of further specification of the net avoidable cost methodology, attention is drawn to telecommunications and postal legislation as guidance.[139] There is also, for the first time, some specificity with respect to the allocation of common costs, but with sufficient flexibility to accommodate any objective, rationally defensible method. There is also greater nuance introduced in relation to the position on the rate of return, with departures from the safe harbour identified in the 2012 SGEI Decision where the SGEI provider faces a meaningful commercial risk.[140]

The 2011 SGEI Framework also provides that the act of entrustment itself must include a mechanism for avoiding and repaying any over-compensation. While the 2011 SGEI Framework carries forward the 2005 approach with respect to entrustment, it introduces an important new requirement targeting open-ended mandates. It stipulates that in principle, entrustment should not extend beyond the period necessary to depreciate the most significant assets underpinning SGEI delivery.[141] Quite obviously many SGEIs may be provided using already highly depreciated assets (at least in accounting terms) so absent significant justified capital expenditure, lengthy concession periods may be difficult to justify. From a government failure perspective this is a significant intervention, considering the sharpening of the position on tendering also included in the 2011 SGEI Framework.[142]

The 2011 SGEI Framework introduces a very significant change with respect to tendering. This links compatibility to actual or prospective compliance with the applicable procurement rules.[143] The impact of this requirement cannot be understated, even if a Member State avoids initial compliance through promising future adherence. Furthermore, its potential effects must be assessed considering

[137] 2005/C297/04, §16.

[138] 2012/C8/03, §23.

[139] ibid, §26.

[140] ibid, §38. This is where the SGEI provider is wholly indemnified through after-the-fact compensation.

[141] ibid, §17.

[142] A similar requirement does not appear in the 2012 SGEI Decision.

[143] 2012/C8/03, §19.

that open-ended entrustment is no longer acceptable. Given the ambiguity of the drafting, on one view, the tendering requirement arises independently of the literal scope of the pertaining procurement rules.[144] Such an interpretation has, however, encountered significant objections, which Geradin has justified with reference to the General Court's judgment in *SIC*.[145] Those are that in *SIC* the General Court appeared to rule out that non-compliance with tendering (absent a sectoral obligation) could preclude reliance on Article 106(2), and that in any event, the appropriate remedy for such non-compliance was regular enforcement action by the Commission. Separately, and maybe more importantly, there may be objections to the Commission effectively amending procurement law through Article 106(2) enforcement.

As against these objections, the Commission's approach in paragraph 19 of the 2011 SGEI Framework possibly reflects two distinct but congruent considerations. First, and as alluded to in Chapter 1, occasionally Article 106(2) has been deployed dynamically to take account of possible changes in circumstances over time. As such, the Commission's reserve position of possibly extracting a future compliance commitment on procurement may be both defensible and realisable in practice. Second, the Commission also has the possibility of calibrating the 'most economically advantage tender' requirement in a way that addresses essential Member State concerns. While two prominent sectors, namely land transport and public service broadcasting, remain outside the scope of the 2011 SGEI Framework, and even considering the safe harbours contained in the 2012 SGEI Decision for other sectors, if the new procurement requirement included in paragraph 19 has teeth, then it is likely to have far-reaching consequences for SGEI provision.[146] It may result in greater recourse to market mechanisms for the resolution of government failures in the design and calculation of SGEI compensation.[147]

Finally, in the 2011 SGEI Framework, the Commission reserves its discretion to impose additional requirements where the competitive distortions may affect the development of trade contrary to the overall interests of the Union.[148] This may serve to operationalise the requirements of the second sentence of Article 106(2).[149]

[144] From a literal perspective, the word 'applicable' in §19 may be crucial.

[145] Geradin, D, 'Public Compensation for Services of General Economic Interest: An Analysis of the 2011 European Commission Framework' (2012) 2 *European State Aid Law Quarterly* 51. Case T-442/03 *SIC* [2008] ECR II-1161, §§145–47, which relies on T-17/02 *Fred Olsen* [2005] ECR II-2031, §§ 238–39. Despite that, §238 of *Fred Olsen* appears to admit of the possibility of guidelines (at least concerning Art 107) having such an effect. While the 2011 Framework could be regarded as an implementation of Art 106(2), it is not an Art 106(3) Directive or Decision. Alternatively, while it may be treated as a set of guidelines on the application of Art 107 when deploying Art 106(2) as the specific test for compatibility, not even the procedural assimilation of Art 106(2) within the State aid rules (as typified by *Banco Exterior*) could be said to have extinguished Art 106(2).

[146] In particular, considering that open-ended entrustment is effectively prohibited.

[147] See Bartosch, A, 'Editorial' (2004) 1 *European State Aid Law Quarterly* 1, commenting in the immediate wake of *Altmark* on the unlikelihood of the Member States ever taking that course unilaterally.

[148] 2012/C8/03, §2.9.

[149] There are significant parallels with the attempts as part of the Refined Economic Approach to specify the requirements concerning competition and the development of trade for State aid purposes.

From a proportionality perspective, the 2011 SGEI Framework contains an important stipulation with respect to entrustment connected with special or exclusive rights. While acknowledging that Article 106(1) remains the primary vehicle for dealing with those matters, the Commission states that where the exclusive rights provide for advantages not properly assessed according to the net cost methodology, then the aid itself might not be deemed compatible.[150] Although one step removed from the justification for the underlying special or exclusive rights, this raises the question of whether such grants are not capable of being interrogated on the same basis as direct PSO compensation.

The Residual Position on Necessity and Proportionality under Article 106(2)

With relatively few cases reaching the European Courts on these issues since *Altmark*, it is difficult to point to any emerging trend. Judgments such as *AG2R Prévoyance* from 2011 tend to confirm that the generally permissive nature of proportionality review that was characteristic of the second phase is still enduring.[151] As against that, in *Hanner*, and relying on *Dusseldorp*, Advocate General Léger asserted that the least restrictive means must be deployed for the purposes of proportionality review under Article 106(2).[152] It will, however be recalled that the Court held that Article 106(2) could not be used to exempt a violation of Article 37. In *AG2R Prévoyance*, exclusive rights had been vested in an undertaking with respect to the provision of supplementary cover for workers in the French bakery sector. At issue in the case was the lack of a mechanism that could be used by particular employers so as to secure an exemption permitting them to purchase cover elsewhere for employees. In considering that issue, the Court implicitly endorsed the necessity of exclusive rights on the basis that competition would mean that AG2R Prévoyance would 'run the risk of defection of low-risk insured parties'.[153] As a result, it would end up with an increasing share of bad risks. This is presented as conjecture only, there being no evidence relied upon by the Court as to the gravity of that risk.[154] The possible homogeneity of risk profiles raised a general question about the necessity for exclusive rights, but at minimum it may have pointed to the need for an exemption mechanism. Despite that, the Court was not prepared to insist on such a requirement.[155] As a result, even the veneer of domestic supervision that was deemed adequate in *Albany* was found to have been permissibly jettisoned by the French authorities in *AG2R Prévoyance*.

A much stricter approach to proportionality review is apparent in the 2016 judgment of the Court in *ANODE* concerning regulation for certain providers

[150] 2012/C8/03, §57.
[151] C-437/09 *AG2R Prévoyance* [2011] ECR I-973.
[152] C-438/02 *Hanner* [2005] ECR I-4551, Opinion of 25 May 2004, §157.
[153] *AG2R Prévoyance* [2011] ECR I-973, §77.
[154] Again, the elementary issue of the homogeneity of risk profiles is not considered properly.
[155] §§75–81.

of gas tariffs to consumers and SMEs in France. The Court indicated that under Directive 2009/73, any measures departing from tariffs set on a free market basis had to be proportionate and verifiable, while also respecting the principle of equal access to consumers for competing undertakings. By way of introduction to its proportionality review, the Court, in reality dealing with what would be necessity review under Article 106(2), undermined fatally the claim that the intervention could in any way be said to be necessary to ensure security of supply, there being no link back to the long-term contracting that was said to characterise underlying supply arrangements. With respect to territorial cohesion, which was also relied upon, the Court was less scathing but still clearly sceptical. In particular it emphasised that the national court would have to investigate whether the measure was appropriate, such, for example as price intervention with respect to 'customers in remote areas identified according to objective social criteria'.[156] Equally, the Court was concerned about the open-ended nature of the intervention and about the apparently discriminatory nature of the measure. Overall, and although commendable, the result is probably more attributable to the specificity of the Directive in aid of disapplication review.

(c) Efficiency

Efficiency under Article 106(2) so as to Avoid State Aid Control

It is perhaps efficiency, and in particular the issue of productive efficiency, that has witnessed the greatest change in the period since *Altmark*. That has come about gradually, with a general ratcheting up of pressure on the Member States to move towards tendering and to impose safeguards against inefficiency.[157] The 2005 SGEI Decision began that process tentatively by noting that in the context of determining a reasonable profit, the Member States were free to introduce incentives in relation to quality and productive efficiency.[158] That approach is carried forward into the 2012 SGEI Decision, although the Commission is more prescriptive and requires that there must be 'balanced sharing' with respect to productive efficiency incentives where they are introduced.[159] It also clarifies that gains in productive efficiency should not lead to deterioration in the quality of output.[160]

Efficiency under Article 106(2) for State Aid Compatibility

The 2005 SGEI Framework replicates the 2005 SGEI Decision by including the same provision with respect to the possible incentivisation of improvements in

[156] §59.
[157] Clearly, the desire is that Member States will resort to tendering.
[158] Art 4 of Commission Decision 2005/842/EC.
[159] Art 5(6) of Commission Decision 2012/21/EU.
[160] ibid, recital 22. Obviously this then requires much greater surveillance of the nature of output by the SGEI provider.

productive efficiency. In the 2011 SGEI Framework the Commission tightens the position in relation to efficiency. It unveiled an important new requirement by obliging the Member States to 'introduce incentives for the efficient provision of SGEIs of a high standard, unless they can duly justify that it is not feasible or appropriate to do so'.[161] Understandably, Member States are allowed a broad discretion, with the Commission citing non-limiting examples, subject to a requirement of independent verification.[162] Furthermore, the link to quality, and in turn the need for adequate specificity through entrustment, is emphasised.[163] Separately, over-compensation is only permitted with respect to performance in excess of expected efficiency gains.[164]

The Residual Position on Efficiency under Article 106(2)

In the aftermath of *Altmark*, litigation before the General Court, in particular, has confirmed the general permissibility of a much less exacting approach to efficiency in line with the approach in *FFSA* in the second phase. In *M6 and TF1*, the principle that compensation should not exceed the net costs of service provision under Article 106(2) was endorsed, with the Court also confirming that the issue of whether it could be performed at lower cost was in principle irrelevant.[165] According to the General Court the more general issue of the provider's efficiency was of no consequence for the purposes of Article 106(2) in the absence of EU rules.[166] While the result might in part be explained as driven by the subject matter, namely PSB, the principle was also applied by the General Court in its 2012 judgment in *Brussels Hospitals*.[167] In that case, the Court acknowledged that it had been confronted by a 'theoretical' argument to the effect that bad administration should not be compensated through State aid, which the applicant had described as a 'black hole view'.[168] The General Court did not engage with this objection except to repeat the position established in *M6 and TF1*, and by asserting that in line with *FFSA*, the choices made by the Member State with regard to the efficiency of the SGEI provider could not be second-guessed.[169] This may assume a degree of informed planning on the part of the Member States that does not exist in practice. Finally, the third phase shows signs that the manifest failure to meet demand

[161] 2012/C8/03, §39.
[162] ibid, §42.
[163] ibid, §§42, 43.
[164] ibid, §47.
[165] T-568/08 *M6 v Commission*, T-573/08 *TF1 v Commission*.
[166] ibid, §§139–40.
[167] T-137/10 *Brussels Hospitals* ECLI:EU:T:2012:584, §298. The argument appears to have been far from theoretical. As Hancher and Sauter point out, the possibility of comparing cost information between public and private hospitals was at least viable, considering the commonality of many regulatory obligations. See Hancher, L and Sauter, W, 'This Won't Hurt a Bit: the Commission's Approach to Services of General Economic Interest and State Aid to Hospitals' (2012) *TILEC Discussion Paper* 012, 20.
[168] T-137/10 *CBI*, §298.
[169] ibid, §300. The Court states that this was the position 'as EU law now stands'.

doctrine still exists. It is referred to by the Court of Justice in its judgment in *AG2R Prévoyance* where it mentions lack of evidence of the relevant fund not meeting the requirements of customers.[170] The manifest failure to meet demand doctrine was also directly relied upon by the Commission in its condemnation under Article 106(1) in conjunction with Article 102 of the conferral of exclusive rights over hybrid mail (and an associated failure to meet demand for a derivative service) on the Slovakian postal incumbent.[171]

E. Conclusions

In this chapter I have set out the extent of government failure tolerated in disapplication review under Article 106(2). The underlying argument is that with greater laxity in its enforcement, the extent to which government failure is tolerated increases. The division of the analysis into three phases demonstrates the variability of the position across those periods. The first phase was characterised by a strong underpinning presumption with respect to the efficacy of markets and the desirability of their integration. As illustrated by *Ahmed Saeed*, that in turn led to a pronounced disinclination to displace the competition rules. Although government failure may not have been a prominent or conscious concern, its prevention and mitigation was the inevitable result. Simplifying matters, the critical conflict that Article 106(2) was intended to address never reached a resolution point in the first phase. Without suggesting a reverse of the adage that hard cases make bad law, it is clear that in many of the first-phase cases the strict exception approach came at a relatively low political price to the Court.[172]

Although the EU Courts continue to refer to Article 106(2) as a 'strict exception', that ceased to be the reality as soon as the liberalisation of network industries began.[173] From the handing down of the judgment in *Corbeau*, Article 106(2) was characterised by progressive laxity, with a corresponding rise in the incidence of government failure. Although several sectors were the subject of extensive regulation in that period, the general approach under Article 106(2) was one of considerable indulgence for SGEI providers. The judgment in *Corbeau* unnecessarily introduced the amorphous 'equilibrium' formula, taking the focus off what was necessary to guarantee SGEI provision as an objective and distinct task.

[170] C-437/09 *AG2R Prévoyance* [2011] ECR I-973, §72. The Court's reliance on this point comes just before its consideration of the SGEI issue.

[171] See Commission Decision C(2008) 5912 final of 7 October 2008, *Slovakian Hybrid Mail*, which was rejected in T-556/08 *Slovenaká Pôsta a.s v Commission* ECLI:EU:T:2015:189.

[172] 'Great cases like hard cases make bad law', *Northern Securities Co. v United States*, 193 US 197, 400 (1904), Justice Holmes dissenting.

[173] Buendía Sierra observes that as an exception Art 106(2) is 'in theory' to be interpreted strictly. Buendía Sierra (n 37) 855.

That was a crucial failure from a government failure perspective. Separately, the judgments in *Deutsche Post* and *TNT Traco* meant that the position in *Ahmed Saeed* on transparency and proof was effectively reversed. Necessity review was attenuated and proportionality obscured by the emergence of ongoing uncertainty as to the applicable standard. The second phase also saw an unqualified retreat by the Court on efficiency. During that period, the Commission had further recourse to its Article 106(3) powers but its generic interventions remained timid and served as a limited corrective to the change of direction led by the Court of Justice. Article 106(2) ceased to be a significant constraint on government failure for SGEIs.

The third phase of the analysis is focused on the post-*Altmark* environment for the operation of Article 106(2). This comprises a picture of considerable complexity and change brought about mainly by legislative intervention and soft-law guidance. The approach of the Commission reflected in the Almunia Package raises several difficulties. The first concerns those areas where Article 106(2) is implicated but which do not involve public service compensation, whether classified as State aid or not. It would appear that they continue to be governed by a permissive derogation version of Article 106(2). The difference between this and the 2011 Framework is not just significant, arguably it is unsustainable. To take one example, the received interpretation of *FFSA* prevents any assessment of efficiency, even by the Commission, which is completely at variance with the multifaceted intervention and prescriptiveness introduced by the 2011 SGEI Framework on this issue. Moreover, the justification for this differential treatment is not apparent either for this or any other of the elements of disapplication review considered in this chapter. This hardly assists with the overall clarity of Article 106(2) or, for that matter, overcoming its contingency. The possible resolution of this profound anomaly raises difficult legal, political and institutional challenges that I consider in the next chapter.

7

Contours of a Better Exemption

A. Introduction

This book is my contribution to the law on SGEIs through the exposure of government failure so as to provide a new understanding of Article 106(2). At its core is the investigation of the rigour of market feasibility and disapplication review. In addition, and by way of a consideration of the investigation of market feasibility, I have incorporated the concept of market failure. The concept of market feasibility has been used to assess the justifications for intervention to create, frame and regulate public services. I have also dissected disapplication review over time using a framework grounded in the fundamentals of government failure but adapted to the specifics of Article 106(2) and informed by parallel developments under Article 107.

The following are the elements of this chapter. First I set out in very broad terms the previous chapters' exposition of government failure and highlight the important incidental findings, not least concerning contingency and the underlying nature of manifest error control. I then reflect on the implications of this work for a possible reformulation of Article 106(2). That is followed by proposals for the reformulation of Article 106(2) and impinging doctrines.

B. Government Failure Redux

1. The Problem of Government Failure Under Article 106(2)

Concentrating on telecommunications, environmental protection and broadcasting, I have demonstrated the nature of government failure in SGEI verification. In particular, I have shown the consequences of varying degrees of attention to the investigation of market feasibility in different contexts. In telecommunications old market failures have been overtaken by concerns of a more distributional or cohesional kind concerning the availability of high-speed broadband networks. There, a quasi-market failure approach has been adopted representing a pragmatic response to insuperable political pressures. At the same time, and somewhat ironically, the scope of permissible SGEIs under Article 106(2) has shrunk, yet again illustrating the provision's contingency. By contrast, the position concerning environmental protection highlights the potential for market failure analysis to penetrate generalised SGEI claims, in the process exposing and mitigating government failure. The elevation of market failure-derived principles such as that of the 'polluter pays' to the constitutional realm has underpinned that rigour. By contrast, broadcasting and in particular PSB, demonstrates how constitutional change can be used to oust any proper investigation of market feasibility. Provider-directed political action has resulted in a regressively more favoured position for PSB entities under Article 106(2). What is routinely presented as the triumph of higher-order values over market mechanisms is little more than privileging the providers of undifferentiated output often otherwise accessible to audiences. Constitutional change has triggered a judicial disavowal of market feasibility constraints and in turn given rise to widespread government failure in PSB provision. All the time, much more pressing concerns for pluralism and diversity in the sourcing and presentation of news and current affairs are not being tackled.

Separately, I have provided an empirical demonstration of government failure in disapplication review over three time phases. The early stages of Article 106(2)'s application were characterised by a reflexive concern to ensure that its application did not undermine the internal market project given the breadth of the exemption. As such, Article 106(2) acted as a brake on government failure with respect to SGEIs. That, however, was in the context of resolving cases where the issues of necessity and proportionality were not engaged in a critical way. As soon as the Court was confronted with difficult distributional and cohesion issues in cases such as *Corbeau*, it became clear that Article 106(2) would not continue to be operated as a strict exception. The second phase of disapplication review was also characterised by a retreat by the Court of Justice on the issues of information and proof. More generally, the Court abandoned any general presumption against the ousting of markets, driven in part by being confronted with more difficult distributional and cohesion questions. By contrast, the third phase, running from the *Altmark* judgment, is characterised by the partial revival of Article 106(2) as a strict exception through the adoption of progressively stricter frameworks in respect of its application to funding for PSOs falling outside the companion exemption decisions.[1] The gap in terms of strictness between the second phase of disapplication review beginning with *Corbeau* and the regime now prescribed for PSOs in the 2011 SGEI Framework is striking. The variance in the position with respect to efficiency is especially vivid given that the Court had effectively sanctioned a hands-off position on this issue under Article 106(2). The formalisation of that variance can serve only to draw more attention to the default position under Article 106(2).

[1] Commission Decision 2005/842/EC, Commission Decision 2012/21/EU. Under the Almunia Package, there is also the possibility of falling within Commission Regulation (EU) 360/2012 on de minimis aid for SGEIs.

2. Implications of the Exposure of Government Failure

The following are the implications of what I have established both in terms of findings that flow directly from the exposure of government failure through to ancillary findings generated through its revelation. Each is fundamental in terms of proposing a reorientation of the provision.

(a) A Single Strict Proportionality Standard Under Article 106(2) is not Viable

The fundamental challenge inherent in the operation of Article 106(2) as an optimised protection against government failure is the need for prescriptiveness to that end. This is borne out by the experience of several of the regulated sectors, among which the situation in relation to telecommunications has featured prominently in this work. More recently, the need for such specificity is reflected in the Monti-Kroes and Almunia packages. All of this underscores the prescience of one of the early rationales for denying Article 106(2) direct effect, namely that it required implementation by the Commission through recourse to its Article 106(3) powers.[2] The alternative is that the regular legislative processes be relied upon, as was the case in several sectors, with Article 106(2) implemented through detailed sectoral rules.

Although prescriptiveness can be used to optimise Article 106(2) from a government failure perspective, even without that, Article 106(2) could have been operated much more effectively to prevent suboptimal or inefficient public service provision. While the Court's initial characterisation of Article 106(2) as a strict exception may have been naive to some degree, at least for the first phase leading up to *Corbeau*, it showed an awareness of the criticality of information asymmetries and tailored disapplication review accordingly. In particular, through directing in *Ahmed Saeed* that a negative inference be drawn from the lack of appropriate evidence, the Court was ensuring that Article 106(2) could not be played as an opaque trump card.

In more general terms, absent detailed legislative prescription, there are two fundamental limitations on the ability to deploy Article 106(2) in a strict government failure-correcting manner. The first concerns the potential impact of the outcome of disapplication review on the fiscal position of the Member State, and the second concerns the question of the value judgements that may be inherent in the choice of means used to deliver a particular SGEI. Either may have implications for the selection of the least restrictive means, at least from an economic perspective. While occasionally the issue of fiscal impact has been acknowledged by the Court in the context of free movement analysis as a relevant (but by no

[2] For example, Opinion of AG Mayras in C-127/73 *BRT v SABAM II* [1973] ECR 313.

means dispositive consideration), it is frequently just as significant in SGEI design. In cases such as *Ambulanz Glöckner* it was to the fore in the Court of Justice's Article 106(2) assessment.[3]

With respect to the fiscal constraint, the optimal (that is, the least distorting in economic terms) method of implementing a distributional goal may involve direct financial assistance to users so that they are in a position to secure an SGEI on market terms that would otherwise be unaffordable. The alternative may be regulation, which internalises the costs of SGEI provision within a sector, without requiring direct financing from taxation. As a result there is a 'fiscal constraint' that will always limit proportionality review such that in practice it may not be feasible to insist on the deployment of the least restrictive means possible.[4] This is to be contrasted with the position for PSO compensation. Member States are prepared to provide monetary transfers and the EU concern is that such compensation is not excessive to the point of giving rise to unwarranted competition and trade distortions.

The second difficulty presented by proportionality review (and in particular, any insistence on the systematic deployment of the least restrictive means) concerns the value judgements and possible political implications of the choice of means of achieving redistribution.[5] Frequently, SGEI design generates difficult questions about the optimal means of effecting distribution, and in particular, whether an SGEI would be much more efficacious if it was more limited and less generally available.[6] That question is reflected in lively academic disagreement concerning whether the breadth of entitlements (for example, their universality) has an impact on ongoing political support for the provision of public services in particular.[7] As a result, while the Commission may be able to point to a more progressive system of redistribution, if that involves a departure from an equally pressing Member State concern, it is difficult to see how the Commission can impose such an approach absent EU legislation precluding that choice or an identifiable pan-European consensus on these issues. This will be referred to as the 'eligibility' constraint.

[3] See, for example, C-372/04 *Watts* ECR I-4325, §72.

[4] With many Member States facing acute deficit problems, proportionality review under Art 106(2) that results in new ongoing costs for the Member States is unlikely to be welcome.

[5] See Lewinsohn-Zamir, D, *In Defense of Redistribution Through Private Law* (2006–07) 91 *Minnesota Law Review* 326, which although dealing with a private law context, nevertheless is an insightful consideration of the nature and effects of alternative means of redistribution going beyond a mere consideration of outcomes.

[6] See generally, Le Grand, *The Strategy of Equality—Redistribution and the Social Services* (Allen & Unwin, 1982), for the argument that certain public services are disproportionately accessed by and benefit the middle classes.

[7] See Moene, K and Wallerstein, M, 'Targeting and Political Support for Welfare Spending' (2001) 2(1) *Economics of Governance* 3–24. Against this, the universality of benefits is then effectively secured by an in-kind inducement to those who do not need the assistance rather than being grounded in a wider political consensus built on the nature of the underlying goal.

(b) *The Contingency of Article 106(2) is Irreversible in Significant Respects*

As set out in Chapter 4, the contingency of Article 106(2) flows in part from a number of long-standing doctrinal inventions by the Court of Justice. Among them, the public authority and solidarity exemptions are very significant. Although both have been shown to be problematic, and each would appear to encroach on territory that Article 106(2) could occupy (in the sense that SGEI claims were viable in many of the cases considered), the question arises as to whether a change of approach would make any meaningful difference to the actual outcome of cases. Although the experience in *Albany* and *AG2R Prévoyance* suggests not, they may be 'staging point' decisions signalling greater rigour in times to come. Separately, it seems that a *modus vivendi* of sorts has been arrived at, at least by the Commission, with respect to the deployment of Article 106(2) in the context of State aid enforcement. Where possible, general interest claims are usually analysed by reference to sectoral guidelines under the State aid rules, with Article 106(2) confined to a sweeper role. While that adds to the relegation of Article 106(2), on administrative grounds alone it is difficult to fault.

Although it may not be feasible to abandon the official authority and solidarity exemptions, it might be possible to at least carve out certain situations from them, in particular where there is an underlying efficiency-derived market failure. Their presence is striking in several of the public authority cases that I have considered. While it is clear that many exercises of public authority do not implicate market failures, where they do then arguably the underlying activity should be treated as economic. That is especially the case where participation in the activity is capable of giving rise to circumstances that by object or effect restrict or distort competition. The position with respect to the solidarity exemption is more complicated since by definition those cases do not usually implicate market failures. Although the argument has been made that those instances are susceptible to scrutiny under Article 106(2), there is usually no avoiding the need for appropriate proportionality review. As previously indicated, in that regard a uniform strict standard is not feasible, although as considered below, such an approach is defensible for new special or exclusive rights, subject to the fiscal and eligibility constraints.

(c) *Greater Deference is Required from the Commission in the Supervision of General Interest Interventions that are not Market Failure Related*

This observation stems in part from my claim that manifest error control is far from marginal and is deferential when it comes to the existence of market failures. That might be justified on the basis that market failure is an objective economic concept, the verification of which is not something where special deference to the Member States is warranted. That stance is much more difficult to sustain with respect to cohesional goals and even more so with respect to distributional objectives. As Majone observes, the making of distributional choices is very closely linked to accountability within domestic political systems.[8] By contrast, market failure questions are more appropriate for technocratic resolution. As a result, absent greater homogeneity across the EU on these issues or harmonising EU legislation, the Commission lacks the political legitimacy to engage in direct second-guessing of a Member State's deliberate distributional choices.[9]

Arguably active supervision of distributional choices made by the Member States has been a strategic blunder on the part of the Commission. In that regard, an approach based on requiring SGEIs to be progressive from an income perspective looks very challenging for the Commission to impose, as it is alleged to have done in litigation concerning *Dutch Social Housing* described in Chapter 1. It is very difficult to regard that level of supervision as marginal. It might be argued that the Commission did no more than to require (through negotiation) that the Netherlands be internally consistent by linking eligibility to thresholds under social welfare law. The problem with this approach is that it may be perceived to relegate the other policy concern of the Netherlands, namely ensuring a wider mix of tenants of varying socio-economic circumstances, and appears to treat it as a less worthy general interest objective. The Commission lacks the political legitimacy necessary to engage in this type of supervision.[10] Intensive scrutiny also appears to be at odds with the sort of value diversity that is recognised in other areas of EU law, not least in relation to the free movement derogation mechanisms.[11] As such, the Commission may need to step back in relation to those issues.

C. Proposals for a Reorientation of the Law with Respect to SGEIs

My primary purpose here is to improve the operation of Article 106(2) as a bulwark against government failure. In making proposals, it is very tempting to point to the avoidable complexity that has been introduced by *Altmark* and by virtue of which Article 106(2) now appears to have several different iterations and intensities depending on the context. While features of Article 106(2) make it an especially capable instrument for curbing government failure and for favouring it for

[8] Majone, G, 'From the Positive to the Regulatory State: Causes and Consequences of Changes in the Mode of Governance' (1997) 17(2) *Journal of Public Policy* 162.

[9] That is not to say that many Commission interventions do not have distributional impacts, but frequently they are secondary effects, no matter how significant. Such interventions appear to be qualitatively different from direct questioning of distributional choices.

[10] See *contra*, Heide-Jørgensen, C, 'Private Distortions of Competition and SSGIs' in Neergaard, U, Szyszczak, E and van de Gronden, JW (eds), *Social Services of General Interest in the EU* (Springer, 2013) 305–06, where she describes the approach of the Commission as 'flexible'.

[11] On that issue see, Lenaerts, K, 'Defining the Concept of "Services of General Economic Interest" in Light of the "Checks and Balances" Set Out in the EU Treaties' (2012) 19(4) *Jurisprudencija* 1247–56, 1255, fn 35, relying on the judgment in Joined Cases C-570/07 and C-571/07 *Pérez and Gómez* [2010] ECR I-4629.

that purpose in certain situations over the alternatives, there can be no simple retreat from the configuration created by *Altmark*. By contrast, with respect to issues such as the public authority and solidarity exceptions, a change in direction by the Court alone could serve to widen the ambit of Article 106(2) as a guard against market failure.

In considering a reorientation of Article 106(2), it should also be borne in mind that much of its substance has been implemented in many sectors, both through Article 106(3) interventions and also by means of ordinary legislation. That, to all intents and purposes, may explain the outcome in *ANODE*, where the specificity of the Directive at issue in that case is striking. This is accounted for not so much by the express cross-reference to Article 106(2) as by the express safeguards built into Directive 2009/73/EC. They represent Article 106(2) in its strict form through requiring that appropriate means must be deployed, that they be tailored to the achievement of the general interest, be proportionate, and respect the principle of equal opportunity of access to customers. The difference in approach to disapplication review between *ANODE* and the *Electricity and Gas Cases*, long treated as the *fons et origo* of Article 106(2) jurisprudence, is striking. It is no exaggeration to say, leaving procedural differences aside, that Directive 2009/73/EC was the defining difference. While Article 106(2) does not need implementing legislation to be a meaningful block on government failure, clearly legislative specificity is necessary to realise something approaching its full potential.

With respect to public services the Commission has comprehensively targeted the 'low hanging fruit' in the form of PSO compensation through the adoption of the Monti-Kroes and Almunia packages. The issue of the granting of special or exclusive rights is a significant area where (assuming no sectoral legislation) Article 106(2) may be engaged and where greater strictness may be justified. As a result, a proposal previously made by Buendía Sierra concerning them is endorsed below. Similarly, the issue of price regulation in markets where SGEIs are recognised will continue to be a significant issue. That is why the *ANODE* judgment of the Court is so potentially significant, not least if it can infuse Article 106(2) more generally with more of the vitality that has been previously lost. In saying this, the current constitutional smörgåsbord for SGEIs and related services of general interest probably will defer indefinitely the kind of plain speaking by the Court that should be the response to incoherent, slogan-based SGEI claims.

1. Clarify the Nature of Manifest Error Control under Article 106(2)

While the Commission may prefer to avoid any formal elaboration of its overall approach to SGEI verification, that clarification is now becoming essential, if only to preserve the legitimacy of Article 106(2) as a curb on government failure. The Commission's stance on market failures under Article 106(2) mirrors that under Article 107(3)(c). It is based mainly on a small number of efficiency-limiting market failures taking known forms, the verification of which is strict, and in no sense marginal. That is justified but the Commission needs to become more explicit in policy pronouncements and guidance that this is its approach. Already there are signs that the Member States are frustrated by the seeming randomness of outcomes under the manifest error test for Article 106(2). Understandably, they tend to emphasise what the Court of Justice has emphasised about their margin of appreciation, often backed up by pre-emption-type claims concerning the lack of EU legislative competence.[12] If unaddressed, this consternation may reignite the constitutional debate on SGEIs, leading to much worse from a government failure perspective than the current accumulation of constitutional platitudes. As a result, the Commission needs to become much more explicit about the role of market failure under Article 106(2).

If the Commission is to clarify the role of market failure under Article 106(2) then it must necessarily become more exacting about its use of the term 'market failure'.[13] It is essential, as I have revealed, that the verification of the existence of market failures is subject to very strict supervision under the manifest error test. While the Commission has been quite precise (and orthodox) in its deployment of market failure concepts under the State aid rules, in certain areas—including for broadband funding—it has used market failure terminology more loosely. In particular, it has rolled up the realisation of cohesion goals into the concept of market failure. Clarification of the nature of the manifest error test and, in particular, confirmation of the actual position with respect to market failures would also necessitate the clarification of the position as to other general interest objectives. Furthermore, it entails confirming the issues on which deference might be complete, partial or, as has been shown for market failures, non-existent.[14] This could debunk Article 106(2) control of SGEI verification as marginal, but in any event that characterisation is no longer credible.

2. Establish Market Feasibility Testing as the Basis of SGEI Verification

This is essential in mitigation of government failure. A claim that a market failure exists is a technical claim that a market is not capable of existing or functioning on

[12] See, for example, the arguments advanced by Germany in T-295/12 *Germany v Commission*, §§43ff, by way of challenge to Commission Decision 2012/485/EU *Tierkörperbeseitigung*.

[13] That is not to underestimate the difficulty of that task in some cases. See in that regard the consideration of market failure versus security of supply with respect to Lithuanian gas imports in SA.36740, *Aid to Klaipedos Nafta—LNG Terminal* C(2013) 7884 final. At §207 the market failure is translated as the failure of the market to invest, suggesting that the analysis may be less faithful to the neoclassical tradition than appears to be the case at first glance. By contrast, see Commission Decision 2015/658 of 8 October 2014 *Hinkley Point*, where the identification of the market failure on the financing side is more forensic.

[14] A new development in that regard is constraints as to the recognition for SGEIs where they are said to violate 'fundamental' principles of EU law such as technological neutrality. This has been upheld by the General Court in T-541/13 *Albertis* ECLI:EU:T:2015:898, §107.

terms that tend to maximise efficiency. That is distinct from a claim that a market does not operate on terms that are socially or politically acceptable. Nevertheless, the starting point in both instances under Article 106(2) should be to take a view on the performance of markets absent a contemplated intervention. Coherent SGEI analysis requires greater attention to whether outcomes diverge from actual or prospective market outcomes and in turn, whether the particular tasks assigned make a contribution to their realisation.

The need to test SGEI verification by reference to market provision is axiomatic.[15] It is an unavoidable starting point if, as is submitted, Article 106(2) is in substance about the justification for intervention intended to produce outcomes that are different to those produced by markets. The justification for a market counterfactual-based default approach to investigating market feasibility has been explored in Chapter 2 by way of exposition of the indispensability of markets to the Treaty objectives and, as a corollary, the expression of a concern for government failure in the organisation and delivery of public services as *the* purpose of Article 106(2). Testing for market feasibility should not just concern whether a market is not delivering services in a particular way, it should in many cases also entail an identification of any market failures and a consideration of how their targeted elimination would affect the overall position ahead of further intervention.

Testing for market feasibility also avoids questions of the characterisation (exemplified by the stylised delivery characteristic approach) of a measure driving SGEI qualification.[16] The need for a market counterfactual might be regarded as being embedded in the Article 106(2) case law by now. It was expressed in very clear terms, albeit with reference to PSOs for transport, in the *Analir* judgment of the Court back in 1999.[17] It is also an established aspect of academic discourse.[18] Without an unrelenting focus on the issue of market feasibility the concept of SGEI will continue to inhabit a legal universe where the General Court's characterisation of it in *BUPA* as being devoid of controlling principles will continue to hold good.[19] That is a renunciation of the role of the markets under the Treaty and of the construction of Article 106(2) in mitigation of government failure.

The Court's approach to SGEI verification in *ANODE*, where it accepted a generalised claim of 'territorial cohesion' with respect to the setting of certain gas tariffs, is the antithesis of robust market feasibility review. Of course, that was a deliberate ploy by France to take itself within the terms of Article 14 of the Treaty,

[15] For a good example of a more robust approach, see Commission Decision (EU) 2016/633 of 23 July 2014 *Nîmes-Uzès-Le Vigan* on State aid SA.33961 (2012/C) (ex 2012/NN), §589.

[16] That said, the introduction of a reference to 'territorial cohesion' in Art 14 of the Treaty means that as demonstrated by *ANODE*, the stylised delivery approach to SGEI qualification continues to have traction despite its frequent vacuity.

[17] C-205/99 *Analir* [2001] ECR I-1271, §34.

[18] See, for example, Nicolaides, P, 'Compensation for the Net Extra Costs of Public Service Obligations: Complexity and Pitfalls' (2014) 35(11) *European Competition Law Review* 526–27.

[19] T-289/03, *BUPA* [2008] ECR II-81, §165.

which makes express reference to territorial cohesion. Yet, one wonders why the Court should continue to indulge this kind of opportunism. Deferential but assiduous in its task, the Court found it necessary to work to the point of identifying a legitimate general interest, which it then uses to strongly signal the illegality of the actual French measure. Politically, it may be a prudent course for the Court but it only serves to obscure the focus on the fundamental questions. In this case, those concerned what precisely France wished to achieve and, separately, to what extent market outcomes were diverging from those objectives.[20] While the interest may be general, the purpose of the intervention should be specific.

A further advantage of focusing on market feasibility is the interrogation of market failure, either by virtue of claims made during the administrative procedure or of the Commission's own motion. In testing for market failure, the identification of disabling market failures may be a crucial first step in realising the general interest. In that regard, there is much good that could be derived from more general reliance on the conventional concept of market failure so as to widen our current conception of SGEIs. Decisions such as *Netherlands Ecological Reserves I* demonstrate how, in the presence of market failures, the particular tasks entrusted need not take the conventional form often associated with SGEIs. That preoccupation with form is what has underpinned the stylised delivery characteristics approach to SGEI qualification. Instead, the focus should be on how a requirement to fulfil tasks that would not otherwise occur delivers diffuse public benefits even when no conventional elements of service provision are apparent. That is feasible without any degradation of the entrustment requirement and brings with it the possibility of better government failure control under Article 106(2), not least if, as also suggested, the Commission becomes more candid about the strict nature of manifest error control for market failures.

3. Distinguish Between Existing and New Special or Exclusive Rights Underpinned by SGEIs

With respect to new special or exclusive rights underpinned by an SGEI claim, Member States should be required to demonstrate that they have deployed the least restrictive means. That is subject to the fiscal and eligibility constraints referred to above. A significant challenge arising with respect to SGEIs is their typically long-standing nature, sometimes based on open-ended acts of entrustment, in respect of which compliance with a strict proportionality standard may not be feasible. As with many similar problems, a time-based distinction appears to be the only viable solution. For existing SGEIs, it would only be necessary (purely in the

[20] Logically, to take a view on that, free market conditions would either need to operate for a period or be the subject of economic modelling to a high degree of certainty. In that regard, it could not be safely assumed that providers would not spontaneously engage in tariff averaging to some degree.

interests of legal certainty) to show that without the contested measures, it would not be possible to go on providing the SGEI on pre-existing terms. By contrast, the granting of new special or exclusive rights should require a demonstration by the maker of the SGEI claim that subject to the fiscal and eligibility constraints identified above, the least restrictive means had been deployed. In the absence of appropriate proof, that should trigger a reversion to the *Ahmed Saeed*-type approach.

More particularly, in response to at least a prima facie claim as to possible recourse to less restrictive means, the party relying on the SGEI would need to also demonstrate, subject to the fiscal and eligibility constraints identified above as evidence through their manifestation in the underlying political processes, that the least restrictive means had been deployed.[21] I have suggested the stipulation concerning the deliberative process mainly on account of the extent to which SGEI claims are often entirely pretextual and as a deployment of process, namely through a transparency requirement in mitigation of government failure. Quite simply, the gaming that takes place using Article 106(2) is not identified for what it is nearly often enough, although the Commission's censure of Slovakia's conferral of exclusive rights for hybrid mail is a refreshing example. In *Slovakian Hybrid Mail* the argument that the extension of exclusive rights was necessary to underpin the SGEI was rejected as after-the-fact rationalisation (not in any event sustained), considering that this issue did not inform the prior political deliberations on this issue.[22]

The suggestion of distinguishing between existing and new special or exclusive rights is a pragmatic approach first advocated by Buendía Sierra.[23] Specifically, he supported stricter enforcement of the proportionality standard with respect to the grant of new special or exclusive rights. A more lax test would apply in respect of pre-existing SGEIs where the Commission had not acted. Baquero Cruz has objected to such an approach on the basis that Article 106(2) must be the subject of a uniform interpretation, not least because it is not a 'highly technical economic provision' with respect to which the Commission has specific expertise that the Court of Justice does not have.[24] The analysis in Chapter 4 of the reasons for Article 106(2) being denied direct effect, as well as the Commission's exposition of Article 106(2) for PSO compensation post *Altmark* described in Chapter 6,

[21] In effect, this is to suggest that the sort of exercise engaged in by the Commission in the *Electricity and Gas Cases* in terms of the suggestion of alternatives, but condemned by the Court of Justice, should suffice to switch the evidential burden to the party making the SGEI claim. Such a modification is more than defensible given the information asymmetries. Moreover, this is not a case of proving a negative, but simply one of showing that the alternatives suggested by the other side are not less restrictive than the means deployed.

[22] See T-556/08 *Slovenaká Pôsta a.s v Commission* ECLI:EU:T:2015:189, §367.

[23] Buendía Sierra, JL, *Exclusive Rights and State Monopolies under EC Law* (Oxford University Press, 2000) 334–36.

[24] Baquero Cruz, J, 'Beyond Competition: Services of General Interest and European Community Law' in de Búrca (ed), *EU Law and the Welfare State: In Search of Solidarity* (Oxford University Press, 2005) 197–98.

both suggest that Article 106(2) requires detailed and systematic implementation by the Commission. As also revealed in Chapter 6, during the second phase of disapplication review, the Court experienced grave difficulty in applying Article 106(2) with any certitude. By contrast, the Commission, operating over several sectors and with specialist knowledge of the design of economic regulation, has a distinct advantage over the European Courts. As a result, I cannot agree with Baquero Cruz's objection based on Article 106(2) not being a technical provision. Moreover, a uniform interpretation of Article 106(2) is not feasible in practice and in any event is not the case at present under EU law.

There is recent evidence of the Commission taking a strict approach to the grant of new special or exclusive rights although that has been in regulated sectors, where it has adopted that stance for some time and where it has the assistance of extra tools (in the form of sectoral legislation, particularly on transparency).[25] Under this proposal, a strict approach is advocated in all sectors, including those lacking such regimes. While the Commission would carry the legal burden under Article 106(2), as Buendía Sierra points out, ultimately, the party relying on Article 106(2) would need to bring forward the accounting information necessary to assess the SGEI burden and in turn quantify the nature of the benefits accruing from special or exclusive rights.[26]

4. Make Compliance with Relevant Sectoral Legislation a Condition of Article 106(2) Qualification

The availability should be conditional on full compliance with any generally applicable legislation such as the Transparency Directive and any provision on sectoral legislation that is either relevant or controlling for determining qualification under Article 106(2).[27] To be even more blunt, the approach in cases such as *Deutsche Post*, where non-compliance with sectoral legislation was effectively rewarded through permitting reliance on Article 106(2), should not be allowed to stand by the Court. In a situation where a sector requirement could, if it had been complied with, have shone a light on whether disapplication of any other Treaty provision is necessary, then non-compliance therewith (including by reason of transposition failures) in the absence of direct effect should preclude reliance on Article 106(2). To be even more precise, the extension to situations of non-transposition or mis-transposition should apply at least to situations where SGEI providers are public

[25] For an example in the postal sector, see Commission Decision C(2008) 5912 final of 7 October 2008, *Slovakian Hybrid Mail*, which was upheld in T-556/08 *Slovenaká Pôsta a.s v Commission* ECLI:EU:T:2015:189. A further appeal to the Court of Justice was rejected in C-293/15 P *Slovenaká Pôsta a.s v Commission* ECLI:EU:C:2016:511.

[26] Buendía Sierra (n 23) 336.

[27] That would be in line with §18 of the 2011 SGEI Framework applicable to PSOs. That stipulates compliance with Directive 2006/111/EC on Transparency as a condition of eligibility under Art 106(2).

undertakings since that is where the risk of government failure is most acute. That risk, however, cannot also be ruled out in the case of private actors depending on the integrity of the underlying political processes.

5. Revisit the Public Authority and Solidarity Exclusions

Although this is mainly a single actor objective, namely one that is exclusively in the hands of the Court of Justice, I have gone to some lengths to demonstrate how a government failure-directed deployment of Article 106(2), informed in particular by the concept of market failure, could provide a much more satisfactory method of resolving the cases where those exceptions have been applied. That is not to underestimate the nature of that challenge, in particular in relation to the official authority exception, since the problem implicates a conception of the proper or defining role of government at national level. This much is, however, clear: an approach that is based on identifying traditional or usual functions of government is a meaningless classification exercise. Without wishing to understate the difficulty of formulating a replacement theory, a coherent approach might possibly be derived deductively through a focus on a residual set of functions for the state informed by a consideration of subsidiarity within a quasi-federal system, taking account of the feasibility of markets and welfare-enhancing, general interest-directed interventions.

D. Concluding Observations

With this book I have sought to break new ground through the application of mixed legal and economic analyses so as to provide a new understanding of Article 106(2). My purpose is to expose the extent of underlying government failure in its operation. In this instance government failure is concerned with unwarranted or misconceived departures from market mechanisms. It is offered as a contribution to ongoing debates concerning Article 106(2) in the law and economics tradition. Although occasionally proposed, such a study has not been undertaken in a systematic way up to now. I have also sought to flesh out the political dimensions to the operation of Article 106(2); usually it is a ubiquitous but masked presence in all SGEI cases. Capture of the political processes by SGEI providers and their surrogates has led to much of the special pleading that has all too often been successful under Article 106(2). I trust that this study of Article 106(2)'s working from a government failure perspective offers an antidote to scholarship in the field that reflexively decries stricter application of Article 106(2) to public services.

The essential mechanics of Article 106(2) are readily susceptible to a government failure critique because its prevention is their underlying purpose. That is unsurprising given the construction of Article 106(2), even if it has become disconnected from its original moorings. Whether a general interest arises that justifies departure from market mechanisms can only be determined by checking market results against politically desired outcomes. All of this, however, is just one half of the problem. Even where a gap exists and its correction is legitimate, there are crucial questions as to the appropriate means and undesired consequences. That is what usually engages the Treaty, in the sense of giving rise to a violation of a fundamental EU rule, thereby bringing Article 106(2) into play.

As I have demonstrated, the position concerning the investigations of market feasibility is much less embedded than it should be. The position of the Court as represented in judgments such as *ANODE* highlights the seeming constitutional necessity of continuing to pay lip service to vague claims as to the bases for intervention. While the continuing characterisation of SGEIs using stylised delivery characteristics may be an understandable vestige of a slow evolution in economic analysis under Article 106(2), and adroit historic manoeuvring by the Commission, it is now time to end that approach, not least under the 'new' constitutional disposition. The fact that a general interest is at stake does not excuse the need for specificity as to what a Member State seeks to achieve. That said, there is reason to be encouraged. In particular, the approach to PSO compensation under the Almunia Package gets to the heart of the problem from a government failure perspective. In many respects the question is whether the full potential of those measures in mitigation of government failure will be utilised by the Commission and whether in turn that might prompt the Commission into a more active position overall in its application of Article 106(2).

Some of my incidental claims may be surprising, such as the contingency of Article 106(2) or the true nature of manifest error control for market failure claims, while others such as variability of proportionality control may have been assumed, but without having previously been investigated systematically. I have also established the differences between the colloquial interpretation of concepts such as market failure and the much more precise understanding of that construct in economics. Great rigour both in language and method is essential if government failure is to be systematically overcome in the organisation and provision of public services. Moreover, the law on Article 106(2) must be informed to a greater degree by the cutting edge of economic regulation, a process that started with the Monti-Kroes Package. That is possible without the usurpation of the legislative function and can operate at the level of formulating standards of transparency and proof (and the associated issues canvassed in Chapter 6) as classic judicial functions of the EU Courts.

The proposals that I make for the reorientation of Article 106(2) are defined and constrained by the concern to mitigate government failure as that phenomenon is defined in this context. Key to these proposals is greater reliance on first principles, having regard to both the purpose of the Treaty rules and the nature of the exception for SGEIs. Article 106(2) creates a number of difficult but not insuperable challenges from a supervisory perspective within a quasi-federal system of governance. There is significant potential to reduce the incidence and extent of government failure in public service provision through a revitalisation of Article 106(2). The elimination of government failure holds out the promise of better designed, targeted and operated public services. In the process, aspects of Article 106(2)'s documented contingency can be overcome in some but not all its respects. If the underlying purpose of the availability of Article 106(2) is to be respected, then it is the public service mission and not the interests of providers or those with vested interests in them that should be paramount. Whether or not that happens is the real test of adherence to the *service public* tradition. This work is tendered as a practical contribution to that end.

BIBLIOGRAPHY

Adams, R and McCormick, K, 'Research Note—The Traditional Distinction between Public and Private Goods Needs to Be Expanded not Abandoned' (1993) 5(1) *Journal of Theoretical Politics* 109–16.

Akerlof, G, 'The Market for "Lemons"; Quality Uncertainty and the Market Mechanism' (1970) 84(3) *The Quarterly Journal of Economics* 488–500.

Akram, P, '"Consumer Welfare" and Article 82EC: Practice and Rhetoric' (Jul 2008) *CCP Working Paper* 08–25.

Alfonso, A, Schuknecht, L and Tanzi, V, 'Public Sector Efficiency: An International Comparison' (2005) 123(3–4) *Public Choice* 321–47.

Arena, R, 'Subjectivism, Information and Knowledge in Hayek's Economics' (1999) 7(1/2) *History of Economic Ideas*, 9–12 and remainder of parts 1 and 2, 13–253, a special edition on Hayek.

——, 'The Doctrine of Union Preemption in the E.U. Internal Market: Between Sein and Sollen' (2010–11) 17 *Columbia Journal of European Law* 477.

——, 'The Relationship between Antitrust and Regulation in the US and in the EU: An Institutional Assessment' (2011) *Institute for International Law and Justice Emerging Scholar Papers* 19.

Armstrong, M, 'Competition in Telecommunications' (1997) 13(1) *Oxford Review of Economic Policy* 64–82.

—— and Weeds, H, 'Public Service Broadcasting in the Digital World' in Seabright and von Hagen (eds), *The Economic Regulation of Broadcasting Markets: Evolving Technology and Challenges for Policy* (Cambridge University Press, 2007).

Auricchio, V, 'Services of General Economic Interest and the Application of EC Competition Law' (2001) 24(1) *World Competition* 65–91.

Averch, J and Johnson, L, 'Behaviour of the Firm Under Regulatory Constraint' (1962) 52(5) *American Economic Review* 1052–69.

Azoulai, L, 'The Court of Justice and the Social Market Economy: The Emergence of an Ideal and the Conditions for its Realization' (2008) 45 *CML Rev* 1335–56.

Backhouse, R, *The Penguin History of Economics* (Penguin Books, 2002).

Bach, A, 'Case C-185/91, Case C-2/91, Case C-245/91; All on the Interpretation of Articles 3(f), 5(2) and 85(1) EEC Treaty' (1994) 31 *CML Rev* 1357–74.

Baldwin, R and Cave, M, *Understanding Regulation—Theory, Strategy & Practice* (Oxford University Press, 1999).

Baquero Cruz, J, 'Beyond Competition: Services of General Interest and European Community Law' in de Búrca (ed), *EU Law and the Welfare State: In Search of Solidarity* (Oxford University Press, 2005).

——, 'Social Services of General Interest and the State Aid Rules' in Neergaard et al (eds), *Social Services of General Interest in the EU* (Springer, 2013).

Barnard, C and Deakin, S, 'Market Access and Regulatory Competition' in Barnard and Scott (eds), *The Law of the Single European Market* (Hart Publishing, 2002).
—— and Scott (eds), *The Law of the Single European Market* (Hart Publishing, 2002).
Barr, N, *The Economics of the Welfare State*, 4th edn (Oxford University Press, 2004).
Bartosch, A, 'Joined Cases C-147/97 and C-148/97' (2001) 38 *CML Rev* 195–210.
——, 'Clarification or Confusion? How to Reconcile the ECJ's Rulings in *Altmark* and *Chronopost*?' (Oct 2003) CLaSF Working Paper No. 2, http://www.clasf.org/assets/CLaSF%20Working%20Paper%2002.pdf.
——, 'Editorial' (2004) 1 *European State Aid Law Quarterly* 1.
Bator, F, 'The Anatomy of Market Failure' (1958) 72(3) *The Quarterly Journal of Economics* 351–79.
Bauby, P, 'From Rome to Lisbon: SGIs in Primary Law' in Szyszczak, Davies, Andenæs and Bekkedal (eds), *Developments in Services of General Interest* (Asser Press, 2011).
Baumol, W, 'On the Proper Cost Tests for Natural Monopoly in a Multi-product Industry' (1977) 76 *American Economic Review* 809.
Baxter, W, *People or Penguins: The Case for Optimal Pollution* (Columbia University Press, 1974).
Bekkedal, T, 'Article 106 TFEU is Dead. Long Live Article 106 TFEU!' in Szyszczak, Davies, Andenas and Bekkedal (eds), *Developments in Services of General Interest, Legal Issues of Services of General Interest* (Asser Press, 2011).
Bellamy and Child, *Common Market Law of Competition*, 4th edn (Sweet & Maxwell, 1993).
—— and ——, *European Union Law of Competition*, Rose and Bailey (eds), 7th edn (Oxford University Press, 2014).
Bermann, G, 'Proportionality and Subsidiarity' in Barnard and Scott (eds), *The Law of the Single European Market* (Hart Publishing, 2002).
Besley, T, *Principled Agents? The Political Economy of Good Government* (Oxford University Press, 2007).
Bewley, T, 'Why Study General Equilibrium?' in *General Equilibrium, Overlapping Generations Models and Optimal Growth Theory* (Harvard University Press, 2007).
Biondi, A, '*BUPA* v. Commission' (2008) 7 *European State Aid Law Quarterly* 401.
—— and Rubini, L, 'Aims, Effects and Justifications: EC State Aid Law and its Impact on National Social Policies' in Spaventa and Dougan (eds), *Social Welfare and EU Law* (Hart Publishing, 2005).
—— and Eekout, with Ripley eds, *EU Law after Lisbon* (Oxford University Press, 2012).
Black, J, Hashimzade, N, and Myles, G, *Oxford Dictionary of Economics*, 3rd edn (Oxford University Press, 2009).
Block, F, 'The Roles of the State in the Economy' in Smelser and Swedberg (eds), *The Handbook of Economic Sociology* (Princeton University Press, 1994).
Block, W and Barnett II, W, 'Coase and Bertrand on Lighthouses' (2009) 140 *Public Choice* 1–13.
Blum, F and Logue, A, *State Monopolies Under EC Law* (Wiley, 1998).
Boeger, N, 'Solidarity and EC Competition Law' 32(3) *European Law Review* 319–40.
Bovis, C, 'Financing Services of General Interest in the EU: How Do Public Procurement and State Aids Interact to Demarcate between Market Forces and Protection?' (2005) 11(1) *European Law Journal* 79–109.
Bozeman, B, 'Public-Value Failure: When Efficient Markets May Not Do' (2002) 62(2) *Public Administration Review* 145–61.

Bratton W, 'Berle and Means Reconsidered at the Century's Turn' (2001) 26 *Journal of Corporate Law* 737–70.
Breyer, S, 'Analyzing Regulatory Failure: Mismatches, Less Restrictive Alternatives and Reform' (1979) 92(1) *Harvard Law Review* 549–609.
Brothwood, M, 'The Court of Justice on Article 90 of the EEC Treaty' (1983) 20 *CML Rev* 335–46.
Brown A, 'Economics, Public Service Broadcasting, and Social Values' (1996) 9(1) *The Journal of Media Economics* 3–15.
Brown, P, 'The Failure of Market Failures' (1992) 21(1) *The Journal of Socio-Economics* 1–24.
Buchanan, J, 'Market Failure and Political Failure' (1988) 8(1) *Cato Journal* 1–13.
—— and Vanberg, V, 'The Politicisation of Market Failure' (1988) 57 *Public Choice* 101–13.
Buendía Sierra, JL, 'Commentaire de l'arrêt de la Cour de Justice des Communautés européennes du 5 Octobre 1994, affaire C-323/93, "Centre d'insémination de la Crespelle"' (1994) 1(3) EC Competition Policy Newsletter 53–56.
—— *Exclusive Rights and State Monopolies under EC Law* (Oxford University Press, 2000).
——, 'An analysis of Article 86(2) EC, Part IV' in Sanchez Rydelski (ed), *The EU State Aid Regime* (Cameron May, 2006).
——, 'Finding the Right Balance: State Aid and Services of General Economic Interest' in *EC State Aid Law: Liber Amicorum Francisco Santaolalla* (Kluwer, 2008).
——, 'Writing Straight with Crooked Lines: Competition Policy and Services of General Economic Interest' in Biondi and Eekout (eds), *EU Law after Lisbon* (Oxford University Press, 2012).
—— 'Article 106— Exclusive or Special Rights and Other Anti-Competitive State Measures' in Faull and Nikpay (eds), *The EU Law of Competition*, 3rd edn (Oxford University Press, 2014).
—— and Smulders, B, 'The Limited Role of the "Refined Economic Approach" in Achieving the Objectives of State Aid Control: Time for Some Realism' in *EC State Aid Law: Liber Amicorum Francisco Santaolalla* (Kluwer, 2008).
—— and Muñoz de Juan, M, 'Some Legal Reflections on the Almunia Package' (2012) 2 *European State Aid Law Quarterly* 63–81.
—— and JM Panero Rivas, 'The Almunia Package: State Aid and Services of General Economic Interest' in Szyszczak and van de Gronden (eds), *Financing Services of General Economic Interest* (TMC Asser Press, 2013).
de Búrca (ed), *EU Law and the Welfare State: In Search of Solidarity* (Oxford University Press, 2005).
Butler, E, *Public Choice—A Primer* (The Institute of Economic Affairs, 2012).
Cengiz, F, 'Judicial Review and the Rule of Law in the EU Competition Law Regime after *ALROSA*' (2011) 7(1) *European Competition Journal* 127–53.
Chalmers, D, Davies, G and Monti, G, *European Union Law*, 2nd edn (Cambridge University Press, 2010).
Chirico, F and Gáal N, 'A Decade of State Aid Control in the Field of Broadband' (2014) 1 *European State Aid Law Quarterly* 28–38.
Craig, P, *EU Administrative Law*, 2nd edn (Oxford University Press, 2012).
Coase, R, 'The Marginal Cost Controversy' (1946) 13(51) *Economica New Series* 169–82.
——, 'The Regulated Industries; Discussion, with Ernest W Williams, Jr.' (1964) 54(3) *The American Economic Review*, Papers and Proceedings of the Seventy-sixth Annual Meeting of the American Economic Association 192–97.

——, 'The Economics of Broadcasting' (1966) 56(1/2) *The American Economic Review* 440–47.

Cremona (ed), *Market Integration and Public Services in the European Union* (Oxford University Press, 2011).

Cygan, A, 'Public HealthCare in the European Union: Still a Service of General Interest?' (2008) 5 *International & Competition Law Quarterly* 529–60.

Davies G, 'Article 86, the EC's Economic Approach to Competition Law, and the General Interest' (2009) 15(2) *European Competition Journal* 549–84.

——, 'The Price of Letting the Courts Value Solidarity: The Judicial Role in Liberalising Welfare' in Ross and Borgmann-Probel (eds), *Promoting Solidarity in the European Union* (Oxford University Press, 2010).

Dawson, M and de Witte, F, 'Constitutional Balance in the EU after the Euro-Crisis' (2013) 76(5) *Modern Law Review* 817–44.

Devroe, W and Cleynenbreugel, P, 'Observations on Economic Governance and the Search for a European Economic Constitution' in Schiek, Liebert and Schneider (eds), *European Economic and Social Constitutionalism after the Treaty of Lisbon* (Cambridge University Press, 2011).

Di Lorenzo, J, 'The Myth of Natural Monopoly' (1996) 9(2) *The Review of Austrian Economics* 43.

Dolfsma, W, 'Government Failure—Four Types' (2011) XLV(3) *Journal of Economic Issues* 593.

Dollery, B and Worthington, A, 'The Evaluation of Public Policy: Normative Economic Theories of Government Failure' (1996) 7(1) *Journal of Interdisciplinary Economics* 27–39.

Dollery, L and Wallis, J, 'The Theory of Market Failure and Equity-Based Policy Making in Contemporary Local Government' (2001) 27(4) *Local Government Studies* 59–70.

Donders, K, 'State Aid and Public Service Broadcasting—How Future Proof is the Remit of Public Broadcasting Organisations?' (2009) 1 *Institute for European Studies Working Paper*.

Drexl, J, 'Competition Law as Part of the European Constitution' in Von Bogdandy and Bast (eds), *Principles of European Constitutional Law* (Hart Publishing, 2010).

Dryzek, J, 'Foundations for Environmental Political Economy: The Search for Homo Ecologicus' (1996) 1(1) *New Political Economy* 27–36.

Dufour, J-M, 'Market Failure, Inequality and Redistribution' (2008) 6(1) *Ethics and Economics*.

Durlauf and Blume (eds), *The New Palgrave Dictionary of Economics* (online edition, 2008).

Eccles, R and Kuipers, P, 'Postal Services Regulation in Europe' in Crew and Kleindorfer (eds), *Progress Towards the Liberalization of the Postal and Delivery Sector* (Springer, 2005).

Editorial Comment, 'Public Service Obligations: A Blessing or a Liability?' (1996) 33 *CML Rev* 395–400.

Edwards, D and Hoskins, M, 'Article 90: Deregulation and EC Law: Reflections Arising from the XVI FIDE Conference (1995) 32 *CML Rev* 157–86.

Esping-Andersen, G, 'Welfare States and the Economy' in Janoski, Alford, Hicks and Schwartz (eds), *The Handbook of Political Sociology* (Cambridge University Press, 2005).

Esteva Mosso, C, 'La compatibilité des monopoles de droit du secteur des telecommunications avec les norms de concurrence du Traité CEE' (1993) 29 *Cahier de Droit Européen* 445.

Farber, D and Frickey, P, 'The Jurisprudence of Public Choice' (1987) 65(5) *Texas Law Review*.

Faull and Nikpay (eds), *The EU Law of Competition*, 3rd edn (Oxford University Press, 2014).

Fiedziuk, N, 'Towards a More Refined Economic Approach to Services of General Economic Interest' (2010) 16(2) *European Public Law* 271–88.

——, 'Services of General Economic Interest and the Treaty of Lisbon: Opening Doors to a Whole New Approach or Maintaining the Status Quo' (2011) 36(2) *European Law Review* 226–42.

——, 'Putting Services of General Economic Interest up for Tender: Reflections on Applicable EU Rules' (2013) 50 *CML Rev* 87–114.

Foster, N, 'The Free Movement of Persons: Wider Issues and EU Citizenship' in Foster, *Foster on EU Law*, 2nd edn (Oxford University Press, 2009).

Freedland, M, Craig, P, Jacqueson, C and Kountouris, N, *Public Employment Services and European Law* (Oxford University Press, 2007).

Friederiszick, W, Röller, LH and Verouden, V, 'EC State Aid Control: An Economic Perspective' in Rydelski (ed), *The EC State Aid Regime; Distortive Effects of State Aid on Competition and Trade* (Cambridge University Press, 2006).

——, —— and ——, 'European State Aid Control: An Economic Framework' in Paolo Buccirossi (ed), *Handbook of Antitrust Economics* (MIT Press, 2008).

Gal, M and Faibish, I, 'Six Principles for Limiting Government-Facilitated Restraints on Competition' (2007) 44 *CML Rev* 69–100.

Gardner, A, 'The Velvet Revolution: Article 90 and the Triumph of the Free Market in Europe's Regulated Sectors' (1995) 16 *European Competition Law Review* 78–86.

Geradin D, 'Public Compensation for Services of General Economic Interest: An Analysis of the 2011 European Commission Framework' (2012) 2 *European State Aid Law Quarterly* 51.

—— and Petit, N, 'Judicial Review in European Competition Law: A Quantitative and Qualitative Assessment' (2010) No. 2011–008 *TILEC Discussion Paper*, http://orbi.ulg.ac.be/bitstream/2268/143359/1/GERADIN_PETIT_Judicial%20Review.pdf.

Gerlach, C and Pikio, D, 'Aid to Broadcasting, Culture and Sport' in Werner and Verouden (eds), *EU State Aid Law Control* (Wolters Kluwer, 2017).

Giubboni, S, *Social Rights and Market Freedom in the European Constitution* (Cambridge University Press, 2009).

Graham, A and Davies, G, *Broadcasting, Society and Policy in the Multimedia Age* (University of Luton Press, 1997).

Grespan, D, 'A Busy Year for State Aid Control in the Field of Public Service Broadcasting' (2010) 1 *European State Aid Law Quarterly* 79–85.

Gromnicka, E, 'Services of General Economic Interest in the State Aids Regime: Proceduralisation of Political Choices' (2005) 11(3) *European Public Law* 429–61.

——, 'Services of General Economic Interest—from Application of Competition Rules to Europeanisation of Public Services, paper presented at the Conference 'The Treaty of Rome—a golden anniversary—50 years on?' (Warsaw, Mar 2007) www.cels.law.cam.ac.uk/events/Gromnicka.pdf.

Gyselen, L, 'Case Law, Case C-67/96 and Case C-219/97' (2000) 37 *CML Rev* 425–48.

Hammer, J, 'Balancing Market and Government Failure in Service Delivery' (2013) 18:SE *The Lahore Journal of Economics* 1–19.

Hammer P, 'Antitrust beyond Competition: Market Failures, Total Welfare and the Challenge of Intramarket Second-Best Tradeoffs' (2000) 98(4) *Michigan Law Review* 849–925.

Hancher, L, 'Case Law—Case C-320/91 P, *Procureur, du Roi v. Paul Corbeau*, Judgment of the full Court, 19 May 1993' (1994) 31 *CML Rev* 105–22.

——, 'Community State, State, and Market' in Craig and de Búrca (eds), *The Evolution of EU Law* (Oxford University Press, 1999).
——, 'Case Note on C-17/03 VEMW, APX en Eneco N.v. v DTE' (2006) 43 *CML Rev* 1125–44.
——, 'Long-term Contracts and State Aid—A New Application of the EU State Aid Regime or a Special Case' (2010) 2 *European State Aid Law Quarterly* 285–302.
—— and Slot, PJ, 'Article 90' (1990) 11(1) *ECL Rev.*
—— and Buendía Sierra, JL, 'Cross-Subsidization and EC Law' (1998) 35(4) *CML Rev* 901–45.
—— and Sauter, W, 'One Step Beyond? From Sodemare to Docmorris: The EU's Freedom of Establishment Case Law Concerning Health Care' (2010) 47 *CML Rev* 117–46.
—— and Larouche, P, 'The Coming of Age of EU Regulation of Network Industries and Services of General Economic Interest' in Craig and de Búrca (eds), *The Evolution of EU Law* (Oxford University Press, 2011).
—— and Sauter, W, *EU Competition and Internal Market Law in the Health Care Sector* (Oxford University Press, 2012).
——, Ottervanger and Slot (eds), *EU State Aids*, 4th edn (Sweet & Maxwell, 2012).
—— and Sauter, W, 'This Won't Hurt a Bit: the Commission's Approach to Services of General Economic Interest and State Aid to Hospitals' (2012) *TILEC Discussion Paper* 012.
Hardin, G, 'The Tragedy of the Commons' (1968) 162 *Science* 1243.
Haslinger, B, 'Part III' in Säcker and Montag (eds), *European State Aid Law—A Commentary* (CH Beck, Hart and Nomos, 2016).
Hatzopoulos, V, 'The Economic Constitution of the EU Treaty and the Limits between Economic and Non-economic Activities' (2012) 23 *European Business Law Review* 973–1007.
Hayek, FA, *The Constitution of Liberty* (Routledge reprint, 2010).
Heide-Jørgensen, C, 'Private Distortions of Competition and SSGIs' in Neergaard et al (eds), *Social Services of General Interest in the EU* (Springer, 2013).
Helm, D and Jenkinson, T, 'The Assessment: Introducing Competition into Regulated Industries' (1997) 13(1) *Oxford Review of Economic Policy* 1–14.
Héritier, A, 'Market Integration and Social Cohesion: The Politics of Public Services in European Regulation' (2011) 8(5) *Journal of European Public Policy* 825–52.
Hoff K, 'Market Failures and the Distribution of Wealth: A Perspective From the Economics of Information' (1996) 24(4) *Politics & Society* 411–32.
Holcombe R, 'Why Does Government Produce National Defence?' (2008) 137 *Public Choice* 11–19.
Holmes, J, 'Fixing the Limits of EC Competition Law: State Action and the Accommodation of the Public Services' (2004) 57 *Current Legal Problems.*
——, 'The Competition Rules and the Acts of Member States' in Bellamy and Child, *European Union Law of Competition*, 7th edn (Oxford University Press, 2014).
Hoornaert, L, 'Conference Report' (2013) 4 *European State Aid Law Quarterly* 773–77.
Hovenkamp, H, 'Antitrust After Chicago' (1985) 84(212) *Michigan Law Review* 241–42.
Jääskinen, N, 'The New Rules on SGEI' (2011) 10(4) *European State Aid Law Quarterly* 599–600.
Johnston, A, 'Other Exception Clauses' in Oliver (ed), *Oliver on Free Movement of Goods in the European Union*, 5th edn (Hart Publishing, 2010).
Karayigit, M, 'The Notion of Services of General Economic Interest Revisited' (2009) 15 *European Public Law* 575–95.

Katsirea, I, *Public Broadcasting Law: A Comparative Examination of Public Service Obligations in Six Member States* (Wolters Kluwer, 2008).
Kaul, I, Grunberg, I and Stern, M (eds), *Global Public Goods: International Cooperation in the 21st Century* (Oxford University Press, 1999).
Kaupa C, 'The More Economic Approach–A Reform Based on Ideology' (2009) 3 *European State Aid Law Quarterly* 311–22.
Keech, W, Munger, M and Simon, C, 'The Anatomy of Government Failure' *Duke PPE Working Paper* 13.0216.
Kerf, M and Geradin, D, 'Controlling Market Power in Telecommunications: Antitrust v Sector Specific Regulation—An Assessment of the United States, New Zealand and Australian Experiences' (1999) 14(3) *Berkeley Technology Law Journal* 919.
Kersting, C, 'Social Security and Competition Law—ECJ Focuses on Article 106(2)' (2011) 2(5) *Journal of Competition Law and Practice* 475.
Kleiman, M and Teles, S, 'Market and Non-Market Failures' in Moran, Rein, and Goodin (eds), *The Oxford Handbook of Public Policy* (Oxford University Press, 2006).
Kliemann, A and Stehmann, O, 'EU State Aid Control in the Broadband Sector—The 2013 Broadband Guidelines and Recent Case Practice' (2013) 3 *European State Aid Law Quarterly* 493–515.
Kociubinski, J, 'Services of General Economic Interest—Towards a European Concept of Public Services' (2011) 1(2) *Wroclaw Review of Law, Administration & Economics* 49–64.
Kornai, J, Maskin, E and Rolan, G, 'Understanding the Soft Budget Constraint' (2003) 41(4) *Journal of Economic Literature* 1095–136.
Krajewski, M, 'Providing Legal Clarity and Securing Policy Space for Public Services through a Legal Framework for Services of General Economic Interest: Squaring the Circle?' (2008) 14(3) *European Public Law* 377–98.
—— and Farley, M, 'Limited Competition in National Health Systems and the Application of Competition Law: the AOK Bundesverband Case' (2004) 29 *European Law Review* 842–50.
—— and ——, 'Non-economic Activities in Upstream and Downstream Markets and the Scope of Competition Law after *FENIN*' (2007) 32 *European Law Review* 111–24.
Krueger, A, 'The Political Economy of the Rent Seeking Society' (1974) 64(3) *The American Economic Review* 291–303.
Laffont, JJ and Tirole J, 'Setting the Stage' *Competition in Telecommunications* (MIT, 2001).
Lane, J, The Principal-Agent Approach to Politics: Policy Implementation and Public Policy-Making (2013) 3(2) *Open Journal of Political Science* 85–89.
Ledyard, J, 'Market Failure' in Durlauf and Blume (eds), *The New Palgrave Dictionary of Economics* (online edition, 2008).
Lee, M, 'Environmental Economics: A Market Failure Approach to the Commerce Clause' (2006–07) 116 *The Yale Law Journal* 456–91.
Le Grand, J, *The Strategy of Equality—Redistribution and the Social Services* (Allen & Unwin, 1982).
——, 'Quasi-Markets and Social Policy' (1991) 101(408) *The Economic Journal* 1256–67.
——, 'The Theory of Government Failure' (1991) 21(4) *British Journal of Political Science* 424–42.
Lenaerts, K, 'Defining the Concept of "Services of General Economic Interest" in Light of the "Checks and Balances" Set Out in the EU Treaties' (2012) 19(4) *Jurisprudencija* 1247–56.
Lewinsohn-Zamir, D, 'In Defense of Redistribution Through Private Law' (2006–07) 91 *Minnesota Law Review* 326.

Liebert, U, 'Reconciling Market with Social Europe? The EU under the Lisbon Treaty' in Schiek, Liebert, and Schneider (eds), *European Economic and Social Constitutionalism after the Treaty of Lisbon* (Cambridge University Press, 2011).

Lipsey, G and Lancaster, K, 'The General Theory of Second Best' (1956–57) 24(1) *The Review of Economic Studies* 11–32.

Littlechild, S, 'Privatisation, Competition and Regulation' (2000) *Institute of Economic Affairs*, Occasional Paper 110.

Livingstone, S, Lunt P and Miller L, 'Citizens and Consumers, Discursive Debates During and After the Communications Act 2003' (2007) 29(4) *Media Culture and Society* 613–38.

Lynskey, O, 'The Application of Article 86(2) to Measures Which do Not Fulfil the Altmark Criteria; Institutionalising Incoherence in the Legal Framework Governing State Compensation of Public Service Obligations' (2007) 30(1) *World Competition* 153–64.

Maillo, J, 'Article 86 EC: Services of General Interest and EC Competition Law' in Amato and Ehlermann (eds), *EC Competition Law; A Critical Assessment* (Hart Publishing, 2007).

Majone, G, 'From the Positive to the Regulatory State: Causes and Consequences of Changes in the Mode of Governance' (1997) 17(2) *Journal of Public Policy* 139–67.

Mankiw, G, *Principles of Economics*, 4th edn (South-Western College Publishers, 2006).

Marenco, G, 'Public Sector and Community Law' (1983) 20 *CMLR* 495–527.

Massey, P and O'Hare P, 'Competition and Regulatory Reform in Public Utility Industries: Issues and Prospects' (1996) XXVII, Part III *Journal of the Statistical and Social Inquiry Society of Ireland* 71–135.

Mastroianni, R, 'Public Services Media and Market Integration' in Cremona (ed), *Market Integration and Public Services in the European Union* (Oxford University Press, 2011).

McAuslan, JPWB (ed), *The Court of Justice of the European Communities* (Modern Legal Studies, 1989).

McKean, R, The Unseen Hand in Government (1965) 55(3) *The American Economic Review* 496–506.

Moene, K and Wallerstein M, 'Targeting and Political Support for Welfare Spending' (2001) 2(1) *Economics of Governance* 3–24.

Mosca, M, 'On the Origins of the Concept of Natural Monopoly: Economies of Scale and Competition' (2006) 15(2) *The European Journal of the Theory of Economic Thought* 317–53.

Mossialos et al (eds), *Health Systems Governance in Europe* (Cambridge University Press, 2010).

Mrozek, J, 'Market Failures and Efficiency in the Principles Course' (Fall 1999) *Journal of Economic Education* 411–19.

Muller, T, 'Efficiency Control in State Aid and the Power of Member States to Define SGEIs' (2009) 1 *European State Aid Law Quarterly* 39–46.

Musgrave, M, 'A Multiple Theory of Budget Determination' (1956/57) New Series, Bd. 17, H. 3 *FinanzArchiv/Public Finance Analysis* 333–43.

——, 'Merit Goods', *New Palgrave Dictionary of Economics* (Basingstoke, 2008).

Neergaard, U, 'Services of General Economic Interest under EU Law constraints' in Schiek, Liebert and Schneider (eds), *European Economic and Social Constitutionalism after the Treaty of Lisbon* (Cambridge University Press, 2011).

——, Szyszczak, E, van de Gronden, J and Krajewski, M (eds), *Social Services of General Interest in the EU* (Springer, 2013).

Negroponte, N, *Being Digital* (Alfred A. Knopf Inc., 1995).

Neven, D and Verouden, V, 'Towards a More Refined Economic Approach in State Aid Control' in Mederer, Peraresi and Van Hoof (eds), *EU Competition Law—Volume IV: State Aid* (Claeys & Casteels, 2008).
Nicolaides, P, 'The Enforcement of Competition Rules in Regulated Sectors' (1998) 21 *World Competition* 5–28.
—— 'The Application of EU Competition Rules to Services of General Economic Interest: How to Reduce Competitive Distortions' in Eekhoff (ed), *Competition Policy in Europe* (Springer Verlag, 2003).
——, 'Competition and Services of General Economic Interest in the EU: Reconciling Economics and Law' (2003) 2 *European State Aid Law Quarterly* 183–210.
——, 'Compensation for Public Service Obligations: the Floodgates of State Aid' (2003) 24(11) *European Competition Law Review* 561–73.
——, 'State Aid, Advantage and Competitive Selection: What is a Normal Market Transaction?' (2010) 1 *European State Aid Law Quarterly* 65–78.
——, 'Compensation for the Net Extra Costs of Public Service Obligations: Complexity and Pitfalls' (2014) 35(11) *European Competition Law Review* 525–33.
Nicolaides, P, *Critical Analysis of Developments in State Aid* (Lexxion, 2016).
Niejahr, M in Säcker and Montag (eds), *European State Aid Law—A Commentary* (CH Beck, Hart and Nomos, 2016).
Nordlander, K and Melin, H, 'Switching to Action: Commission Applies State Aid Action Plan to Digital Switchover' (2006) 2 *European State Aid Law Quarterly* 257–68.
Nugent, N, *The Government and Politics of the European Community* (Macmillan, 1991).
O'Hare, M, 'A Typology of Government Action' (1989) 8(4) *Journal of Policy Analysis and Management* 670–72.
O'Neill, J, 'Ecological Economics and the Politics of Knowledge: the Debate between Hayek and Neurath' (2004) 28 *Cambridge Journal of Economics* 431–47.
Ogus, A, 'W(h)ither the Economic Theory of Regulation? What Economic Theory of Regulation?' in Jordana and Levi-Faur (eds), *The Politics of Regulation* (Edward Elgar Publishing, 2004).
Oliver, P (ed), *Oliver on Free Movement of Goods in the European Union*, 5th edn (Hart Publishing, 2010).
Ølykke, G and Møllgaard, P, 'What Is a Service of General Economic Interest?' (1 Dec 2013) Published online *European Journal of Law & Economics*.
Orbach, B, 'What Is Government Failure?' (2013) 30(44) *Yale Journal on Regulation*.
Ostrom E, et al, 'Revisiting the Commons: Local Lessons, Global Challenges' 1999) 284(5412) *Science* 278–82.
Oxford Dictionary of Economics, 3rd edn (Oxford University Press, 2009).
Pappalardo, A, 'State Measures and Public Undertakings: Article 90 of the EEC Treaty Revisited' (1991) 12(1) *European Competition Law Review* 29–39.
Paolucci, F, Den Exter, A and Van de Ven, W, 'Solidarity in Competitive Health Insurance Markets: Analysing the Relevant EC Legal Framework' (2006) 1(2) *Health, Economics, Policy and Law* 107–26.
Peacock, A, 'Public Service Broadcasting Without the BBC?' (2004) 133 *Occasional Papers—The Institute of Economic Affairs* 33–53.
Pigou, AC, *The Economics of Welfare* (Macmillan & Co, 1920).
Pierce, R and Gellhorn, E, *Regulated Industries*, 4th edn (West Group, 1999).
Posner R, 'Natural Monopoly and its Regulation' (1969) 21(3) *Stanford Law Review* 548–643.

——, 'Taxation by Regulation' (1971) 2(1) *The Bell Journal of Economics and Management Science* 22–50.
Potschka, C, 'Broadcasting and Market-Driven Politics in the UK and Germany: The Peacock Committee in Comparative Perspective' (2013) 19(5) *International Journal of Cultural Policy* 595–609.
Prosser, T, 'Public Service Law: Privatisation's Unexpected Offspring' (2000) 63(4) *Law and Contemporary Problems* 63–82.
——, 'Services of General Economic Interest in Community Law: From Single Market to Citizenship Rights' (15 Dec 2003) *Lecture delivered to the Dipartimento di Diritto dell'Economica*, http://kavehh.com/my%20Document/Essex/SGEI/Rome_lecture_Dece03.pdf.
——, 'Competition Law and Public Services: From Single Market to Citizenship Rights' (2005) 11(4) *European Public Law* 543–63.
——, 'Regulation and Social Solidarity' (2006) 33(3) *Journal of Law and Society* 364–87.
——, 'EU Competition Law and Public Services' in Mossialos et al (eds), *Health Systems Governance in Europe* (Cambridge University Press, 2010).
——, *The Regulatory Enterprise: Government Regulation and Legitimacy* (Oxford University Press, 2010).
Raboy, M and Price, W, *Public Service Broadcasting in Transition: A Documentary Reader* (Kluwer Law International, 2003).
Rand, A and Entwistle, T, *Public Service Efficiency: Reframing the Debate* (Routledge, 2014).
Randall, A, 'Property Rights and Social Microeconomics' (1975) 15 *Natural Resources Journal* 729.
——, 'The Problem of Market Failure' (1983) 23 *Natural Resources Journal* 131.
Rawls, J, *A Theory of Justice* (Belknap, 1971).
Reich, N, 'Competition between Legal Orders: A New Paradigm of EC Law?' (1992) 29 *CML Rev* 861–96.
——, 'The "November Revolution" of the European Court of Justice: *KECK, MENG* and *AUDI* Revisited' (1994) 31 *CML Rev* 459–92.
Reinhardt, U, 'Can Efficiency in Health Care Be Left to the Market?' (2001) 26(5) *Journal of Health Politics, Policy and Law* 967–92.
Reith, JCW, *Into the Wind* (Hodden & Stoughton, 1949).
Renzulli, A, 'Services of General Economic Interest: The Post-*Altmark* Scenario' (2008) 14(3) *European Public Law*.
Roemer, J, 'An Anti-Hayekian Manifesto' (1995) I/211 *New Left Review* 112–29.
Ross, M, 'Article 16 E.C. and Services of General Interest: From Derogation to Obligation?' (2000) 25(1) *European Law Review* 22–38.
——, 'Promoting Solidarity: From Public Services to a European Model of Competition' (2007) 44 *CML Rev* 1057–80.
——, 'A Healthy Approach to Services of General Economic Interest? The BUPA Judgment of the Court of First Instance' (2009) 34(1) *European Law Review* 127–40.
——, 'Solidarity—A New Constitutional Paradigm for the EU?' in Ross and Borgmann-Prebil (eds), *Promoting Solidarity in the European Union* (Oxford University Press, 2010).
Ruccia, N, 'The Legal Framework of Services of General Economic Interest in the European Union' (25 Nov 2011) *Conference on Competition and Regulation in Network Industries*, www.crninet.com/2011/c9a.pdf.
Rydelski, M (ed), *The EC State Aid Regime; Distortive Effects of State Aid on Competition and Trade* (Cambridge University Press, 2006).

Sagoff, M, *The Economy of the Earth*, 2nd edn (Cambridge University Press, 2008).
Sadeleer, N, *EU Environmental Law and the Single European Market* (Oxford University Press, 2014).
Samuleson, P, 'The Pure Theory of Public Expenditure' (1954) 36 *Review of Economics and Statistics* 387–88.
Sánchez Graells, A, 'Distortions of Competition Generated by Public Buyer Power' (2009) University of Oxford Centre for Competition Law and Policy Working Paper (L) 23, http://papers.ssrn.com/sol3/papers.cfm?abstract_id=1458949.
Santa Maria, A, *European Economic Law* 3rd edn (Wolters Kluwer, 2014).
Sauter, W, 'The Telecommunications Law of the European Union' (1995) 1(1) *European Law Journal* 92–111.
——, The Economic Constitution of the European Union (1998) 4 *Columbia Journal of European Law* 27.
——, 'Services of General Economic Interest (SGEI) and Universal Service Obligations (USO) as an EU Law Framework for Curative Health Care' (2007) 029 *TILEC Discussion Paper* 9, http://papers.ssrn.com/sol3/papers.cfm?abstract_id=1013261.
——, 'Services of General Economic Interest and Universal Service in EU Law' (2008) 33(2) *European Law Review* 167–193.
——, 'Health Insurance and EU Law' (2011) 034 *TILEC Discussion Paper*, http://papers.ssrn.com/sol3/papers.cfm?abstract_id=1876304.
——, 'Proportionality in EU Law—A Balancing Act' (2013) *Cambridge Yearbook of European Legal Studies.*
——, 'Proportionality in EU Competition Law' (2014) *European Competition Law Review* 327–332.
——, 'Public Services and the Internal Market: Building Blocks or Persistent Irritant?' (2014) 022 *TILEC Discussion Paper*, http://papers.ssrn.com/sol3/papers.cfm?abstract_id=2445373.
——, 'Squaring EU Law and Competition Policy: The Case of Broadband' (2013) 021 *TILEC Discussion Paper*, http://papers.ssrn.com/sol3/papers.cfm?abstract_id=2339898.
——, 'The Criterion of Advantage in State Aid; *Altmark* and Services of General Economic Interest' (Apr 2014) 015 *TILEC Discussion Paper*, http://papers.ssrn.com/sol3/papers.cfm?abstract_id=2426230.
——, *Public Services in EU Law* (Cambridge University Press, 2015).
—— and Schepel, H, '"State" and "Market" in the Competition and Free Movement Case Law of the EU Courts' (2007) 024 *TILEC Discussion Paper* 124, www.researchgate.net/publication/228230815_'State'_and_'Market'_in_the_Competition_and_Free_Movement_Case_Law_of_the_EU_Courts.
—— and Van de Gronden, J, 'State Aid, Services of General Economic Interest and Universal Service in Healthcare' (2011) 32(12) *European Competition Law Review* 602–14.
Scharpf, F, 'The Asymmetry of European Integration, or Why the EU Cannot Be a "Social Market Economy"' (2010) 8 *Socio-Economic Review* 211–50.
Sharkey, W, *The Theory of Natural Monopoly* (Cambridge University Press, 1989).
Schiek, Liebert and Schneider (eds), *European Economic and Social Constitutionalism after the Treaty of Lisbon* (Cambridge University Press, 2011).
Schmidt S, 'Commission Activism: Subsuming Telecommunications and Electricity under European Competition Law' (2011) 5(1) *Journal of European Public Policy* 169–84.
Schulte-Braucks, R, 'European Telecommunications Law in the Light of the British Telecom Judgment' (1986) 23 *CML Rev* 39–59.

Schultze, C, *The Public Use of Private Interest* (Brookings Institution Press, 1977).

Schutze, R, 'Supremacy Without Pre-Emption? The Very Slowly Emergent Doctrine of Community Pre-Emption' (2006) 43 *CML Rev* 1023–48.

Schweitzer, H, 'Services of General Economic Interest: European Law's Impact on the Role of Markets and of Member States' in Cremona (ed), *Market Integration and Public Services in the European Union* (Oxford University Press, 2011).

Schwintowski, H, 'The Common Good, Public Subsistence and the Functions of Public Undertakings in the European Internal Market' (2003) 4 *European Business Organization Law Review* 353–82.

Scott, J, 'Mandatory or Imperative Requirements in the EU and the WTO' in Barnard and Scott (eds), *The Law of the Single European Market* (Hart Publishing, 2002).

Sefton, T, 'Distributive and Redistributive Policy' in Moran, Rein and Goodin (eds), *The Oxford Handbook of Public Policy* (Oxford University Press, 2006).

Sharkey, W, 'The Theory of Natural Monopoly' in *Natural Monopoly and the Telecommunications Industry* (Cambridge University Press, 1989).

Shepsle, K and Weingast, B, 'Political Solutions to Market Problems' (1984) 78 *American Political Science Review* 417–34.

Shin, R and Ying, J, 'Unnatural Monopolies in Local Telephone' (1992) 23(2) *The Rand Journal of Economics* 171–83.

Shy, O, 'The Economics of Network Industries' in *Introduction to Network Economics* (Cambridge University Press, 2001).

Slot, PJ, 'Energy and Competition' (1994) 31 *CML Rev* 511–47.

——, 'Case Note on Case C-157/94 Commission of the European Communities v Kingdom of the Netherlands [1997] ECR I-05699; Case C-158/94 Commission of the European Communities v Italian Republic [1997] ECR I-05789; Case C-159/94 Commission of the European Communities v French Republic [1997] ECR I-05815; Case C-160/94 Commission of the European Communities v Kingdom of Spain [1997] ECR I 5851; and, Case C-189/95 Harry Franzén [1997] ECR I-5909' (1998) 35 *CML Rev* 1183–203.

——, 'A View from the Mountain: 40 Years of Developments in EC Competition Law' (2004) 41 *CML Rev* 443–73.

Smelser, N and Swedberg, R (eds), *The Handbook of Economic Sociology* (Princeton University Press, 1994).

Soares, AG, 'Pre-emption, Conflicts of Powers and Subsidiarity' (1998) 23(2) *European Law Review* 132–45.

Sokol, D, 'Limiting Anti-Competitive Government Interventions that Benefit Special Interests' (2009) 17 *George Mason Law Review* 119.

Soriano, LM, 'The Role of the European Court of Justice in the Design of Regulatory Space' (2001) European Union Studies Association Biennial Conference, http://aei.pitt.edu/2187/1/002676_1.pdf.

——, 'How Proportionate should Anti-Competitive State Intervention Be?' (2003) 28(1) *European Law Review* 112–23.

Spaventa, E and Dougan, M (eds), *Social Welfare and EU Law* (Hart Publishing, 2005).

Steemers, J, 'In Search of a Third Way: Balancing Public Purpose and Commerce in German and British Public Service Broadcasting' (2001) 26(1) *Canadian Journal of Communication*.

Steiner P, 'Program Patterns and Preferences and the Workability of Competition in Broadcasting' (1952) 66 *Quarterly Journal of Economics* 194–23.

Stephen, F, 'The Market Failure Justification for the Regulation of Professional Service Markets and the Characteristics of Consumers' in Ehlermann and Atanasiu (eds), *European Competition Law Annual 2004: The Relationship between Competition Law and (Liberal) Professions* (Hart Publishing, 2006).

Stern, N, The Economics of Development: A Survey (1989) 99(397) *The Economic Journal* 597–685.

Stigler, G, 'A Theory of Government Regulation' (1971) 2(1) *Bell Journal of Economics* 3–21.

Stiglitz, J, 'The Invisible Hand and Modern Welfare Economics' (Mar 1991) *National Bureau of Economic Research Working paper* no. 3641, 4.

——, *Whither Socialism* (MIT Press, 1994).

——, 'Redefining the Role of the State' (Mar 1998) Paper presented at the 10th Anniversary of MITI Research Institute Tokyo, http://people.ds.cam.ac.uk/mb65/library/stiglitz-1998.pdf.

——, 'Knowledge as a Global Public Good' in Inge, Grunberg and Stern (eds), *Global Public Goods: International Cooperation in the 21st Century*, United Nations Development Programme (New York, 1999).

——, 'The Contribution of the Economics of Information to Twentieth Century Economics' (2000) 115(4) *The Quarterly Journal of Economics* 1441–78.

——, 'Information and the Change in the Paradigm in Economics' (2002) 92(3) *The American Economic Review* 460–501.

——, 'Moving Beyond Market Fundamentalism to a More Balanced Economy' (2009) 80(3) *Annals of Public and Cooperative Economics* 345–60.

——, Regulation and Failure, in Moss and Cisternino (eds), *New Perspectives on Regulation* (Cambridge University Press, 2009).

Streit, M and Mussler, W, 'The Economic Constitution of the European Community: From "Rome" to "Maastricht"' (1995) 1(1) *European Law Journal* 5–30.

Sunstein, C (ed), *Behavioral Law & Economics* (Cambridge University Press, 2000).

Szyszczak, E, 'Altmark Assessed' in Szyszczak (ed), *Research Handbook on European State Aid Law* (Edward Elgar, 2011).

—— et al (eds), *Developments in Services of General Interest, Legal Issues of Services of General Interest* (TMC Asser Press, 2011).

Thaler, R and Rosen, S, 'The Value of Saving a Life: Evidence from Labour Markets' in Terleyckyj (ed), *Household Production and Consumption* (National Bureau of Economic Research, 1976).

Thatcher, M, 'The Europeanisation of Regulation. The Case of Telecommunications' (Oct 1999) RSC No. 99/22 *European University Institute, Working Paper*, www.uned.es/113016/docencia/spd%20-%20doctorado%202001-02/Regulaci%F3n/thatcher%20-%20regulation%20europe%20EUI%201999.htm.

Thierer, A, 'Unnatural Monopoly: Critical Moments in the Development of the Bell System Monopoly' (1994) 14(2) *Cato Journal* 267.

Tridimas, T, 'Proportionality in Community Law: Searching for the Appropriate Standard of Scrutiny' in Ellis (ed), *The Principle of Proportionality in the Laws of Europe* (Hart Publishing, 2012).

van Bael and Bellis, *Competition Law of the European Union*, 5th edn (Kluwer, 2010).

van Buiren, K, Gerritsen, M, and van Der Voort, J, 'The Prohibition of Overcompensations to Services of General Economic Interest' (2014) 1 *European State Aid Law Quarterly* 61–66.

van de Gronden, J, 'Purchasing Care: Economic Activity or Service of General (Economic) Interest?' (2004) 254(2) *European Competition Law Review*.

——, 'The Internal Market, the State and Private Initiative: A Legal Assessment of National Mixed Public-Private Arrangements in the Light of European Law' (2006) 33(2) *Legal Issues of European Integration* 105–37.

——, 'Financing Health Care in EU Law: Do the European State Aid Rules Write Out an Effective Prescription for Integrating Competition Law with Health Care?' (2009) 6(1) *The Competition Law Review* 5–29.

——, 'Free Movement of Services and the Right of Establishment' in Neergaard et al (eds), *Social Services of General Interest in the EU* (TMC Asser Press, 2013).

—— and Sauter, W, 'Taking the Temperature: EU Competition Law and Health Care' (2011) 38(3) *Legal Issues of Economic Integration* 213–41.

van Vliet, H, 'State Resources and *PreussenElektra:* When is a State Aid Not a State Aid?' in Gadea (ed), *EC State Aid Law* (Kluwer, 2008).

Vedder, H, 'Of Jurisdiction and Justification. Why Competition is Good for 'Non-Economic' Goals, But May Need to be Restricted' (2009) 6(1) *The Competition Law Review* 51–75.

Veetil, V, 'Concepts of Rationality in Law and Economics: A Critical Analysis of the Homoeconomicus and Behavioral Models of Individuals' (2011) 31(2) *European Journal of Law and Economics* 1–16.

Velijanovski, C, 'Economic Approaches to Regulation' in Baldwin, Cave and Lodge (eds), *The Oxford Handbook of Regulation* (Oxford University Press, 2010).

Vining, A and Weimer, D, 'Government Supply and Government Production Failure: A Framework Based on Contestability' (1990) 10(1) *Journal of Public Policy* 1–22.

Vogelsang, I and Mitchell, B, *The Local Telecommunications Landscape in Telecommunications Competition—The Last Ten Miles* (MIT Press, 1997).

von Bogdandy, A and Bast, J, *Principles of European Constitutional Law* (Hart Publishing, 2010).

von Wendland, B, 'Public Funding for Research Infrastructures and EU State Aid Rules—Key Issues, Case Examples and State Aid Reform' (2013) 3 *European State Aid Law Quarterly* 523–42.

de Waele, H, 'The Role of the European Court of Justice in the Integration Process: A Contemporary and Normative Assessment' (2010) 6(1) *Hanse Law Review* 3–26.

Wahl, N, 'Standard of Review—Comprehensive or Limited?' in Ehlermann and Marquis (eds), *European Law Annual 2009* (Hart Publishing, 2011).

Wehlander, C, *Services of General Economic Interest as a Constitutional Concept in EU Law* (Springer, 2016).

Weimer, D and Vining, R, 'Rationales for Public Policy—Distributional and Other Choices' in *Policy Analysis—Concepts and Practice* (Longman, 2011).

Weimer, D and Vining, A, *Policy Analysis: Concepts and Practice* (Longman, 2011).

Wiedemann, V, 'Public Service Broadcasting, State Aid, and the Internet: Emerging EU Law' (2004) 4 *European State Aid Law Quarterly* 597.

Williamson, O, 'The Economics of Organisation: The Transaction Cost Approach' (1981) 87(3) *American Journal of Sociology* 548–77.

Winston, C, *Government Failure versus Market Failure* (AEI-Brookings Joint Centre for Regulatory Studies, 2006).

Winterstein, A, 'Nailing the Jellyfish: Social Security and Competition Law' (1999) 20(6) *European Competition Law Review* 324–33.

Wolf Jr, C, 'A Theory of Nonmarket Failure: Framework for Implementation Analysis' (1979) 22(1) *Journal of Law and Economics* 107–39.

——, 'Markets or Governments: Choosing Between Imperfect Alternatives' (Sep 1986) N-2505-SF *A Rand Note, prepared for the Alfred P. Sloan Foundation.*

——, 'Market and Non-Market Failures: Comparison and Assessment' (1987) 7(1) *Journal of Public Policy* 43–70.

Zerbe Jr. R and McCurdy, H, 'The Failure of Market Failure' (1999) 18(4) *Journal of Policy Analysis and Management* 558–78.

INDEX

www.ingramcontent.com/pod-product-compliance
Ingram Content Group UK Ltd.
Pitfield, Milton Keynes, MK11 3LW, UK
UKHW021908150926
475560UK00003B/249

9 781509 912759